The terms of structuralist and post-structuralist theory have been widely debated within the field of music analysis in recent years. However, very few analyses have attempted to address the musical works which seem most obviously to escape the categories of conventional analysis: the repertoire of large orchestral works of the turn of the century. This first book-length study of its kind uses a semiotic theory of signification in order to investigate different types of musical communication. Musical meaning is defined on several levels: from structures immanent to the work, through narrative alongside other contemporary non-musical texts. Ideas from Eco, Barthes and Derrida are deployed within the context of close analysis of the score in order to unite specifically analytical insights with cultural hermeneutics. This book is a contribution both to the 'New Musicology' and to Mahler studies in general.

CAMBRIDGE STUDIES IN MUSIC THEORY
AND ANALYSIS

GENERAL EDITOR: IAN BENT

MAHLER'S SIXTH
SYMPHONY

TITLES IN THIS SERIES

1 *Haydn's 'Farewell' Symphony and the Idea of Classical Style
Through Composition and Cyclic Integration in his Instrumental Music*
James Webster

2 *Ernst Kurth: Selected Writings*
edited and translated by Lee A. Rothfarb

3 *The Musical Dilettante: A Treatise on Composition by J. F. Daube*
edited and translated by Susan Snook Luther

4 *Rameau and Musical Thought in the Enlightenment*
Thomas Christensen

5 *The Masterwork in Music
Volume 1: Heinrich Schenker*
edited by William Drabkin

MAHLER'S SIXTH SYMPHONY

A STUDY IN MUSICAL SEMIOTICS

ROBERT SAMUELS
University of Lancaster

PUBLISHED BY THE PRESS SYNDICATE OF THE UNIVERSITY OF CAMBRIDGE
The Pitt Building, Trumpington Street, Cambridge, United Kingdom

CAMBRIDGE UNIVERSITY PRESS
The Edinburgh Building, Cambridge CB2 2RU, UK
40 West 20th Street, New York NY 10011–4211, USA
477 Williamstown Road, Port Melbourne, VIC 3207, Australia
Ruiz de Alarcón 13, 28014 Madrid, Spain
Dock House, The Waterfront, Cape Town 8001, South Africa

http://www.cambridge.org

© Cambridge University Press 1995

This book is in copyright. Subject to statutory exception
and to the provisions of relevant collective licensing agreements,
no reproduction of any part may take place without
the written permission of Cambridge University Press.

First published 1995
First paperback edition 2004

A catalogue record for this book is available from the British Library

Library of Congress cataloguing in publication data
Samuels, Robert, 1962-
Mahler's sixth symphony: a study in musical semiotics / Robert Samuels.
p. cm. – (Cambridge studies in music theory and analysis: 6)
Includes index.
ISBN 0 521 48166 X hardback
1. Mahler, Gustav, 1860–1911. Symphonies, no. 6, A minor.
2. Symphonies – Analysis, appreciation. 3. Music – Semiotics.
I. Title. II. Series.
MT130.M25S2 1995
784.2'184–dc20 95–41314 MN

ISBN 0 521 48166 X hardback
ISBN 0 521 60283 1 paperback

THIS IS FOR ALISON

CONTENTS

Foreword by Ian Bent		*page* xi
Preface		xv
1	Music, theory and signification	1
2	Motive as sign: an analysis of the Andante	18
3	Coding of musical form: the Finale	64
4	Genre and presupposition in the Mahlerian scherzo	91
5	Musical narrative and the suicide of the symphony	133
6	Coda	166
	Bibliography	168
	Index	173

FOREWORD BY IAN BENT

Theory and analysis are in one sense reciprocals: if analysis opens up a musical structure or style to inspection, inventorying its components, identifying its connective forces, providing a description adequate to some live experience, then theory generalizes from such data, predicting what the analyst will find in other cases within a given structural or stylistic orbit, devising systems by which other works - as yet unwritten - might be generated. Conversely, if theory intuits how musical systems operate, then analysis furnishes feedback to such imaginative intuitions, rendering them more insightful. In this sense, they are like two hemispheres that fit together to form a globe (or cerebrum!), functioning deductively as investigation and abstraction, inductively as hypothesis and verification, and in practice forming a chain of alternating activities.

Professionally, on the other hand, 'theory' now denotes a whole subdiscipline of the general field of musicology. Analysis often appears to be a subordinate category within the larger activity of theory. After all, there is theory that does not require analysis. Theorists may engage in building systems or formulating strategies for use by composers; and these almost by definition have no use for analysis. Others may conduct experimental research into the sound-materials of music or the cognitive processes of the human mind, to which analysis may be wholly inappropriate. And on the other hand, historians habitually use analysis as a tool for understanding the classes of compositions — repertoires, 'outputs', 'periods', works, versions, sketches, and so forth — that they study. Professionally, then, our ideal image of twin hemispheres is replaced by an intersection: an area that exists in common between two subdisciplines. Seen from this viewpoint, analysis reciprocates in two directions: with certain kinds of theoretical inquiry, and with certain kinds of historical inquiry. In the former case, analysis has tended to be used in rather orthodox modes, in the latter in a more eclectic fashion; but that does not mean that analysis in the service of theory is necessarily more exact, more 'scientific', than analysis in the service of history.

The above epistemological excursion is by no means irrelevant to the present series. Cambridge Studies in Music Theory and Analysis is intended to present the work of theories and of analysts. It has been designed to include 'pure' theory –

that is, theoretical formulation with a minimum of analytical exemplification; 'pure' analysis – that is, practical analysis with a minimum of theoretical underpinning; and writings that fall at points along the spectrum between the two extremes. In these capacities, it aims to illuminate music as work and process.

However, theory and analysis are not the exclusive preserves of the present day. As subjects in their own right they are diachronic. The former is coeval with the very study of music itself, and extends far beyond the confines of Western culture; the latter, defined broadly, has several centuries of past practice. Moreover, they have been dynamic, not static fields throughout their histories. Consequently, studying earlier music through the eyes of its own contemporary theory helps us to escape (when we need to, not that we should make a dogma out of it) from the preconceptions of our own age. Studying earlier analyses does this too, and in a particularly sharply focused way; at the same time it gives us the opportunity to re-evaluate past analytical methods for present purposes, such as is happening currently, for example, with the long-despised hermeneutic analysis of the late nineteenth century. The series thus includes editions and translations of major works of past theory, and also studies in the history of theory.

The very notion of a semiotic analysis of Mahler's Sixth Symphony seems a contradiction in terms. How could a work in four such mighty movements, a work so extensive and so massive in its sonic fabric, yield up its secrets to a method that we associate with single lines and tiny time-spans? The answer lies in both the character of the analysis and the nature of the overall enterprise.

As to the analysis: to be sure, the apparatus commonly associated with semiotics – segmental arrays, tables of occurrences, paradigmatic indices, parallel music examples, and the like – is to be found here. And yet the reader is never overwhelmed by them, for Samuels communicates by other means as well. For a start, he uses motivic music examples, voice-leading graphs, and form-analytical tables, though not in order to dilute or popularize his semiotic method, nor yet to engage in 'multiple methodologies', but always to deepen and intensify the semiotic reading itself. More to the point, he constructs a sustained verbal discourse that leads irresistibly from beginning to end of the volume, through five highly differentiated yet intimately interlinked chapters, engaging with each of the salient issues of this problematic musical structure in turn and bringing all of them forward to his conclusion.

Samuels' analysis reaches steadily outwards as it proceeds. It takes particular musical events and looks at them within a series of ever larger contexts: their immediate surroundings, the broader settings of section, movement and symphony, the Mahlerian symphonic output as a whole, the stock of material that constituted musical consciousness at Mahler's time, and the totality of contemporaneous extramusical consciousness. In technical terms, it looks at events 'intratextually', and then 'intertextually' in increasing orbits of reference, ultimately situating the work within 'cultural intertexts'. The outcome is a narrative analysis of the Sixth Symphony which does not (to use Samuels' words) 'claim to have discovered

Mahler's intended "programme" for the symphony, nor even an unconscious programme latent within the musical text and waiting to be discovered'.

As to the nature of the enterprise: Robert Samuels' discourse takes the reader on a voyage of discovery that goes beyond Mahler's music to explore the signifying power of music itself, grappling with such fascinating and troublesome concepts as the personal musical language-pattern distinctive to a given composer (idiolect), genre in music, irony, parody, cliché and kitsch in music, and the capacity of music to carry multiplicity of meaning (polysemy). It treats musical works as texts, and sees them as located within the network of relationships that constitutes all cultural products. In the course of the journey, it enlarges the domain of musical semiotics, situating narrative within it as one of its 'codes'. With its stylish prose and its many eloquent descriptions of music, it makes an adventurous read.

Ian Bent

PREFACE

This book has been a very long time in the making. The debts, both personal and professional, to which it bears witness can neither be adequately repaid or enumerated. Those who have commented on the ideas or text of individual chapters include Kofi Agawu, Andrew Brown, Geoffrey Chew, Jonathan Dunsby, Jean-Jacques Nattiez, Alan Street, Alastair Williams and John Williamson. I also owe thanks to Paul and Christine Banks; Henri-Louis de La Grange and the Bibliothèque Gustav Mahler, Paris; Stephen Watson of Skate Press, Cambridge, for the creation of the font for the rhythmic notation within the text; and all my colleagues at Lancaster University.

Three people above all others have, however, ensured that this labour has finally come to its end. The first is the supervisor of the doctoral dissertation from which this book sprang, Derrick Puffett, whose encouragement and acutely perceptive comments were constant throughout the time I was his student. The second is Anthony Pople, who has not only commented on the text, but has also, as my Head of Department, greatly helped me to assign to it the time needed for its completion. Lastly, of course, I cannot begin to describe the part played by Alison over the years that we have both lived with this project. Without her, the best of what follows would not have been written at all.

1

MUSIC, THEORY AND SIGNIFICATION

Analysis of music, at least in the century or so of its modern history as an intellectual discipline, has tended to assume that musical works can and do bear meaning. The definition of what sort of meaning this might be, however, has been neglected, perhaps from a fear of the aesthetic and epistemological complications that the issue raises. Comparisons of music with language, or of music with literature, have only recently advanced beyond the simple mapping of the terms of description of one sort of human expression onto another, without first establishing the grounds on which the comparison can be made. However, the body of thought which has sought to define a general theory of signification (that is, structuralist and post-structuralist semiotics) has often found it difficult to deal with music as an instance of a mode of human communication. Musical works seem by turns to be anomalous amongst the arts because of their lack of linguistic articulation and referential content, or to hold the key to understanding the intractable questions of deconstructive intertextuality. It is no accident that on the one hand, Paul de Man's famous discussion of Jacques Derrida's epistemology, 'The Rhetoric of Blindness', should rely on music as a metaphor for textual signification (de Man 1983: 126-31); nor that on the other hand, there is no discussion of an individual musical work to be found anywhere amongst Derrida's or de Man's essays.

This book is a semiotic study, in the sense that it seeks to define a theory of music analysis which is based on the premise that music can be considered as a system of signs. The definition of what constitutes a musical sign, however, and therefore in what sense music can be said to communicate, is a topic which has attracted the attention of numerous theorists in the twenty-five years or so that semiotics has been the subject of musicological investigation. The purpose of this chapter is to set out the model of semiotic theory which is the basis of the method used in the remainder of the study. Therefore, a general understanding of sign functioning is detailed first, which is then compared with attempts to forge a specifically musical semiotics. Finally, a methodological model is proposed for the analysis which is to follow.

This book is also a monograph on Mahler's Sixth Symphony, a work whose size and complexity make it a daunting prospect for any attempt at systematic analysis. Finished in 1904, it is the most unremittingly bleak of the symphonies. The contrast between its mood and the personal happiness of the recently married composer during the summers in which he wrote it has always puzzled enthusiasts; perhaps as a result, several of Alma Mahler's anecdotes concerning the score have come to have prominent places in the 'Mahler myth' via endless recounting in biographies, programme notes and record sleeves. Every Mahlerian can enumerate the three 'blows of Fate' which befell Mahler in the year following the première of the Sixth (actually three years and two symphonies after its composition), mirroring (to Alma's mind, at least) the three hammer-blows notated in the Finale. Others of Alma's stories include the account of Mahler's distress after that première, when he was reportedly found wringing his hands and asking, 'What have I done?' Perhaps the most poignant interpretative narrative is Alma's assertion that the irregularly barred Trio sections of the Scherzo depict the games played by their children on the shore of the lake where they spent the summers.

The point of reminding the reader of these stories is not to suggest that the game of analysis-by-biography is justified. They do, however, gesture towards the gap between description of musical process (harmony, melody and so forth) and description of the communicative potential of the work. This study arose from an initial desire to explain the tremendously powerful effect that the Symphony has always exerted on listeners, and to explain this effect in terms that could address both the sequence of notes on the page and the accumulation of programmatic anecdote and interpretation that has surrounded it. It is, ultimately, a comment on the achievement of *fin-de-siècle* art that this project has entailed the theoretical framework which is detailed below.

THEORIES OF THE SIGN: SAUSSURE, PEIRCE, ECO

The body of contemporary theory known as semiotics can be held to begin with the ideas of Ferdinand de Saussure and Charles Saunders Peirce. Although contemporaries, they produced their work in isolation from each other, and much of the subsequently tangled history of semiotic theory derives from these twin origins, in Switzerland and America, and from the fact that in the case of both men, their influence has been almost entirely posthumous. Saussure began with the project of comparative linguistics, and his *Cours de linguistique générale* is concerned primarily with the study of language as a symbolic system; this science Saussure called 'sémiologie'. Peirce, by contrast, who preferred the term 'semeiotic', attempted the definition of a general theory of signs, in which language has no privileged place, being only one of the most complex of many instances of modes of communication.

Saussure defines the sign as the union of signifier (*signifiant*) and signified (*signifié*). Immediately, there is an important difference between this and previous linguistic theories. Instead of a set of objects and concepts located in the world (or the human consciousness), and a range of possible vocal sounds which can label them, Saussure conceives of both the linguistic materials and the perceived phenomena as undifferentiated before the advent of language. The linguistic sign 'simultaneously cuts into both planes' to create meaning (Saussure 1916: 120). The 'cutting up' of the 'plane of content' and the 'plane of expression' proceeds by the creation of a system of oppositions and relations in each. The relativity introduced to the study of language by this move is the radical feature of Saussure's theory. The idea that the relation between a word and its object is arbitrary can be found in Plato; but the idea that meaning itself *only* exists in virtue of the relations between things is entirely new. 'In language, there are only differences, without positive terms', Saussure writes (1916: 166). This reverses the relation between language and experience: the fact that the Inuit have four different words for 'snow' means that a range of conceptual oppositions are available to them which are not present in English.

Saussure's basic armoury of concepts proceeds in binary oppositions. First, he distinguishes 'synchronic' analysis from 'diachronic'. Synchronic analysis attempts to reconstruct the totality of relations between signifiers in a system at a given moment of time; diachronic analysis traces the evolution of signifiers through time. Secondly, language exists both as an abstract system of rules, which Saussure terms 'langue', and as particular instances of spoken or written utterance, which he terms 'parole'. Thirdly, the analysis of language must be both 'paradigmatic' and 'syntagmatic'. Paradigms are groups of signs which may theoretically substitute for one another, whereas syntagms are allowable ('grammatical') sequences of signs. All of these terms have passed into the vocabulary of semiotic analysis.

Peirce's formulation of sign function is slightly different. In place of *signifiant* and *signifié*, he uses the terms 'representamen' and 'object'; and he invents a third term, the 'interpretant', to name the component of the sign which acts to unite the two halves of the Saussurean opposition. Conceptually, these three elements of the sign have the same epistemological status, and they are even interchangeable. The most famous consequence of this is Peirce's recognition that an interpretant may come to function as a representamen in a new sign, requiring an interpretant in its own right. The concept of the 'interpretant' is crucial in this model, for it names the element in the process of creating meaning which is omitted by Saussure. Peirce insists that meaning is created by the receiver of the message, rather than being self-evident; we 'make sense' of a text. In this, Saussure agrees. But Peirce also realises that, as soon as this third component is created, it can in turn be taken up in a new process of making meaning.

An example may help here. The word 'snow' was discussed above as being united, in English, with a certain sort of precipitation (indeed, a range of different sorts of precipitation). That brief discussion is an interpretant which unites the representamen 'snow' with an object (a range of sorts of precipitation). In the present paragraph, I return to this example to explain that it illustrates a certain technical point; so that now, the earlier passage is no longer an interpretant, but a representamen held to refer to a new object (the theoretical concept of Peirce's triangle). This process can clearly be repeated *ad infinitum*.

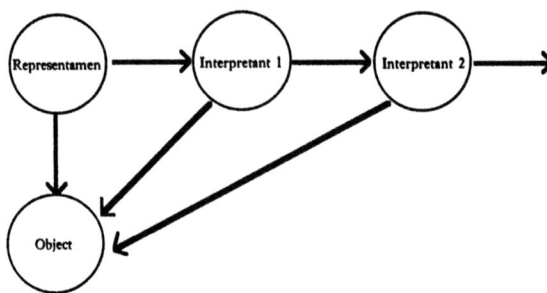

Figure 1.1

This never-ending sequence of interpretants leads to 'unclosed semiosis', summed up in Peirce's diagram given as figure 1.1.

Throughout this book, the term 'interpretant' will always be used in this specifically Peircean sense, although the terms 'representamen' and 'object' will generally be replaced by 'signifier' and 'signified'. Peirce's definition of the interpretant is a theoretical notion which has had far-reaching ramifications. It relativises the concept of truth itself, since it implies that no fixed, final meaning can ever be established except by an arbitrary closure of this process. Peirce's claim that 'man is a sign' leads ultimately to the post-structuralist claim that 'the world is the general text'. Writing always engenders more writing; the refusal to accept this fact of human communication is called 'ideology' by Derrida and other analysts of the textual nature of meaning. On the other hand, the assertion that all meaning is susceptible to further interpretation does not imply that meaning disappears altogether. The lack of a final, definitive reading sharpens the conflict between ideologically motivated analyses. Jonathan Culler explains:

> While it does enjoin scepticism about possibilities of arresting meaning, of discovering a meaning that lies outside of and governs the play of signs in a text, it does not propose indeterminacy of meaning in the usual sense: the impossibility or unjustifiability of choosing one meaning over another. On the contrary, it is only because there may be excellent reasons for choosing one meaning over another that there is any point in insisting that the meaning chosen is itself also a signifier that can be interpreted in turn. (1983: 189)

On the face of it, this description of the semiotic process should be eminently transferable to the discussion of music. The unfixed, endlessly fluid possibilities of connection and substitution between musical motives, for example, are not unlike Peirce's unclosed triangle. However, this merely locates the problem of assigning meaning to music within the larger problem of assigning meaning to utterances in general. It does nothing to suggest how to make the decision as to what constitutes a musical representamen or signifier. This perhaps accounts for the relatively late interest in semiotics on the part of musicologists; as Umberto Eco comments, 'until a few years ago contemporary musicology had scarcely been influenced by the current structuralist studies, which are concerned with methods and themes that it had absorbed centuries ago' (1977: 10).

The observation, however, that the value of a musical unit is determined by its relationships to others within the work and style in hand, creates a problem if it is taken to exemplify Saussurean relativism. If music is treated as 'pure structure', in the way that Eco seems to imply here, then it is unable to signify beyond itself. Yet this is a disappointing conclusion for the music analyst. The technical armoury of Schenkerian voice-leading, pitch-class set theory, and other analytical systems have developed powerful means for describing musical structure: what one might term the 'syntactics' of music. But the positivism of such twentieth-century approaches has also led to a search for modes of analysis which have more to say concerning music's capacity to communicate. More to say, in other words, about its function as a genuine system of articulated signs. Joseph Kerman's plea for a more 'humane' approach to analysis (Kerman 1981) is a notable example of the conviction that there must be ways of uniting musical structure with human signification without returning to the nineteenth-century aesthetic of expression.

This is the possibility held out by the semiotics of music. If musical signs can be identified, and their signifying structures brought to light, then the concern for a 'correct' reading of structure which is so much a feature of Anglo-American analysis can be replaced by a more open-ended inquiry into the possible multiple meanings which the musical text can carry. Most importantly, such a project seeks to unite the two, in order to give an account of how meaning arises from structures immanent to the work.

From the start, there have been several methods by which a semiotic inquiry may proceed. Culler summarises the difference between Saussure and Peirce thus:

By conceiving semiotics on the model of linguistics, Saussure gave it a practical programme, at the cost of begging important questions about the similarities between linguistic and non-linguistic signs that would eventually lead to a critique of his model. But by attempting to construct an autonomous semiotics, Peirce condemned himself to taxonomic speculations that denied him any influence until semiotics was so well developed that his obsession seemed appropriate. (Culler 1981: 23)

Both practical and theoretical elaborations of semiotic method have left a plethora of technical terms and diverse applications which has touched every one of the human sciences. Not only language, but other cultural systems such as fashion, advertising or tourism can be treated as semiotic. In addition, the definition of what constitutes a 'text' widens to obliterate the traditional boundaries between forms of writing. Literature, philosophy and history become part of the general enterprise of studying the articulation of human experience. In order to assess the place of music in this field, it is necessary to elaborate the concepts of Saussure and Peirce a little further. The theory which presents the most useful definition of a semiotic method, for the purposes of this study, is that of Umberto Eco.

Eco's *Theory of Semiotics* (1977) is one of the most sustained expositions of a general theory of signs. Central to his thought is the concept of the 'code'. In earlier theory, the code is the body of knowledge that the receiver of a semiotic message must possess to be a competent user of the system. This idea is found, for instance, in Georges Mounin's *Introduction à la sémiologie* (1970). Mounin emphasises a lexical attitude to language, in which the meaning of a signifier is 'decoded' and therefore mastered; an example would be the meaning of a road sign understood by looking it up in the highway code. Taken to its logical conclusion, this produces the rather silly view that literature, for instance, is not a system of signs, because it cannot be decoded in this way (this is pointed out by Culler, 1975: 20). Eco refines the term significantly, by describing the structured articulation of all three components of the Peircean sign as codes. Meaning is produced by the 'play of two systems of differences', which the user of a semiotic system creates. Eco calls these systems of differences 's-codes', which he divides into four types:

1 elements coordinated by internal rules: a 'syntactic system.'
2 elements coordinated on a plane of content.
3 a set of behavioural responses.
4 combinations of a syntactic system with 2 or 3.

The term 's-code' is one which will recur in this book. It denotes any collection of objects, ideas, musical stimuli or whatever that can be grouped together and described as structured in some way. Thus a harmonic structure, a pattern of motivic repetition, a given musical form and an explanatory narrative can all be described as arising from s-codes of different sorts. An associated term is the 'seme', which denotes any individual element within an s-code (such as a chord or motive). The appeal of the s-code as a theoretical concept is that it is tremendously flexible, making no distinction in principle between the sorts of things that can be taken as signifiers and those which can function as signifieds. Eco's intention is to 'empty' the notion of the sign altogether. Meaning arises from the 'sign-function' that a term derives from the play between s-codes, and the receiver of a message must engage in 'sign production', by bringing her own s-code into relation with the s-code of the signifier. This emphasis on the activity of 'sign production' is crucial: texts (of any sort) do not simply 'have' meaning; rather, the user of an interpreting s-code literally 'makes sense' of the text. The fact that signifiers can possess different meanings in different contexts (or for different interpreters) is no longer a problem from this perspective: 'the value [of a sign] resides in the nature of the coding correlation which a given code establishes' (Eco 1977: 42). This has led to a concern in recent theory with the study of what Michael Riffaterre calls 'text production' (Riffaterre 1979). The idea that the text has to be constructed by the reader, rather than existing as an already present entity, is a striking consequence of Eco's position, and one which further emphasises the role of ideology in cultural practices. In his later writings, Eco has appeared to shift ground somewhat from the denial that the concept of 'intention' is a useful one in constructing meanings (or deciding between alternative meanings) within a text. Whilst still refusing to countenance the 'intentions of the author' as legitimate grounds for preferring a given reading, he is concerned, both in *Semiotics and the Philosophy of Language* and in the recent essays in *Interpretation and Overinterpretation*, to limit the process of semiosis in certain ways. There may be infinite potential meanings to a text, but their proliferation proceeds according to specific paths (rooted, at the outset at least, in the text itself) and not entirely randomly. As Eco succinctly puts it, 'If there is something to be interpreted, the interpretation must speak of something which must be found somewhere, and in some way respected' (1992: 43). This 'something' is indicated by what Eco terms 'the intention of the text', and it serves as a warning to the more ludically minded of contemporary theorists. It gives grounds for defending the use, for instance, of knowledge about the cultural circumstances of a text's production in deciding the import of any particular signifying structure found in a text. Even authorial statements or biographical data may in fact be incorporated, as it were retrospectively, into this perspective.

To return, however, to the fluidity of Eco's 'sign production' as the basic semiotic activity: considered in this way, what is contentious in literary study seems hardly so in music. Indeed, a unique feature of music as a semiotic system is the fact that not only signifieds, but the signifiers themselves have to be constructed by the receiver of the message (the listener); all music analysis has to confront the infinitely variable possibilities for significant patterning within a score from the outset of the enterprise.

Much of Eco's *Theory of Semiotics* is devoted to an attack on the concept of the 'iconic sign'. An 'icon' is a sign with a perceptible resemblance between signifier and signified; onomatopoeia in language, or bird song in music. Eco seeks to prove that these apparently 'given', self-evident signs rest on conventional (and therefore arbitrary) coding relations just as much as other forms of sign. In other words, typologies of sign function are more important than typologies of signs themselves: the signified is fixed by the code, and not *a priori*.

Wlad Godzich comments on the importance for music semiotics of the fact that it is the code which carves out and identifies the signifiers in a semiotic text. If the s-codes of the internal organisation of a system and its 'plane of content' are not givens, but determined by the act of understanding, then meaning can genuinely arise by correlating musical signs with each other, in 'intra-s-code semiosis' (Godzich 1978: 130). Eco's own comment on music as a semiotic system follows this logic: if a musical unit signifies not only itself, but the set of its possible antecedents and consequents, then the two systems of differences required by the semiotician are identified (Eco 1977: 88). Eco does not consider music in any detail; nevertheless, his theory suggests that semiotic analysis of music will focus on the codes brought to bear on a piece by the listener, rather than on the structure of the work *per se*. Eco's observations on the dialectic between 'code' and 'message' are also particularly relevant to music. He points out that a message containing elements not previously used within the system can cause the code itself to be restructured. Chomsky calls this 'rule-changing' rather than 'rule-governed' activity when applied to linguistics. Eco describes the case of a message which appears to escape any existing code as requiring a '*ratio difficilis*' to interpret it. This state of affairs is familiar in music: for instance, the New Music of the Second Viennese School, which cannot be interpreted via the code of tonal organisation, nevertheless bears the marks of that code.

The general contours of a semiotic method are now a little clearer. It is necessary, however, to turn in more detail to the history of the application of semiotic thought to music before an analytical method can be constructed.

SEMIOTICS AND MUSIC

The central figure in the application of semiotics to music is Jean-Jacques Nattiez. His *Fondements d'une sémiologie de la musique* (1975) was the first extended attempt to define the field, and his theoretical position has remained recognisably the same, although much refined and adapted, since its publication. Nattiez's theory rests on the communicative chain composer → piece → listener. Analysis, he contends, must situate itself in relation to these three stages of musical production. This produces a threefold project, which he terms the 'tripartition', and which was invented by the theorist Jean Molino (see Molino 1990). The three components are: 'poietic' analysis, of the relationship of the composer to the work; 'neutral level' analysis, of structures immanent to the work; and 'esthesic' analysis of the relations of the work to the listener. These are summarised in figure 1.2.

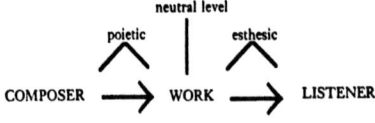

Figure 1.2

Nattiez's 'first definition' of musical semiotics gives as its aim 'to describe and to explain the nature of the *relational phenomena* which music exhibits' (Nattiez 1975: 27-8). The Augustinian *aliquid stat pro aliquo* is accepted as the universal definition of a sign. In practice, the understandable concern to be as precise in method as possible leads Nattiez to be concerned initially to describe relations only between units segmented in a given musical score. As a result, the issues of relations between musical texts, or extramusical reference, lie more or less outside the scope of his individual analyses. Although he mentions the study of compositional method as an example of poietic analysis, and refers to research into cognition as an instance of an esthesic method, the bulk of *Fondements* is taken up with the definition of the neutral level, a concept which has been much debated ever since. It remains at the centre of Nattiez's thinking, as his most recent description of the theory shows:

The symbolic form is embedded physically and materially in the form of a *trace* accessible to the five senses ... Molino proposed the name 'neutral level' or 'material level' for this trace. An objective description of the neutral level can always be proposed – in other words, an *analysis* of its immanent and recurrent properties. (1991:12)

At first glance, this seems straightforward enough. However, the attempt to bring scientific rigour ('objective description ... can always be proposed') to the musical work uncovers a theoretical problem. Nattiez is quite clear that the neutral level is a *construct* of the analyst; he has often quoted Otto Laske's description of it as a 'methodological artefact' (Laske 1977: 222, quoted for instance in Nattiez 1989: 36). As such, it comprises structures discovered by explicit procedures prior to any analytic comment, for what 'makes this descriptive level "neutral" is that the tools used in the segmentation of phenomena ... are exploited systematically to their furthest conclusion, and are exchanged only when new hypotheses or new difficulties lead to the proposal of new ones' (1975: 54).

Even in this first formulation, there is an uneasy tension between a supposedly mechanistic technique and the admission that results may modify method. The important feature of the neutral level is that it is *provisional*. It is constantly displaced, as its contours change in the course of the analysis; Nattiez even describes it as 'dirty'. Nevertheless, there is a persistent implication that, in some sense, it exists prior to its discovery by the analyst. Nattiez argues that the rigorous application of a technique of segmentation will inevitably produce units which appear not to have a poietic or esthesic function. As an example, he discusses Pierre Boulez's analysis of *The Rite of Spring*. The fact that the configurations which Boulez discovers would have been incomprehensible at the time that the work was composed does not, in Nattiez's view, invalidate the analysis: 'A certain analytical technique will uncover [*faire apparaître*] a given, circumscribed level of organisation in the musical message: *there is no a priori, definitive pertinence of the segmented configurations; there is only relative pertinence*' (1975: 406).

On the one hand, then, the neutral level is provisional and constantly displaced; but here, it appears to be 'given' and 'circumscribed'. The concept is, in fact, double: a pre-existent 'neutral level' is assumed to exist, independently of composer or listener. The analyst's 'neutral level' is a model of this, which is constantly called into question by its own findings.

Objections to the epistemological status of the neutral level have been reiterated ever since the publication of *Fondements*. Jonathan Dunsby refers to it as the 'deeply obscure aspect of Nattiez's semiotics' (1983: 31), and a systematic attack on it was first formulated by Allen Keiler (1981). Nattiez is a subtle and inventive thinker, and his reaction to these attacks has been to maintain his position via an insistence on the pragmatic nature of the tripartition. In his revision of the theory (1987, 1991), Nattiez refers scrupulously to 'the neutral level of analysis' rather than 'analysis of the neutral level', to try and avoid the objections outlined above. However, it is hard to deny that the existence of the level at all, even as a 'methodological artefact', must ultimately subscribe to what Derrida calls the 'metaphysics of presence': the belief in a plenitude of meaning within the material work. This need not, of course, be an untenable position at all; but it does indicate that Nattiez's semiotics remains an example of the classic structuralist enterprise which equates meaning with objective structure. To describe Nattiez, who began his theoretical speculations from the perspective of ethnomusicology and has frequently attested his admiration for the Belgian anthropologist Claude Lévi-Strauss, as a structuralist hardly constitutes a criticism. Derrida's development and revision of structuralism, however, deserves to be considered for its implications for such a theory.

The method represented by the neutral level is important: Nattiez is a relativist in the sense that he does not believe in any final, decidable meaning for the musical message. He rejects the idea that the last word can ever be had on the analysis of a work. But instead of accepting this as evidence for the endless deferral of meaning represented by Derrida's term *différance*, and concentrating on the vested interests present in any analytical presupposition, Nattiez constantly tries to reclaim the right to make normative judgments (see, for example, 'Analyses and truth' in Nattiez 1991: 233-8). Eco's contention, that signs are produced by the receiver of the message, is in effect an equally semiotic alternative to Nattiez's theoretical position. According to the Ecovian concept of 'sign-function', the neutral level can only ever be the product of the analyst's s-code in its engagement with the s-code of the work. Eco, too, would not deny that musical works possess structure. But the analytical discovery of this structure is always mediated. In comparing the tripartition with Peirce's semiotic triangle, Nattiez equates the neutral level with the representamen, 'which can only be grasped by interpretants distributed between the esthesic and the poietic' (1975: 57). The point is an important one. Both esthesic and poietic analysis *follow* a neutral level description, although poietic structures must be assumed to *precede* the work. In fact, all analysis is esthesic: the immanent structures of the work, and the compositional strategies that created it, can only be reconstructed after the event, according to an analytical model; hence the 'dirtiness' of the neutral level.

Although so far the discussion has been entirely theoretical, there are clear implications for analytical method in Nattiez's construction of the tripartition. Indeed, a large portion of *Music and Discourse* is concerned with describing existing analytical techniques in terms of a sixfold model that expands Molino's three categories. Nattiez's own approach to the analysis of musical detail is instructive as an attempt to reproduce the assumed objectivity and categorisation of his theory in analytical terms.

Nattiez's basic method is to attempt to segment the musical score according to strict criteria, and then derive paradigms of signifiers from the results. A method of segmentation is proposed, starting with the simplest possible criteria for recognising potential signifiers. These are then ordered according to their similarity to each other (an assumption is made that similarity indicates potential substitution). The result is generally a table of columns, each one containing a paradigm class. Consideration of the data contained in the table then leads to a refinement of the segmentation criteria, and the process starts again.

A paradigmatic approach to analysis was first attempted by Nicolas Ruwet, in the analysis of troubadour songs (1966, reprinted in Ruwet 1972 and 1987). Taking as his principle for segmentation the simplest possible criterion, that of repetition, Ruwet first identifies the largest blocks that are repeated, and then subdivides them, according to the same criterion. This method is reversed by Nattiez, who first seeks to identify small repeated units, and then moves from these to the consideration of larger structures. His most extended analysis is an essay on Varèse's *Density 21.5* (Nattiez 1982). This begins with the characterisation of the neutral level as 'a descriptive inventory containing the most exhaustive inventory possible of all types of configurations conceivably recognisable in a score' (1982: 244).

This is an enormous claim, and it engenders one of the most remarkable *tours de force* in the whole literature of musicology: 111 pages of analysis of a sixty-bar monodic flute piece. Inevitably, as Nattiez himself recognises, even this does not achieve the apparent goal quoted above. Apart from the fact that a virtually infinite number of 'configurations' can be found, the analysis has in practice constantly to rely on analytical assumptions of one sort or another. Nattiez's great achievement in this study is to render these assumptions much more explicit than was the case in earlier styles of analysis. The pertinence of symmetry, the functional equivalence of different-sized intervals, the opposition of consonant and dissonant intervals; all are invoked at some stage of the argument (as is capably, if unsympathetically, exposed by Jonathan Bernard, 1986). Furthermore, the discovery of the syntactic rules governing the piece must, as Nattiez admits, depend on some concept of style (1982: 300). However, this is not to dismiss this analysis as futile. The impracticality of adopting an approach that attempts to rid itself of presuppositions does at least show the extent to which previous analytical techniques had relied on unquestioned beliefs. The task that confronts a proposed semiotics of music is to incorporate a recognition of the need for assumptions into the analytical project, without allowing the ideological closure that those assumptions imply. The next stage of the argument in this chapter is to propose a context for analysis which adheres to these principles. This requires the return to the concept of the code found in Eco's theory.

THE CODE AS A MODEL FOR ANALYSIS

A taxonomic approach to the segmentation of paradigm classes fails in its assumption of neutrality. This suggests that it would be more profitable to begin the definition of a semiotic method for music analysis from the basis of the code brought by the listener to the work. Certain characteristics of an s-code are clear: it consists of a set of structured relations between units which carve out signifiers from the musical text. At the same time, it does not have to be shared by composer and listener in order to function. A semiotic analysis is interested in the signifying potential of the text, which does of course change in the course of its reception history. While comments made by the composer may be useful in formulating a code, they are never authoritative; they inform the listener's activity, but remain part of his esthesic information. The listener, indeed, is an indispensable theoretical construct for a semiotic music analysis, as the reader is for literary analysis. The 'death of the author' proclaimed by Roland Barthes is simultaneously the 'birth of the reader' (1977: 142-8). By asking the question of how the listener 'makes sense' of the musical work, the analysis acknowledges both the arbitrary nature of the creation of musical signs, and the existence of signifying structures within the work.

There is a famous text which attempts a thoroughgoing exposition of the codes required by a literary work, and that is Barthes' *S/Z*. It takes the form of a line-by-line analysis of *Sarrasine*, a novella by Balzac. Barthes simply divides up the text into convenient short chunks ('lexies'), and then proceeds to identify signifying units which are identified in each chunk by the codes. There is no sense of Ruwet's or Nattiez's rigour in the segmentation: 'the cutting up, admittedly, will be arbitrary in the extreme; it will imply no methodological responsibility, since it will bear on the signifier, whereas the proposed analysis bears solely on the signified' (1974: 13).

Each signifying unit constitutes a seme. Barthes proposes five codes for the analysis of the story. These are:

1 The *hermeneutic* code: this identifies enigmas, their suspense and resolution.
2 The *semic* code: this collects features of characters, objects and places, in order to recognise them. For instance, the title, 'Sarrasine', contains the seme 'femininity' in its final 'e'.
3 The *symbolic* code works in a similar way to the semic code, enabling thematic readings to be established.
4 The *proairetic* code governs the reader's construction of plot.
5 The *referential* code incorporates cultural knowledge into the text (such as trees that resemble 'the Dance of the Dead').

These codes do not appear to be exhaustive (see Culler 1983: 33-5, and chapter 5 below), and neither do they suggest a direct adoption into music. It is notable, however, that Barthes turns to the metaphor of the orchestra in order to describe how they work, even using music notation in a diagram representing the interplay of the codes as the 'full score' of the text (Barthes 1974: 28-30). The basic point is that the codes operate simultaneously, although each has a course in the work that can be charted individually, like an instrument in an orchestra. An important distinction drawn by Barthes is that between 'sequential' and 'non-sequential' codes: 'We can attribute to two lines of the polyphonic table (the hermeneutic and the proairetic) the same tonal determination that melody and harmony have in classical music; the readerly text is a *tonal* text ... and its tonal unity is basically dependent on two sequential codes' (1970: 29-30).

The point is a simple one: some codes rely on the order in which events occur to make sense (a character cannot be rescued, for instance, before being captured). Others do not: we build up a picture of someone's moral character, for example, by collecting together descriptions of them wherever they occur in the text. These second sorts of code are described as non-sequential. One of the most important things about identifying these latter is the way in which meaning is created, as it were, in fragments scattered through the text which the reader brings together.

A sequential code, such as the construction of plot, reinforces the integrity of the narrative. Codes whose signifiers refer irrespective of their sequence (as cultural reference does in literature, or motivic working in music), tend to undercut the 'readability' of the text. The ultimate consequence of privileging non-sequential codes is in the modernist novelist, such as James Joyce, whose texts force their reader into an act of construction, or writing. Barthes terms these 'writerly' texts, 'textes scriptibles', rather than the classic 'readerly' texts, 'textes lisibles', of the nineteenth-century realist novel.

This is an extremely suggestive approach to the analysis of a text. For one thing, it gives a context for considering previous methods of analysis: these amount to partial representations of the text, whose selectivity indicates ideological choice. In the realm of music, the obvious example of this is a Schenkerian voice-leading graph. This amounts to a sequential code, and the insistence by Schenker on the primacy of tonal structure as evidence of aesthetic worth is a result of this particular view of semiotic hierarchy. Barthes' study is extremely subtle. On the one hand, it appears to be a scientistic, even positivistic method, which comments on every single word of the novella in turn; and on the other, its real theoretical substance is arguably found not in the paragraphs of commentary, but in the asides and excurses on the nature of signs that alternate with the analysis of the 'lexies'. And the effect of this complete analysis is paradoxical. Time and again Barthes indicates moments of fissure or unclosure in the text, especially in the action of the non-sequential codes. It is as if the self-imposed discipline of accounting for a completed work impels him to find it unfinished. In particular, the code foregrounds the intertextual nature of meaning: the story relies for its coherence on texts outside itself. This is a situation common to story and reader: ' "*I*" is not an innocent subject that is anterior to texts ... the *I* that approaches the text is itself already a plurality of other texts, of infinite or, more precisely, lost codes (whose origins are lost)' (1970: 16).

Perhaps the most significant aspect of the method employed in *S/Z* is that Barthes never used it again. The adoption of an arch-structuralist objectivity is a role assumed by Barthes, to be understood alongside the many different methodologies adopted by him in other texts. The use of the code as a tool for analysis serves to emphasise the textuality of the story. In the analysis of music, too, one should expect to discover the limit points of codes, the moments of excess or absence in the musical text that reflect its temporal and textual nature. A piece of music is an event that happens to the listener, not an 'object to be dismantled or a site to be occupied', to use Barthes' phrase in *S/Z*. The code serves both to articulate the experience of listening to music, and to resist the hypostatisation of form that is a consequence of positivistic analysis.

With these considerations in mind, it is time to turn to the question of analytical procedure. It is clear by this stage that semiotics does not constitute an analytical method. It is, rather, an orientation for analysis, a kind of 'meta-analytical' discourse. If the idea of the code is made primary in the analysis of music, and if the code dictates the segmentation of musical signs, then it follows that different analytical techniques will become appropriate in the context of different codes. The example mentioned above, of a voice-leading graph, indicates that the results of existing analytical techniques can be made to serve new ends.

The crucial decision concerns what is taken to constitute a code. Several recent studies have addressed this issue in some form. The solution of both Robert Hatten's and William Dougherty's explicitly semiotic studies is to define codes in terms of stylistic procedures. Hatten uses an opposition between what he terms 'style' and 'strategy'. Style consists of elements such as scales, rhythms, and harmonic rules, which are organised oppositionally. Strategy, on the other hand, is the specific configuration deployed within a piece. Thus a work will generally be 'in' a style, but at the same time play 'against' it strategically (Hatten 1982). Whilst this dialectic accounts for much of the signifying process of works, it does not easily enable music to be considered in a genuinely intertextual manner, as a 'mode of signification' to be considered alongside other means of cultural production. What is needed is a conceptualisation that can more easily incorporate codes made up of extramusical structures.

One way of distinguishing between Barthes' codes in *S/Z* is in their scope of reference. The hermeneutic code clearly refers only within the text in hand, while the proairetic makes use of concepts of plot archetype drawn from the history of the novel as a genre. The broadest range of reference is that of the referential code, which creates interpretants outside the text altogether.

To generalise from this, a semiotic theory capable of addressing the question of musical signification needs to define referential codes according to the size of the body of texts which their operation presupposes. This might be termed their 'signifying scope', with one extreme represented by features which refer only to a part of the work in hand (or, indeed, are unique, unrepeated occurrences), and the other extreme represented by universal or near-universal reference (examples might be the Schoenbergian 'basic motive' or the Schenkerian *Ursatz*). There is a general progression from 'introversive semiosis', finding relations within the work in hand, to 'extroversive semiosis', which relates the work to an intertextual space.

A precedent for this model does indeed exist, in the work of Gino Stefani (especially Stefani 1987 and 1989). He also arranges codes in order of referential scope, and recognises that these codes overlap: in fact, the process of attaining musical competence is one of applying the codes successively. Stefani describes the codes he identifies as follows (the list is taken from Stefani 1989: 8):

1 The general code: made up of perceptual schemes, the 'universals' of music.
2 The code of social practices: language, religion etc.
3 Musical techniques: scales, tonality, formal repertoire, etc.
4 Styles: individual composers, periods of common practice.
5 Opus: the work in hand.

The shortcoming of this model is that it presents the codes as discrete (although overlapping) entities: the boundaries of reference are fixed in advance. The model of *S/Z* implies that the delimitation of the code is not a pre-ordained category, and Eco's concept of 'sign production' suggests that the responsibility for the very creation of the codes themselves resides with the listener rather than the composer, or even the compositional tradition.

To sum up, the semiotic theory which will direct the following analyses proposes that, for music as a signifying system, the listener engages in a sign-producing activity which consists of delimiting semiotic codes according to different ranges of reference amongst potential signifying units. In other words, not only the codes, but the signs themselves are created by the act of listening. A given 'signifying scope' creates a certain sort of signifying unit within the musical text, and hence a certain sort of structure. Thus the consideration of different sorts of musical signification will demand varying analytical techniques in order to 'produce the text', and will give rise to multiple structures according to the code suggested.

In general, then, the analytical method for the following chapters will follow the following pattern: first, a certain sort of coding strategy on the part of the listener will be suggested; then potential signifying units for such a code will be identified as rigorously as possible; finally, the resulting structure will be examined as a semiotic phenomenon. Before specific codes are suggested and these decisions justified, however, it is necessary to examine in more detail the choice of Mahler's Sixth Symphony as a test case for this enterprise.

SEMIOTICS AND MAHLER

Mahler is the natural choice for the project of developing a broad conception of semiotic analysis for several reasons. Firstly, there is a marked difference in scale between the sixty bars of solo flute that make up *Density 21.5*, and the enormous score, lasting well over an hour in performance, of Mahler's Sixth Symphony. Added to this is the undoubted semiotic richness of the work: commentators on Mahler, both supporters and detractors, have always been able to find distinctive features in the score to support their claims. A Mahler symphony is so complex, indeed, that an approach based on the general issues of musical meaning and the musical articulation of experience is the only mode of analysis that can hope to unite discussion of musical detail with an overall view of the work. Finally, the reception history of Mahler's works testifies to their ability to find value in the postmodern culture that seems remarkably distant from their origin in *fin-de-siècle* Vienna. From work cycles in major concert halls, to their appearance in the novels of Milan Kundera, the ability of Mahler's symphonies to bear out the composer's dictum, 'My time will come', is quite astonishing. Whatever else this proves, the signifying potential of the works cannot be doubted. Within this general context, the Sixth Symphony stands out as an ideal candidate for study. In common with the other middle-period instrumental symphonies, it also shows a conscious engagement with music of the past, which provides many points of departure for considering its potential as a signifying structure.

Before progressing to the consideration of the Sixth Symphony, however, it is necessary to take account of a theorist whose name will recur throughout the following chapters. This is Theodor Adorno, whose monograph on Mahler (1960) has been a touchstone of criticism ever since its publication. Adorno's ability to anticipate critical fashion is truly uncanny; to read his comments from a semiotician's perspective is to be impressed time and again with the sureness of his instincts concerning the large issues of meaning and cultural value invoked by the music. Adorno's discussion of the score itself is always limited, drawing on a fairly ordinary stock of motivic and thematic analytical techniques. But his interpretive comments, which initially seem to be wild extrapolations of philosophical import, rest on exactly the sort of referential nexus identified in the previous section of this chapter.

A particular example of this is Adorno's construction of a typology of Mahlerian form. He identifies three characteristic devices, which he labels 'Breakthrough' (*Durchbruch*), 'Suspension' (*Suspension*), and 'Fulfilment' (*Erfühlung*). Breakthrough refers to the sense of arrival or epiphany which represents a Utopian image of integration (Adorno's first example is the end of the introduction to the First Symphony). This can be created in many different ways, including the use of orchestration (as in this example); but its semiotic definition has to do with the confrontation of the music with material which appears to come from 'outside' it. Suspension, by contrast, refers to those passages of 'musical prose' (to use Schoenberg's term) which abandon metre to give the illusion of the arrested progress of time. Fulfilment, finally, is used in the sense of culmination which does not give in to the 'inauthentic' representation of a wholeness not justified by the course of the music. Adorno's terms are typical of his method: they illuminate sparse moments of the works whilst invoking a global critique of Mahler's 'metamusical' preoccupations. The philosophical and the analytical are inseparable in Adorno's method. What is frustrating about his discussion is that the criteria for the recognition of the formal types are extremely informal. To bring a greater degree of methodological consistency to such comments is one of the projects made possible by a semiotic analysis.

Because the central concern of this book is the investigation of musical signification within the Sixth Symphony, it would be inappropriate simply to discuss each movement of the work in the order in which they are played in performance. The arrangement of the following chapters is therefore based on a succession of coding strategies, moving from introversive to extroversive reference. Chapter 2 considers motivic organisation, in a way not dissimilar to the paradigmatic analysis of melody by Ruwet and Nattiez. Chapter 3 compares immanent structures with coded expectations, in a consideration of issues of form. This implicit comparison with other works continues in chapter 4, which investigates genre. Finally, chapter 5 addresses the relationship of the work to wholly cultural signifieds, by confronting the question of musical narrative.

This arrangement means that, although each chapter focuses on a different movement, these are not discussed in order. Neither is there any claim that this study constitutes a complete discussion of the work. At every turn, the inquiry finds multiple and interrelated structures. This introductory chapter has been intentionally brief, because it is a methodological premise of this study that specific analytical techniques, and the theory that articulates them, can only arise in the context of confrontation with the individual work. Whilst a range of techniques is used, including Schenkerian graphs and Schoenbergian motivic annotation, the concern throughout the study is to identify the articulation of signs that gives each code its signifying power.

2

MOTIVE AS SIGN: AN ANALYSIS OF THE ANDANTE

Like several other of Mahler's symphonic slow movements, the Andante of the Sixth Symphony appears isolated from the rest of the work. Its tonality, melodic profile and mood (for want of a better term) all oppose the content of the other three movements, and in addition exhibit a closure of gesture which encourages the view of the movement as almost a separable *Charakterstück*. This isolation, which to some extent could be remarked in the Adagietto of the Fifth Symphony or the *Nachtmusiken* of the Seventh, is the more noticeable because of the high degree of cross-reference and gestural unclosure in the first movement, Scherzo and Finale. There is a clear connection between the Andante and the compositional methods of the *Kindertotenlieder* and *Rückert-Lieder*, a comparison which is explicitly betrayed by the occurrence of a cadential figure from the song *Nun will die Sonn' so hell aufgeh'n* at the end of the opening melody (bar 9). Although this song is not entirely autonomous (the *Kindertotenlieder* are constructed as a genuine 'multi-piece'), the self-containment of the symphonic song or song-cycle genre is clearly a referent of the symphonic slow movement.

There are, of course, many ways in which the Andante can be accommodated to a narrative of the work as a whole, and indeed even the explicit connections between it and the other movements are more numerous than at first seems the case. The choice of key, a tritone away from the A of the other movements and in the major mode rather than the minor, seems a self-conscious choice of opposition, and hence connection, to the rest of the Symphony. However, this is to run ahead of the methods of this study; these issues will be addressed in chapters 4 and 5. It is the relative autonomy of the movement that makes the Andante the ideal starting-point for the investigation of semiotic codes in the Sixth Symphony. This chapter will consider the production of signs which are composed entirely of signifiers with a material trace — in other words, structures of pitch, duration, timbre and so forth — and whose referential scope is entirely 'intramusical', and initially even 'intratextual', requiring no interpretant (to use Peirce's term) drawn from outside the work in hand.

The most often-discussed musical process which fulfils these criteria is, of course, that of motivic repetition and development. A motivic analysis will identify motives within the musical text, derive them from each other, and assign value to the patterns of recurrence and deviation which result. The signs so constructed are held to refer within the text itself, or possibly to an ideal motivic shape that may

Motive as sign: the Andante

be inferred from the text (Schoenberg's *Grundgestalt*); the pattern of motivic repetition may also become a signifier of an extramusical idea (most obviously, for Schoenberg at least, that of 'unity').

The problem with Schoenberg's own writings, for a semiotic analysis of motive, is their informality. His own definition of what constitutes a 'motive' is variable; from 'any rhythmicized succession of notes' in *Fundamentals of Musical Composition* (1967: 9), to 'certain parts [of a piece of music], the smallest, which always recur' in the essay 'Problems of Harmony' (1975: 279), to the example of an analysis such as that in 'Brahms the Progressive', where the motives appear to be entirely intervallic (1975: 398-441). This is because the 'unity, relationship, coherence, logic, comprehensibility and fluency' (Schoenberg 1967: 8), which are held to be the result of motivic integration in any given piece, are actually believed to be present before the analysis begins; the purpose of extracting motives from the text is to demonstrate something which is already known, namely its structural coherence and (hence) aesthetic worth. For this reason, the abstract concepts of *Grundgestalt* and, indeed, *Gedank* are never fully defined; they are analytical hypotheses created to investigate compositional practice (this point is lucidly discussed by David Epstein, 1979: 17-21, and Alexander Goehr, 1982). In terms of a semiotic description of the analytical process, this theoretical prejudice might just be seen as a strong conception of sign production. But the method is too partial in its operation: it is not possible to separate the analytical and aesthetic presuppositions of the analyst from the empirical data to which they refer. Indeed, this is what makes it justifiable to claim that more can be learned about Schoenberg than about Brahms from the analysis of the String Quartet Op. 51, no. 2 referred to above. If the working of a genuinely semiotic code is to be identified, then the structures within the work which are to be taken as signifiers must be identified according to explicit criteria before the consequences of applying different interpretants to them are assessed.

Having said that, it is not practicable to attempt to account for every conceivable intervallic or rhythmic pattern in any relatively complex piece of music, and certainly not in a movement of a Mahler symphony. The 111 pages of Nattiez's analysis of *Density 21.5* are more a warning than a model for the would-be semiotic analyst. For this reason the analyses in this chapter are complete, but not exhaustive. In other words, each paradigmatic table includes every musical pattern that fulfils the criteria for that table, but the tables in aggregate do not attempt to cover even every note of the movement once, let alone 'all types of configurations conceivably recognizable' in the score (Nattiez 1982: 244). A process of selection is therefore made before a paradigmatic analysis is attempted; but this process carries no interpretive weight in regard to the information generated.

PARADIGMATIC ANALYSIS OF MOTIVE

For the purposes of this chapter, the term 'motive' is used to refer to musical features that can be organised non-sequentially according to recurrence. That is, the differences and similarities between discrete musical units are ordered in paradigm classes according to explicit criteria. Concepts such as motivic transformation or development are not used, in order to avoid the prejudgments inherent in Schoenberg's metaphors of organic growth. This relatively wide definition of motive accords with Barthes' definition of a non-sequential code, and provides the data that can justifiably be taken to constitute one of Eco's s-codes, since its extraction from the text proceeds according to explicit criteria. The starting hypothesis for the analysis is that a code which identifies motivic patterns and derives them from one another has interpretative validity in the music of this period. Such issues as the relative merits of considering surface features (rather than reductively deduced patterns) as motivic, or the importance of reference outside the work in hand, will arise in the course of the analysis. In what follows, the 'motivic code' is suggested as an analytical hypothesis along with several others also composed of structures of pitch, rhythm and so forth, with which it interacts. One such other is a 'melodic code', which identifies thematic melodic statements; this is sequential in Barthes' sense, as is a 'harmonic (or voice-leading) code', which assigns traditional harmonic and contrapuntal functions to the music. The motivic code itself can arguably be split into sub-codes, as shall be seen; but what defines it at the outset is the nature of the signification of its units, rather than their symbolic form (i.e., whether they are intervallic or rhythmic, reduced or surface features, etc.).

One problem that does not beset this form of analysis is the generation of data. As remarked above, a process of selection is necessary before a paradigmatic approach can be brought to bear on such a complex score; further, in the interests of producing tables of a manageable size, this chapter will begin by considering the first 55 bars of the Andante. The movement as a whole falls into a readily identifiable slow rondo form, in which this section forms the first A section. The interaction of motive, melody and form will be discussed at the end of this chapter. For now, the overall divisions can briefly be summarised as follows:

Section	Bars	Key	Description
A	1–55	E♭ major and G minor	small ABA form with two contrasting themes
B	56–84	mainly E minor	motivically fragmented texture
C	85–99	E major	Wagnerian pastoral (*Naturlaut*)
A	100–114	E♭ major	short middle section
B	115–145	C♯ major, A major, A minor	motivically fragmented texture
A	146–173	C minor, B minor, B major	based on themes from the A section; climax or *Höhepunkt*
A	174–201	E♭ major	coda

The first A section therefore represents roughly one quarter of the whole of the movement; and the material of what follows largely repeats or transforms what is presented within this opening. The melodic or formal organisation of these bars is relatively straightforward: an opening melody in E♭, a contrasting theme at bar 22

Motive as sign: the Andante

in G minor, and an altered return of the E♭ melody at bar 28. The section ends with unison Gs on string harmonics acting as a pivot modulation from E♭ to E minor at the double bar line (bar 56). For the analysis below, then, it is enough to note that this section presents a relatively self-contained sequence of musical material which can legitimately be considered as a group of signs.

To start with the beginning, Table 2.1 presents a paradigmatic inventory of the motive which opens the melody. Two sets of criteria have been used to construct the table: sequences of notes in the rhythm ♩ ♫ and with identical first and third pitches; and sequences of notes in the rhythm ♫ ♩♩ with identical second and third pitches. Because of the close similarity of the first occurrences of each set of motives (compare the first three entries in column II), these are taken as being part of the same signifying group.

The graph arranges the data into ten columns according to interval size and direction:

Column	Interval	Direction	No.
I	diminished seventh / augmented sixth	ascending / descending	13
II	major / minor sixth	ascending / descending	14
III	augmented fifth	ascending / descending	12
IV	perfect fifth	ascending / descending	1
V	perfect fifth	descending / ascending	7
VI	tritone	descending / ascending	2
VII	perfect fourth	ascending / descending	2
VIII	perfect fourth	descending / ascending	3
IX	major / minor third	ascending / descending	5
X	major / minor third	descending / ascending	3
			(42)

The choice of diatonic intervals reflects the notation of the piece (obviously enough), but also an assumption of diatonic equivalence; that is (for instance), it assumes that because units II-1 and II-2 are a diatonic transposition of each other, they may be taken as instances of the same paradigm, despite the fact that they contain different numbers of semitones. Where units fulfil the paradigmatic criteria for more than one column, this has been indicated by bending the column line and inserting an '=' sign (for instance, the viola line of bar 19 occurs as both V-5 and VI-5). Six units are included twice in this way, so that the true total of units in the table is 36. Literal, immediate repetitions are indicated only by two bar numbers (units II/V-18 and V/VIII-17), for economy of space. Musical material that does not fulfil the criteria of the table, but bears some resemblance to the units which do, has been included in boxes with an arrow to show the connection.

There are a few inconsistencies in the table: units II-4 and II-8 should strictly also appear in a column before column I, since they contain the interval of an octave; similarly, the unit II/V-18 should also appear in two more columns, to take account of the fact that it combines the two patterns of interval direction; these

Table 2.1

Motive as sign: the Andante

Table 2.1 (cont.)

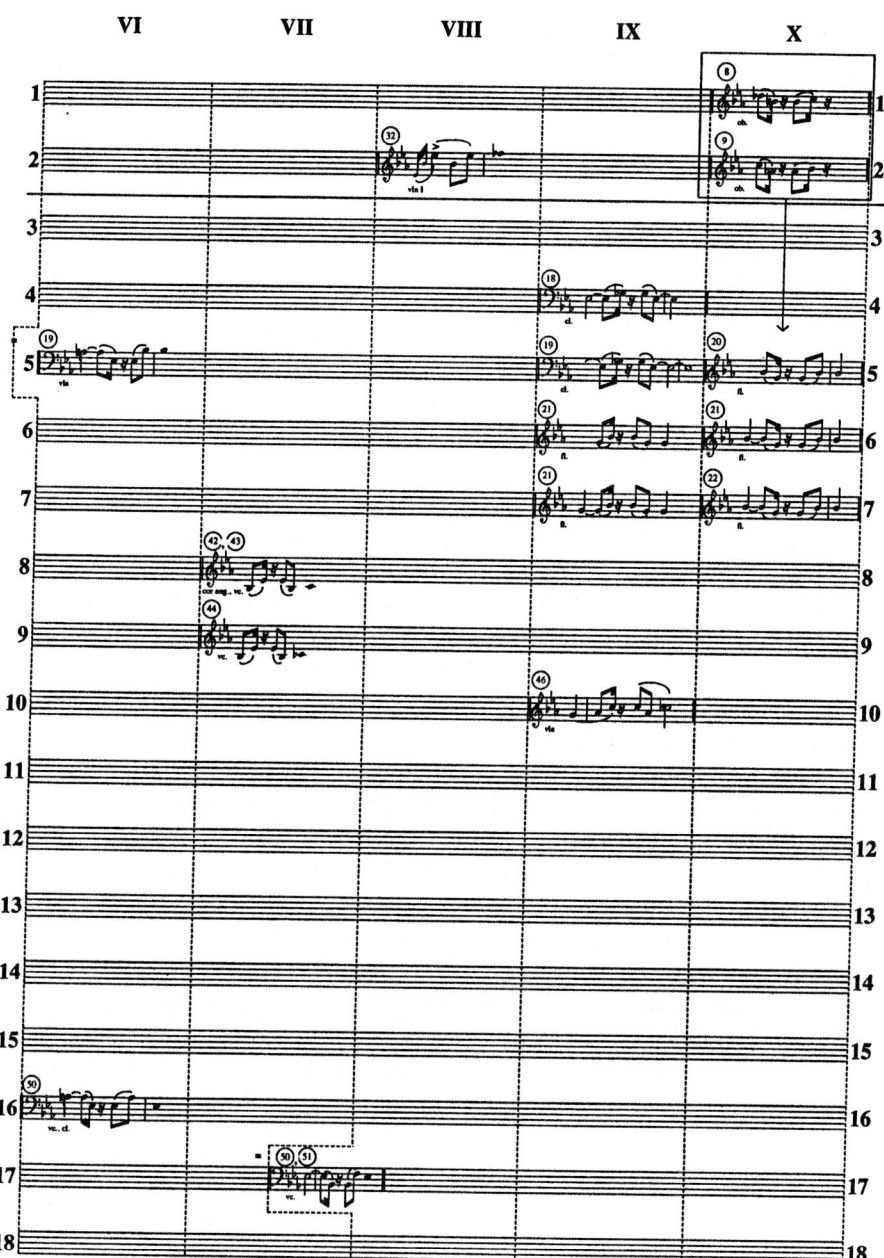

omissions are due solely to considerations of space. More marginal is the case of the oboe line at bars eight to nine (shown boxed as X-1 and X-2), which should arguably appear in a column XI, containing intervals of a diminished third and minor second, although the rhythm of these units is also slightly different from the table's criteria.

Table 2.1 is faithful to Nattiez's description of a 'provisional analysis'. A first hypothesis has been used to segment the data, and this has then been revised by the results to produce the units included in the table. Their relative ordering in sub-paradigms also reflects analytical judgments, such as the equivalence of diatonic interval class, which are made on the basis of observation of the data. This first table therefore already represents several stages of the process of 'neutral' segmentation and revision. Although it differs from Nattiez's own paradigmatic tables, these differences are mainly the result of the difference in scale between the pieces under discussion. The concept of the motivic code is not a feature of Nattiez's method; but as far as segmentation of signifiers goes, this chapter investigates signs of the same type as those proposed by Nattiez and Ruwet.

If the data contained in this table is taken to represent a single motive, then several observations may be made immediately. The relationship between the units of the upper and lower halves of the graph is easy to define: the rhythms are similar, and the interval of a sixth is prevalent in each, its fourteen occurrences accounting for 39 per cent of the units altogether. The distribution of the four units in the upper part of the graph is important: they are the opening of the melody, the opening of its consequent phrase, the opening of the contrasting melody of bar 22, and the opening of the consequent phrase of the E♭ melody at bar 32 (the rhythm is also found at the opening of this melody in bar 27: the boxed unit IV-1). The lower part of the graph shows the linking of these rhythmically identical, but motivically distinct, units to the motivic paradigm; none of the units in the lower half would be identified by the melodic code in the same way, so that the two halves of the graph represent melodic and non-melodic faces of the motive. In other words, the connection between the openings of melodic segments, which is made by the rhythm and the direction of the intervals, is elaborated by the distribution of the other motivic units, which occur mainly as accompaniment or at the ends of melodic phrases. This coincidence of distribution and semiotic coding suggests that the division of the first crotchet beat of the ♩♫ rhythm to create the ♫♪♫ of the lower half is connected with the non-sequential nature of the motivic code; the repetition of the pitch (producing a palindromic figure) reflects the fact that the lower-half units do not have a linear function. This is not only to do with the melodic code; it is further noticeable that the lower-half units tend not to be involved in part movement at the level of voice-leading. This is a good example of the way in which a semiotic analysis constantly finds points at which one code needs to invoke another to explain the distribution of the units it identifies. Here, the two interpretants both concern musical reference within the movement in hand; elsewhere, this is the mechanism by which the resort to codes of wider referential scope is necessitated by the analysis.

Clearly, the high incidence of units (36 within the first 55 bars), and their distributional importance, make this a motive whose 'signifying scope', to use the term described in chapter 1, lies primarily within this movement, and which represents the defining motivic paradigm of the Andante. If this configuration of units would be called the *Grundgestalt* by Schoenberg, its semiotic potential is confirmed by its distribution. It is also immediately tempting to look around the edges of the table, as it were, to make some observations of other motivic structures which associate themselves with this motive. The box at III-1 indicates the way in which the accompanying texture at the beginning becomes motivic if the interval of a sixth is taken to reflect the opening of the theme; this is also true of the prominent linear intervallic pattern of parallel sixths between first and second violins in the opening five bars, especially the chromatic line $G^\flat(F^\sharp)$-$G^\natural$-$A^\flat$ against $A^\natural$-$B^\flat$-$C^\flat(B^\natural)$ in bars four to five. In these cases, ordinary accompanimental or contrapuntal patterns are made motivic (literally 'motivated') by the application of an interpretive code. This is an exemplary case of the unclosed boundaries of musical semiosis; connections are multiple and unpredictable, no matter how stringent the paradigmatic criteria. Another feature tangential to this table is the number of cases of the modal opposition of major and minor thirds, or major and minor sixths, either literally or by implication in chromatic neighbour-note part movement. Some of these cases involve pairs of units which are adjacent in the score (II-3 and III-3, IX-5 and X-5, VII-8 and VII-9); others embody the opposition within a single unit (II-8, II-13 and IX-10). These are not the only moments, even in these opening bars, in which this modal uncertainty can be heard: for instance, the detail of scoring which inserts the clarinets and bass clarinet in bar four seems to be present precisely in order to make the chromatic neighbour note in the violin line (which is in any case spelt as $G^\flat$) sound as a minor third against the low open fifth. However, the association of modal equivocation with the motive of table 2.1 becomes important if the antecedents of this device in the symphony are considered. It can be linked with both the specific motivic feature of the major/minor triad which appears in all the other movements, from bar 59 of the first movement onwards, and with the more general voice-leading mixture of major and minor tonality which is prevalent in the work as a whole. On the one hand, the interpretive strategy required to make this feature of table 2.1 signify relies on a wider referential scope than that which created the table, one which links it with the rest of the symphony. On the other hand, the same strategy suggests that this referential boundary is much more significant, in distributional terms, than, say, that described by the terms 'nineteenth-century symphonies' or 'late tonal practice'. The unclosure of signification within this movement becomes a sign of its integration within the rest of the work.

A widened scope of reference is also involved in the interpretation of the

Example 2.1

remaining boxed units, those shown at X-1 and X-2. These chromatically descending figures, which borrow the rhythm of the table 2.1 motive, in fact serve to make explicit a connection between the Andante and the first movement. At the corresponding point in the form, the end of the opening thematic melody, the same rhythm occurs, also with upward semitones in the second of each pair of notes, but with much wider downward-plunging intervals (see ex. 2.1). The resemblance is striking, and it is hard to resist the narrativising impulse to describe this point in the Andante as a re-writing both of the motivic content and the semiotic significance of the earlier moment, as the violent half-close of the first movement is transformed into a quiet cadence via the figure which, as was remarked above, is borrowed from the *Kindertotenlieder*. According to this interpretive linking of the two passages, the figure from the first movement is first re-written and condensed (metaphorically, 'tamed' or 'neutralised') and then 'written into' the Andante by the lower half of table 2.1, which preserves the rhythm and intervals of the quotation, but disempowers it by removing its sequential nature.

What is instructive in the foregoing analysis is the fact that it demonstrates how any discussion of apparently 'purely musical', abstract motivic shapes is likely to throw up multiple connections in which significance is both undoubted, and yet only describable by resort to metaphor or narrative. The motivic analysis, which reassuringly establishes points of integration between the Andante and the rest of the symphony, is also disturbing: investigation of the 'purely musical' in its own terms consistently turns out to be impossible. Any code, perhaps especially a code which takes abstract structures as its material signifiers, relies on already existing codes which 'unclose' its boundaries.

One thing that even this initial analysis does is give the lie to such a statement as that by the normally perceptive Hans Redlich, that the 'only link between that seemingly erratic third movement and its surrounding movements remains an element of indefinite sound: the cow bells' (1963: 254). On the other hand, the nature of the links which can be demonstrated tend to imply a relationship of negation, of quotation or allusion which opposes the extramusical or metaphorical significance of that to which allusion is made. Whether through recasting of motivic material (as is the case with the major/minor modal opposition) or

Motive as sign: the Andante 27

Example 2.2

through reversal of melodic or harmonic function (as with the downward motion of units X-1 and X-2), the connections rely on a narrative code to give them meaning. The nature that such a code might take, and the sort of narrative implied by the motivic connections, will be explored in chapter 5 below. For now, it is sufficient to remark the truth of the assertion that meaning is always relational, and semiosis always unclosed, even in the case of seemingly straightforward musical repetition and development.

However, to return to the consideration of the paradigms constructed in table 2.1, it is now worth asking whether it is possible to identify any general patterns, of the sort that Nattiez or Ruwet would consider to be clues to the syntagmatic rules (in other words, the grammar) governing the piece. One such observation is that the units of the lower half of the graph tend to occur in pairs, often simply repeating each other (as IX-4 and IX-5), or containing a significant difference, normally a semitonal change (as II-3 and III-3). The units which are exceptions to this rule are II-4 and II-8, which, it has already been noted, deserve parallel entries in a column of their own, since they are the only units to contain the interval of an octave. They are also distinguished from the other units by their distributional location, since they both immediately precede cadences; and they resemble each other in their orchestration (the oboe, a typically Mahlerian sonority in these passages) and in the fact that both of them allude to the major/minor modal opposition. The single entries of the upper half of the table all have the melodic function of opening; this is mirrored, in the case of the single entries of the lower half of the table, by the melodic function of closing. Once again, the two codes interact. Indeed, unit II-8 is an extremely interesting phrase for several reasons: it plays with the direction of its following interval (the B♭ is approached from below by the G♮ and from above by the B♮), and suggests not only the major/minor alternation, but a middleground motivic shape, $\hat{6}$-$\hat{5}$-$\hat{1}$, of more than passing interest (see 'Motives at middleground levels' pp. 48-55, below). These features are summarised by example 2.2.

The mention of the direction of the interval following each unit introduces the question of whether size of intervals is the only (or best) paradigmatic arrangement for this table. In table 2.1, a rough threefold grouping can be observed, around the intervals of the sixth, the fourth and fifth, and the third respectively. The first of these groups, columns I to III, exhibits a great number of chromatically altered notes, in the service of diminished or Neapolitan harmony or the major/minor modal alternation. The motivic interval with which the movement opens, the ascending sixth, is in this manner connected with local harmonic motion. This relative instability contrasts with the harmonic functions of the other two groups. Columns V to VII give the tonic/dominant pedal that underpins the close of each E♭ section. The units which are part of an upper-voice line here are VII-8 and VII-9, which add the sixth degree to the tonic triad, and emphasise harmonic stasis rather than detracting from it. The reappearances of this motive later in the movement are, in all four cases, at crucial moments. The first is at the opening of the first 'B' section, with the decisive modulation to E minor (bars 56-8). The second is in the following E major section (bars 84-99), where, on the F trumpet, it becomes one of the defining features of the Mahlerian *Naturlaut*. This is a point discussed by Theodor Schmitt (1983: 167-8) who takes up the term from Hans-Heinrich Eggebrecht (1981: 127-68). Mahler's own references to the *Naturlaut* in his own works and in Wagner's confirm it as a central image of freedom and Utopian escape. The third appearance of the motive is in the A major section (bars 124-31). Its final occurrence is just before the return to E♭, in the bass of bars 170-1. The semiotic importance both of the motive and of the formal sections in which it occurs will be discussed in the next two sections of this chapter.

The third group, columns IX to X, is confined almost entirely to the five bars of transition from the opening E♭ to the subsidiary G minor. X-5 acts aurally as a clear echo, or antiphonal response, to units VII-5, IX-5 and V-6, preserving the notes common to both keys, G and B♭. Pivot modulations such as these are a favourite device for tonal change between sections, both in this movement and generally in Mahler. Schmitt describes the effect of bars 18-24 as 'meshing' the contrasting theme into the codetta of the opening melody (1983: 145). One unit is anomalous in this grouping of units: IX-10. Since it occurs simultaneously with II-10, acting with it to resolve the pitch C♮ onto both C♭ and D♮ (which then immediately form unit I-11), it can be seen to belong with the column I to III group; in fact, a remarkable consistency of motivic function and interval content is demonstrated across the table.

This general division arising from interval content, however, is not the only possible arrangement of the units in table 2.1. If they are ordered instead according to the direction of the following interval, a remarkable bunching of occurrences is immediately apparent, and is given as table 2.2. Naturally, there are now only three columns, according to whether the interval is ascending (column I), repeated or tied (column II), or descending (column III). The 39 units fall into just five successively longer groups, and it is remarkable how the units which appeared anomalous for one reason or another in table 2.1 are now grouped in a way which makes their semiotic function clear. For instance, the bass and upper-voice figures of the transitional section discussed immediately above now combine to form the only column II group, which derives entirely from the five transitional bars (bars

18–22). Unit IX-10 from table 2.1 indeed joins up, in table 2.2, with the units it accompanies, and is part of a column I group (the unit is now I-21).

The arrangement of the units in table 2.2, by comparison with table 2.1, suggests that intervallic direction is more important than interval content in determining the function of motivic detail in this opening section. This observation is confirmed by the fact that, whilst intervallic direction is sometimes made part of a virtual two-part counterpoint (as in I-19, for instance, where the F♭ and G resolve onto E♭ and A♭), it is sometimes made to contradict the voice-leading (as in III-28). The fact that the cadential descent of the oboe line at bar 40 is harnessed to an ascending motivic shape (discussed above in relation to table 2.1) is also shown to be part of this consistency of organisation; the paradigmatic criteria of the table place it as I-15, whereas a repetition of the B♮ in place of the low G would have made it an anomalous entry as III-15 (shown in brackets).

The pattern of units displayed in this table is related to the melodic organisation of this section, although it is not identical with it. Most obviously, motivic ascent is related to beginning, descent to ending, and repetition to transition; the column II group is drawn from only five bars of the section, as is the final column III group (III-22 to III-14). Indeed, the 'meshing' of the opening section with the contrasting theme is made more apparent by the column II group, which straddles the boundary between the two sections (which occurs at II-9). The first column III group (III-2 to III-4) contains the material identified by Schmitt as an *Abgesang* to the opening section. The two column I groups contain the four melodic gestures which had occurred in the top half of table 2.1; they are now the opening pair of units in each group. It is noteworthy that the point of exchange between the last two groups, bar 48, is the point at which the cantabile melodic line, carried by the first violins and flutes, gives way to the motivically fragmented texture of the codetta.

The fact that the upward motivic direction is maintained throughout the second column I group (I-13 to I-22) serves several purposes, and demonstrates the way in which motivic organisation contributes to the integration of materials. For one thing, it connects the G minor melody with the altered restatement of the E♭ melody that contains the next motivic unit. The fact that this paradigm continues when the open fifth pedal arrives in bars 42 to 44 (units I-16 to I-18) marks these *Naturlaut* figures (discussed above) with the seme 'beginning', and, arguably, suggests their later recurrence.

If this seems a little far-fetched, it at least relates the defining motivic shape of this section to processes of introduction and development which can be demonstrated within the score. The argument for preferring table 2.2 over table 2.1 (if a preference is sought) as a paradigmatic arrangement of the units segmented by these motivic criteria is ultimately a pragmatic one: it gives a more consistent pattern of organisation, and therefore gives greater support to assertions linking its patterning with other codes. However, the analysis just given as a commentary on the findings

Table 2.2

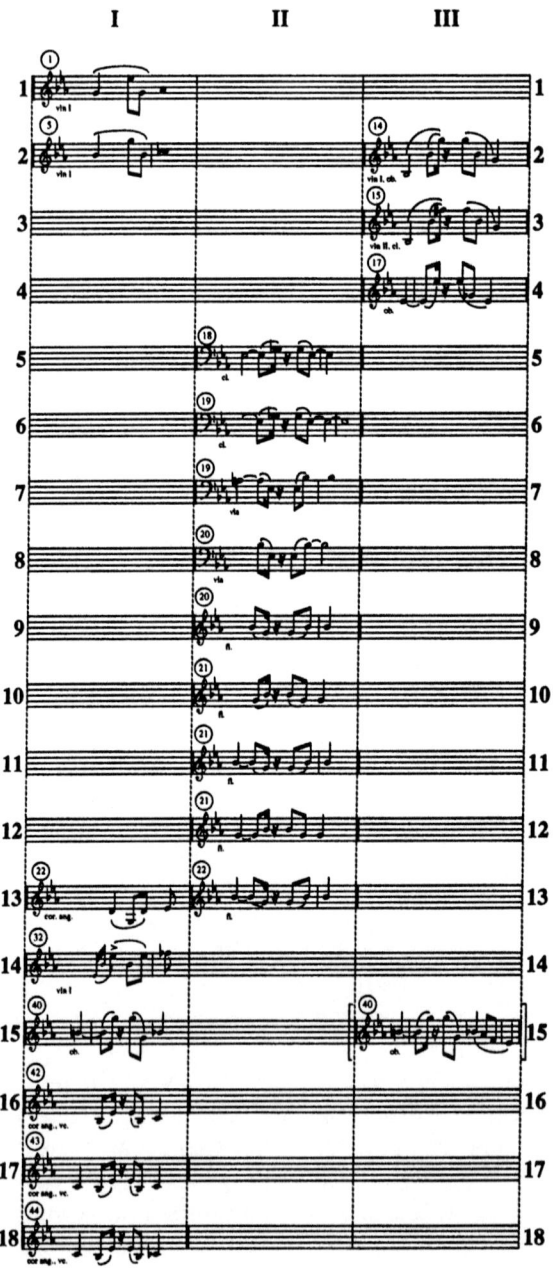

Motive as sign: the Andante

Table 2.2 (*cont.*)

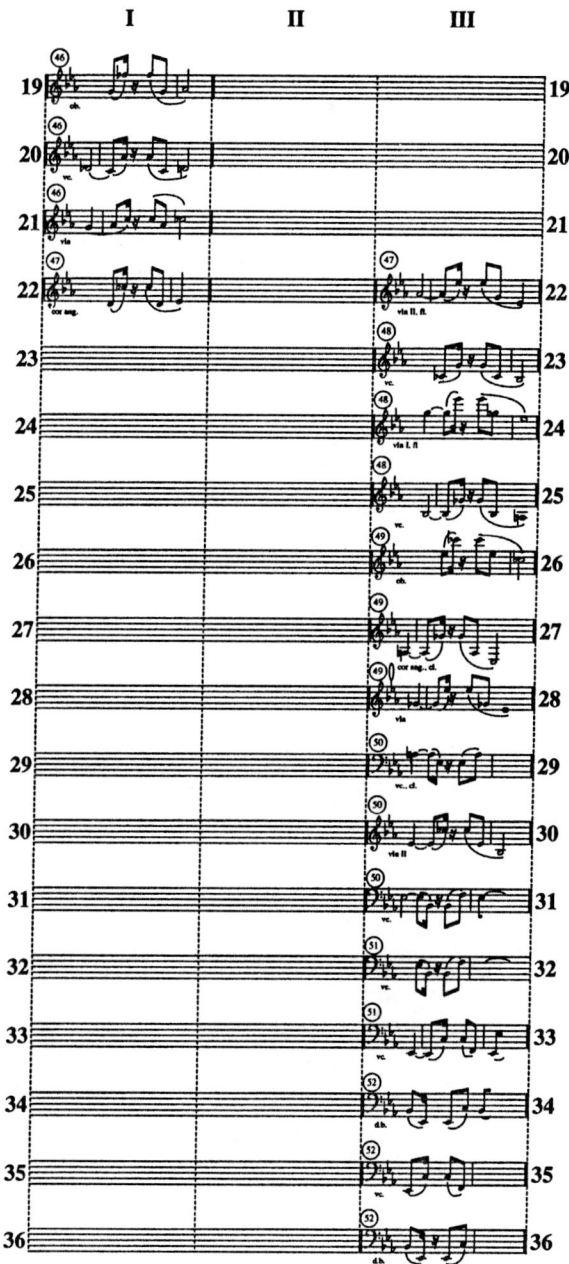

of the two tables cannot simply be thought of as a 'correct' semiotic reading. It is not a description of a communicative structure to be compared with or judged alongside a voice-leading analysis or a programmatic interpretation. Rather, the analysis provides a set of interpretants which unites the musical units defined by the paradigmatic criteria. These interpretants, in other words, treat the motives as a set of conceptually interchangeable signifiers. Further, the motivic code creates interpretants which can unite these signifiers with signifieds which constitute other codes (such as melodic succession). The scope of reference is limited within the text, and it is the contention of the analysis that the structures which can be described by the tables justify the conclusion that this motive serves the semiotic purpose of defining the autonomy of the movement (or, at least, of its opening section), and interacts with other coded musical features to create coherence of organisation. It would be equally possible, however, to use these findings to demonstrate the unclosed nature of any semiosis; the features which extend beyond these boundaries, such as those which connect this movement with the others of the Sixth Symphony, or those which suggest a connection between the *Naturlaut* figures and the Wagner of the *Siegfried Idyll* (a connection convincingly demonstrated by Schmitt, 1983: 168), underline the ultimately arbitrary nature of any discussion of signification, or at least the impossibility of assigning limits to the exercise.

REFERENTIAL SCOPE AND MOTIVIC DISTRIBUTION

It would be a fascinating exercise to trace the motive of tables 2.1 and 2.2 through the rest of the movement; but for the purposes of this chapter, it is necessary to consider other motives, of different signifying potential to this central feature of the Andante. To this end, table 2.3 gives a paradigmatic arrangement of a set of related rhythms.

The criterion for inclusion in the table is the minim covering the second and third beats of the bar; the simplest rhythm to have this form is ♩ ♩ ♩, which makes up column I. Columns II to IV contain different divisions of the first and fourth beats: ♩ ♩ ♫, ♫ ♩ ♫, and ♫ ♩ ♫. Column V is a more debatable inclusion. Its rhythm is ♩ ♩. ♬, a figure which stresses the second beat of the bar. In addition to this resemblance to the other rhythms of the table, the column V units often occur in rhythmic unison with them; the implications of its inclusion will be discussed more fully below.

The first observation to be made of table 2.3, in comparison with tables 2.1 and 2.2, is that there are only 40 units to be found in the entire movement, despite an arguably wider set of criteria for inclusion. Clearly, this is a motive with a different 'signifying scope'. There are two alternatives: either this is a much less important motivic formation, with only limited semiotic potential (or, indeed, simply a random collection of rhythmic values which is insignificant, and does not merit paradigmatic description); or it is a motive with reference outside the piece, of more general scope than the motive of tables 2.1 and 2.2. If it comes as no surprise that

Motive as sign: the Andante

Table 2.3

Table 2.3 (*cont.*)

this study will favour the latter alternative, there are several factors that can be adduced to support the reading. One is the distribution; the units of table 2.3 include some of the most obviously significant melodic moments in the movement. In particular, the melodic lines of nearly all the sections which are not in E♭ are included: the units on staves 10 to 12 in the E minor 'B' section (bars 56-83), unit II-14 which begins the melody of the E major section (bars 84-99), units I-17, II-18 and III-19 in the C major section (bars 115-23), and unit II-20, I-21 and V-21 in the A major section (bars 124-45). But the most important observation to be made concerning the signifying scope of this rhythmic motive is that it is commonly found in other works by Mahler. More than that, it often occurs with the particular paradigmatic alternatives and prevalent intervallic and harmonic patterns that it has in this movement. This can be demonstrated by comparing the units from the E minor and E major sections with the melody which seems to be the model for them, a secondary theme from the first movement of the Second Symphony (a theme which is, significantly, in the same key: see ex. 2.3). In both symphonies, the column I rhythm frequently appears as three notes moving down by step, with an appoggiatura on the first two beats, or a suspension on the second to fourth, or (in typically Mahlerian fashion) both; all these alternatives occur in ex. 2.3.

Another example of memorable appoggiaturas is the melody from the Adagietto of the Fifth Symphony, which is made up of column V rhythms (ex. 2.4). This, then, is a paradigm of units whose reference is intertextual: they are indicators of a 'vocabulary' of gestures which are distinctively Mahlerian. This vocabulary can be described as an 'idiolect', an s-code specific to an individual corpus of texts and which serves to identify them in the manner of a signature, although the power of 'idiolectic' reference goes far beyond the simple denotation of a work as being produced by Mahler rather than by anyone else. The occurrence of these idiolectic

Example 2.3

Mahler, Sixth Symphony, Andante

Mahler, Sixth Symphony, Andante

Mahler, Second Symphony, first movement

Example 2.4

Mahler, Fifth Symphony, Adagietto

units at precisely those moments which are most problematic for a hermetic reading of the form of the Andante is an indication that the codes which seek to account for these moments (the Adornian 'breakthrough' of the E major theme, the *misterioso* 'B' section in C major and A major) must look beyond the Symphony as a whole, not just beyond this movement. In other words, the semiosis of the motivic code suggests a leap to more general codes such as narrative or generic archetypes.

Of course, the basic rhythm of the table, ♩♩♩, is so common in tonal (and, indeed, atonal) practice that it can hardly be claimed as paradigmatic for the Mahlerian idiolect on its own. However, the fact that it is so general implies one of the most significant observations to be made concerning the data of table 2.3. The table, as was remarked above, actually represents a continuum, from the simple (and therefore semiotically neutral) rhythm of column I to the rhythms of columns IV and V, where the paradigmatic shape is inflected in a typically Mahlerian fashion. Column IV, in particular, is a strong idiolectic reference; and it is noticeable that this column is used in the return of the opening melody, at bars 101 and 160, to give motivic differentiation to what was, at bar 2, a very ordinary point of repose.

Empirical proof of the idiolectic status of column IV would of course necessitate a statistical survey of all pieces written up to 1902 in order to show that its rhythm occurred significantly more often in Mahler than anywhere else. If the assertion is accepted without such an exercise, however, the table provides a means of describing the mechanism by which this unequivocally idiolectic paradigm incorporates the other columns into its semiotic scope. Precedents such as the passages given as ex. 2.3 and ex. 2.4 are drawn into the specific referential nexus of the table, despite the general nature of the majority of the units. The situation is in some ways similar to that of Brahms' use of the hemiola, where a feature common enough in Western tonal practice is made distinctive within a particular composer's corpus of works; not just through the frequency of its use, but by distinctive harmonic, rhythmic and melodic features of its deployment. If the units that compose table 2.3 are heard as members of the same paradigm of signifiers, then the limited distributional reference of columns IV and V endows the other columns with a more specific (and therefore more powerful) referential scope. It should be stressed that this idea is not self-evident; it is an analytical assertion made by the creation of interpretants via the motivic code. And, whilst the semiotic process is a general one, it seems particularly applicable to Mahler's music; the way in which simple (or common) rhythmic and intervallic shapes are used to make up textures or melodic lines which are instantly recognisable as Mahlerian is a feature frequently attested by informal criticism of the music from its first performances.

The idea that a specifically Mahlerian paradigm can encompass general motivic shapes is an appealing one. However, a rigorous argument to support the interpretation of table 2.3 just offered would entail a vast statistical sampling of other works. For this reason, the final paradigmatic analysis of motive in this chapter will take an extremely simple set of paradigmatic criteria in order to extract a more significant number of units from the Andante itself, whilst still giving grounds for making observations concerning a Mahlerian idiolect. Table 2.4 therefore takes as its qualifying criterion any sequence of four consecutively descending notes. This basic requirement is refined slightly by selecting only those units which begin on a minim beat, and which cover a whole number of crotchet beats (to avoid trivial overlaps where five or more notes descend consecutively). The units are arranged according to intervallic sequence. This produces a table of eleven columns, which arranges 95 units on 63 staves.

Although there may seem little point in using so general a criterion as consecutive descent to construct a table, the first observation to be made of the results is that certain shapes, especially minim groups of four quavers, are very generally evident. Further, a recurrent shape seems to be the combination of scalic (stepwise) motion with an initial leap of a larger interval. The arrangement of the columns reflects these facts. There are, theoretically, 343 different possible four-note linear intervallic patterns (if diatonic intervals only are used to arrange intervals); the fact that only eleven occur in this movement is already noteworthy. On the other hand, if the units are considered as sequences of steps (intervals of a second) and gaps (other intervals), then seven of the eight possible patterns are represented. These have been used to order the columns as follows:

Motive as sign: the Andante

Column	Step/gap pattern	Intervallic sequence
I	step-step-step	second-second-second
II	step-step-gap	second-second-third
III	step-gap-step	second-third- second
IV	step-gap-step	second-fourth-second
V	step-gap-gap	second-third-third
VI	step-gap-gap	second-third-fourth
VII	gap-step-step	third-second-second
VIII	gap-step-step	fourth-second-second
IX	gap-step-step	fifth-second-second
X	gap-gap-step	third-third-second
XI	gap-gap-gap	third-third-third

Whilst this ordering represents a small range of shapes from amongst those theoretically possible, a much more significant statistical finding is gained from tabulating the distribution of units within the table. This is particularly true if the prevalence of the ♫♫ rhythm is also noted. The numbers of units in the table is as follows:

Column	Number of extracts	♫♫ groups (untied)	♫♫ groups (tied)
I	21	8	2
II	5	3	0
III	1	0	0
IV	1	0	0
V	6	6	0
VI	2	1	1
VII	37	34	1
VIII	16	13	3
IX	2	2	0
X	3	2	0
XI	1	0	1
Total	95	69 (72.6%)	8 (8.4%)

Even more remarkable is the result if the definition of motivic shape according to steps and gaps is accepted:

Intervallic type	Number of extracts
step-step-step	21 (22.1%)
step-step-gap	5 (5.3%)
step-gap-step	2 (2.1%)
step-gap-gap	8 (8.4%)
gap-step-step	55 (57.9%)
gap-step-gap	0
gap-gap-step	3 (3.2%)
gap-gap-gap	1 (1.1%)

38　　　　　　　　　Mahler's Sixth Symphony

Table 2.4

Motive as sign: the Andante

Table 2.4 (*cont.*)

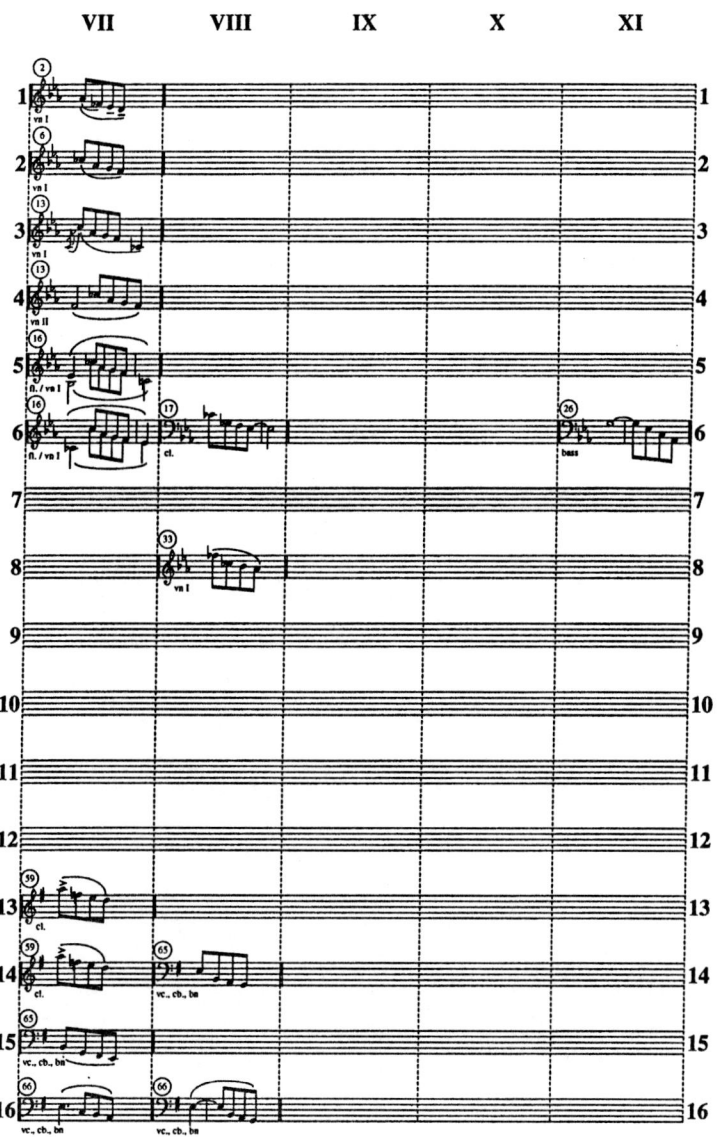

Table 2.4 (cont.)

Motive as sign: the Andante

Table 2.4 *(cont.)*

Table 2.4 (cont.)

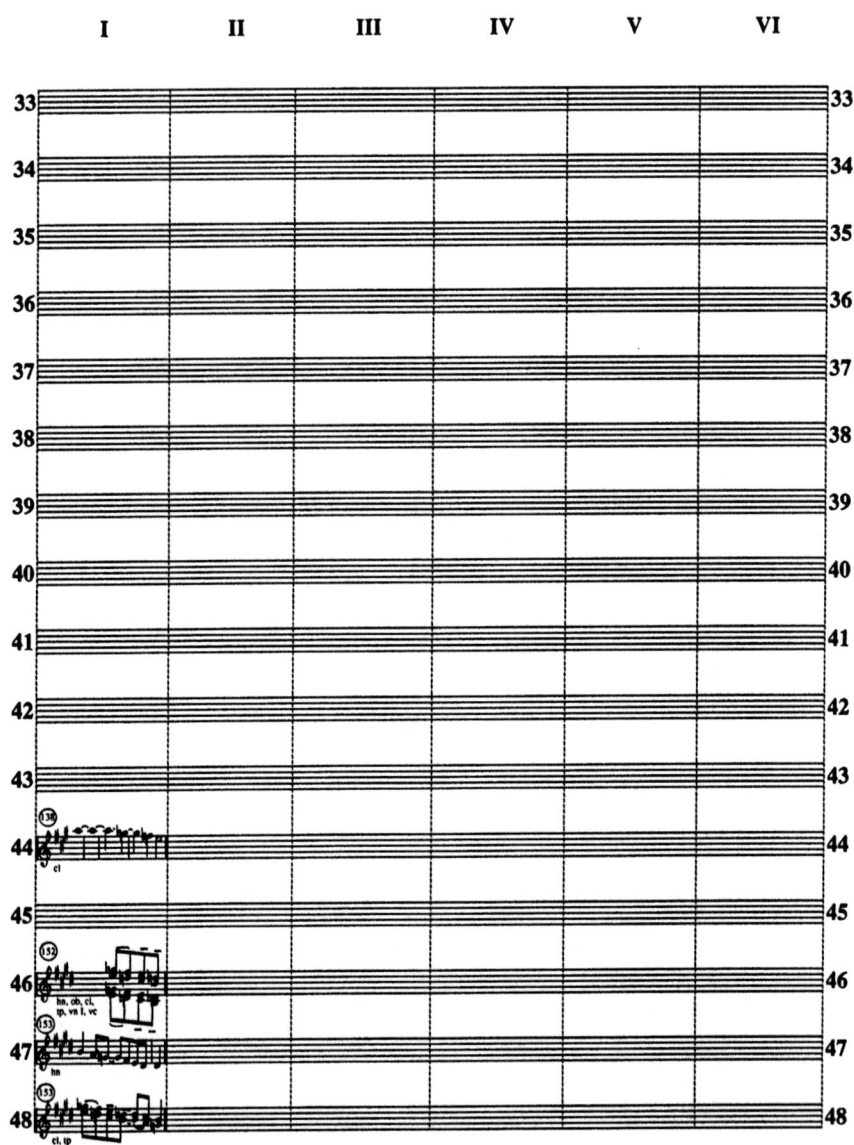

Motive as sign: the Andante

Table 2.4 (cont.)

Table 2.4 (*cont.*)

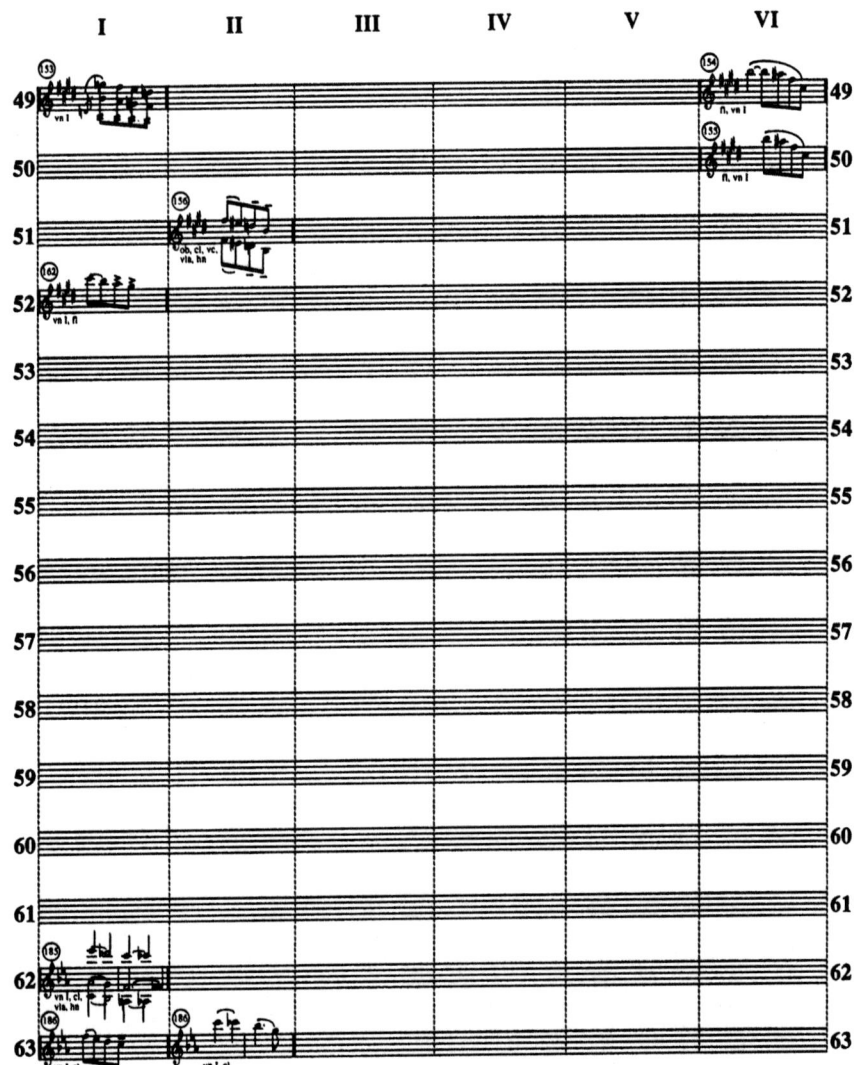

Table 2.4 (cont.)

Statistical tables are always a poor vehicle for communicating facts of musical articulation; but the restriction of means of presenting descending voice patterns within this movement becomes truly remarkable in the light of the above figures. Obviously, columns VII and VIII, which make up the shape gap-step-step and contain more than half the units, constitute a significant motivic shape within this movement. Since VII-1 occurs near the beginning of the opening theme, and since many of the observations concerning the distribution of the table 2.1 units also apply to these columns (their appearance at melodically or formally significant moments, the incorporation of the major/minor modal opposition in VII-3 and similar units), this is not a controversial statement. What is more surprising is the extent to which this table covers almost all the descending intervallic shapes of any sort in the movement. There are only four instances of overlapping units (I-17 & I-18; I-27 & I-28; I-62 & II-63; VII-63 & I-63), and no two extracts form a contiguous descent. In other words, this table demonstrates the fact that within this movement, voices always descend in characteristic ways. Indeed, the only instance of more than seven consecutive descending notes in the whole movement is the chromatic line at bars 98-9, and the climactic cadence on $E^\flat$ at bars 185-6.

Once again, the information represented by this table gives grounds for observations concerning both the specific content of this piece, and the more general procedure of Mahler's music. The two patterns that predominate, making up 78 per cent of the table altogether, are step-step-step (column I), and gap-step-step (columns VI and VII). Evidently, the first of these, straightforward scalic descent, is of completely general occurrence; however, the other, which 'fills in' the gap between two notes of an arpeggaic descent, is much less so. It would be difficult to claim that columns VII and VIII are a specifically Mahlerian paradigm, if it were not for the fact that they are so predominant in the distribution of the units. There is a tendency for descending figures to occur only in these patterns, and it is this distribution which encourages the hearing of these paradigms as references within the Mahlerian idiolect. As with table 2.3, it is the fact that patterns of descent are limited, combined with the fact that descending sequences of notes of any length are extremely rare, that narrows and empowers the referential scope of these units. There is an easy interpretive jump from these observations to the comment that this table gives evidence of Mahler's lack of Brahmsian or Brucknerian self-assurance: confident descending scales are not merely absent, they are replaced with paradigmatically limited, hesitant figures that combine arpeggaic and scalic motion. Once again, the commonest musical features are motivated and made significant by a consistent distribution of motivic reference. The accents on the simple scalic figures I-8 and I-27 are a compositorial underlining of the fact that they have been marked in this way.

The idea that idiolectical methods of descent might be one of the strongest defining elements of a composer's style is one which has been suggested before, notably in Vladimir Jankelevitch's study of Debussy (1976). Undoubtedly, this sort of patterned descent is particularly important in music of the late nineteenth and early twentieth century, where motivic substitutes for the formulaic figures of

Motive as sign: the Andante 47

Example 2.5

eighteenth-century common practice are indispensable. However, it is extremely difficult to make any but the most general comments about a topic that appears to demand the investigation in detail of every piece in a composer's oeuvre. The paradigmatic analysis presented here does at least give statistical and musical support to the analysis of compositorial style within the Andante; it seems likely that the categories of semiotic analysis are the only way to approach this slipperiest of topics.

There are, of course, other motivic shapes that deserve this sort of attention in discussing the Andante. The fact that 81 per cent of the units in table 2.4 have the rhythm ♪♪♪♪ is a point of connection with several groups of figures within the movement. As has just been suggested, there is high correlation between the incidence of this rhythm and motivically defined shapes. In other words, chains of rhythmically undifferentiated quavers are as rare in the Andante (and in the rest of Mahler) as chains of scales or arpeggios. Three groups of four-quaver motivic shapes are given in ex. 2.5.

The pattern of up-down-down in ex. 2.5a is retrograded by the down-down-up of ex. 2.5b; and the distributional linkage of the figures is demonstrated by the fact that these groups appear in the two passages of secondary seventh sequences, ex. 2.5b at bars 73ff and 174ff, and ex. 2.5a at bars 76ff and 176ff; and by the fact that each of these passages is immediately followed by one of the ex. 2.5c extracts. The use of a small number of well-defined four-quaver units is an example of what Adorno describes as 'reification' at work in the movement; the constituent units of the main theme and the contrasting sections become fixed and detachable from their context via the motivic code, as if they were transferable, commodity-like entities. Again, a paradigmatic table using as its basic criterion the ♪♪♪♩ rhythm would not only go a fair way towards explaining the consistency lying behind what Adorno called the 'unrepeating richness' of the Andante; it would also indicate a point of entry to a rich intertextual field within the Mahlerian oeuvre. Further investigation of these structures between works would go some way to giving analytical grounds for the metamusical assertions often made concerning the music. A study such as Eric Hanson's (1986), which makes a convincing case for the association of a consistent metaphysical charge with a recurrent motive across the whole corpus of Mahler's works, is tantalising to the very extent that it is successful; the number of motivic shapes that can be identified in this way is more or less limited to the 'Will to life' motive first discussed by William McGrath (1974), while the number of recurrent motives in the corpus is far greater. The definition of the semiotic character of intertextual reference is the necessary prelude to the justification of narrative or metaphysical readings of works. This is a topic which will return in chapters 4 and 5. For the purposes of the present chapter, however, it is necessary to leave the discussion of motivic shapes found in musical 'surface features', in order to ask whether more abstract configurations also constitute identifiable paradigm sets.

MOTIVES AT MIDDLEGROUND LEVELS

A major criticism of the paradigmatic analyses of Nattiez and other semiologists of music is that the tables deal almost always with surface detail; even the elementary reductions of a Schenkerian foreground graph would disrupt the patterns of repetition and deviation. However, practically all systems of music analysis in this century have operated with some sort of reductive approach, whether it be the hierarchic trees of Fred Lerdahl and Ray Jackendoff (1983), the extraction of detail by the Schoenberg of 'Brahms the Progressive', or the Schenkerian concepts of foreground, middleground and background. Indeed, since one contention of orthodox Schenkerian analysis is that the features which define a given composer's style are by and large the techniques used to elaborate middleground and foreground levels of organisation, no discussion of idiolect can ignore the possibility that motives embedded in deeper levels than the musical surface may also create complexes of sign association. This necessarily entails a more speculative approach to the creation

Example 2.6

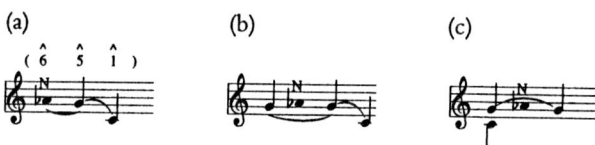

of paradigm classes. The criteria for inclusion have to rest on features obtained by reductive techniques, and are therefore open to question. In addition, it is far from evident how one might answer the question of whether reductions of different scales (for example, within both foreground and middleground) can be regarded as equivalent.

The combination of motivic and Schenkerian perspectives has often been attempted in the discussion of late nineteenth-century music. Allen Forte, in a notable article on the Adagietto of Mahler's Fifth Symphony, argues that the replication of foreground motives at middleground levels accounts in a large part for the hierarchical organisation of the movement (Forte 1985). However, his account is compromised slightly by the fact that all of the motives that he discusses are made up of scalic motion; the issue of how linear voice-leading patterns can be considered as specifically motivic is one which it is not really possible to resolve, at least if other parameters such as rhythm or orchestration are excluded, as they are by a middleground reduction. What is needed is an investigation of a non-linear intervallic pattern which can legitimately be distinguished at middleground levels.

One such candidate has already been suggested in this chapter, and that is the pattern of a falling semitone followed by a falling fifth. This is a figure which recurs in many works by Mahler, and which introduces several complex areas of intertextual comparison. As an intervallic shape, it is obviously a stock-in-trade of late nineteenth-century expression. It consists of a chromatic delay to a linear movement, and is eminently suitable both for motivically fragmented textures and for incorporation into melodic lines of wide intervallic leaps. As a set of scale degrees, on the other hand, it embodies an approach to a $\hat{5}$–$\hat{1}$ movement via a $\hat{6}$–$\hat{5}$ or $\hat{6}^\flat$–$\hat{5}$ neighbour-note formation. These intervallic and harmonic functions combine in the idiolectic deployment of the figure in Mahler's works. It is the motivic face of his treatment of neighbour-notes, particularly of $\hat{6}$–$\hat{5}$ and $\hat{6}^\flat$–$\hat{5}$, which is often the basis for the organisation of relatively large formal sections. Some alternative manifestations of this motive are shown in ex. 2.6. Ex. 2.6a is the simplest form of the motive, and therefore the shape which can be taken as the model for the paradigms to be discussed. The commonest shapes which can be associated with it are ex. 2.6b, which has a complete neighbour-note motion (this is also more easily retrogradable), and ex. 2.6c, which analyses the intervals as a virtual two-part counterpoint. Obviously, there are many cases where a set of intervals in the score can be analysed by more than one of these sets of stems and slurs (or variants of them); and, to repeat the assertion made above, it is the interaction of archetypal intervallic and harmonic patterns that makes this motivic feature interesting.

Example 2.7

(a) Mahler, Fifth Symphony, first movement

(b) Mahler, Third Symphony, first movement

Example 2.8

To illustrate the fact that this motive tends to occur at significant moments in Mahler, ex. 2.7 gives two examples, from near the openings of the Fifth and Third Symphonies. The first is a straightforward foreground occurrence of the figure, in which the downward fifth is extended to cover first an octave, and then an octave and a fifth, a remarkably large leap for a single voice, and one which makes an especially memorable cadential plunge at the end of this introduction. The extract from the Third Symphony is just as clearly an instance of this motivic figure, but here it occurs at a middleground level, over a space of nineteen bars. Again, the downward interval is a compound one, and here the voice-leading follows the pattern of ex. 2.6b, with the B♭ of bar 7 acting as an upper neighbour-note within an octave transfer of the A♮.

Once the search for similar examples of this motive in the Andante of the Sixth Symphony is begun, its prevalence becomes striking. The most obvious example is the contrasting theme of bar 22. Whilst not as direct a statement of the figure as ex. 2.7a, the prominent neighbour-note pair E♭-D, preceded and followed by the fifth D-G, means that all three of the possibilities shown at ex. 2.6 can be applied to the melody (ex. 2.8).

The consideration of this melody as part of an intertextual motivic nexus gives grounds for commenting on several features of its use in the Andante. For a start, it appears as a more or less invariant melody, by contrast with Mahler's normal procedure (which for instance varies the main theme of the Andante each time that it returns). On the other hand, it appears in what seems at first sight to be quite a wide variety of contexts: as the first contrasting theme of the opening section (bar 22); near the beginning of the first 'B' section (bar 60); near the end of the second 'B' section (bar 139); and, shortly after this, at the beginning of the section which moves back to E♭, via C♯ minor and B major (bar 146). If the important feature of the theme is held to be its use of the middleground shape, then this gives a reason for its remaining invariant. The fact that it is taken up by the motivic code rather than a melodic code (which would take account of linear succession) makes the contrast between the themes of bar 1 and bar 22 a semiotic one as well as a thematic one. Indeed, the fact that the major melodic contrast of the movement cannot be assimilated by the normal semiotics of melody, because of its invariance and because it connects strongly to the intertextual motivic code, is a good reason for describing it as 'enigmatic' or 'distant'. It is a form of interruption which, like the theme of the E major section (though by different means), contains the seme of 'the other'. Under a more general code (such as musical narrative), this specifically intramusical semiosis furnishes the material for discussing images of the 'outside'; that is, the Utopian vision towards which Mahler's music has always been held to gesture. Once again, it is only by means of a semiotic understanding of musical signification that extramusical comment and analytical description can be shown to be mutually reinforcing.

Apart from this theme, the other points at which this middleground shape can readily be identified are all, significantly, formal or thematic boundaries of one sort or another. The equivocation between C minor and E♭ major at the end of the opening melody (bar 40) incorporates the motive as a B♭-B♭-E♭ figure, as was noted above in the discussion of unit II-8 in table 2.1. This means of ending a section or effecting a transition is applied consistently in the movement, although a greater degree of reduction is necessary to observe it.

There are four examples, which will be taken in turn. First is the transition between the E minor 'B' section and the E major section. This is extremely interesting, from a motivic point of view, for its combination and recombination of four-quaver figures. It rests on a prominent C♯ in the bass of bars 76 and 78-9, which then falls as C-B-E (giving the middleground shape) during bars 78-84 (a Schenkerian reduction of this is given in ex. 2.9).

Secondly, at bar 114, the transition to the second 'B' section after the brief return of the E♭ melody is accomplished via a whole-tone chord over a D♭ in the bass, which functions both as a chromatic $^4_2$ triad in E♭ and as a chromatic applied dominant in the new key (C major). The new C major tonality is not, however, well-defined, and a sense of harmonic repose is only given by the descent (via units from table 2.3 above) on to an F major triad (supporting a prominent melodic E-D appoggiatura) at bar 121. All of which outlines D♭-C-F in the bass, again giving the middleground motive under discussion (see ex. 2.10).

Thirdly, the transition from the second 'B' section to the final 'A' section at bars 137-149 gives a remarkable set of nested occurrences of the shape. As was noted above, the secondary theme is heard on both sides of the double bar line, in bars 139-41 in A minor, and in bars 146-8, in the bass, in C♯ minor. Just before the first of these, the first violins slide up to a top A♮ on a string harmonic, a pitch which is then reached again by the melodic line of bars 146-8, until it falls to G♯ in bar 149, to be answered immediately by C♯ in the bass. Whilst the C♯ tonality is never stable,

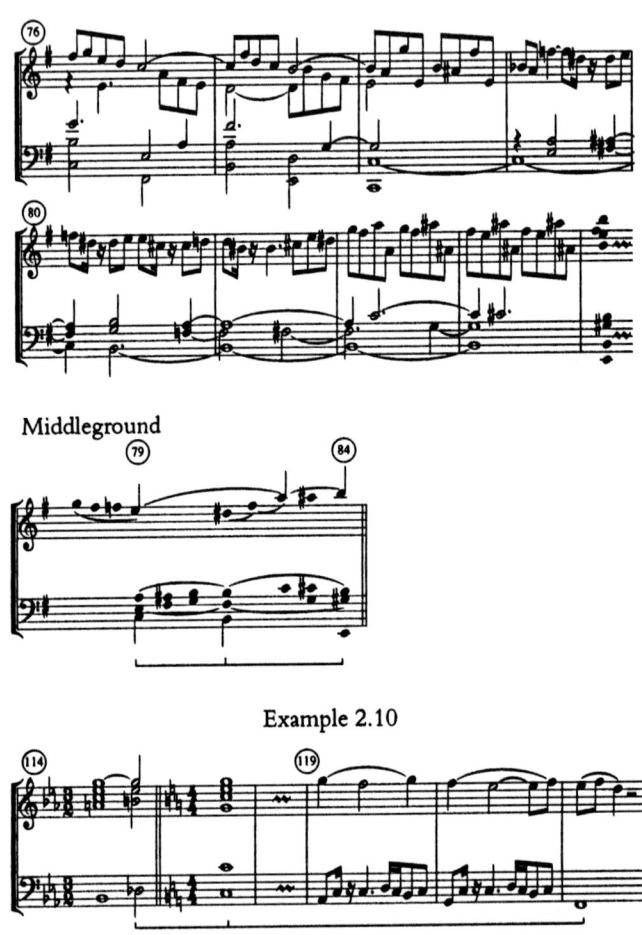

Example 2.9

Middleground

Example 2.10

the middleground motivic shape is readily discernible here; ex. 2.11 shows its occurrences, though here without suggesting voice-leading functions. It is also notable that the A is the stable last note of the motive on one side of the double bar line, and the unstable first note on the other.

The last instance of the shape is found in the final transition to E♭, where it is once again found in the bass. This moment is quite unusual, since the arrival of the tonic note in the bass is delayed until bar 174, a bar after the arrival of the E♭ tonality and high G in the melody, which a Schenkerian view of the movement would have to place as the *Kopfton*. It is approached by another peculiar chord with whole-tone characteristics, made up of F♮ (moving to F♯), E♭ and C♭ in the bass (second half of bar 172); this C♭ then moves to B♭ in the next bar, before it is transferred down to the eventual E♭ by motives from table 2.4 above (see ex. 2.12).

Motive as sign: the Andante

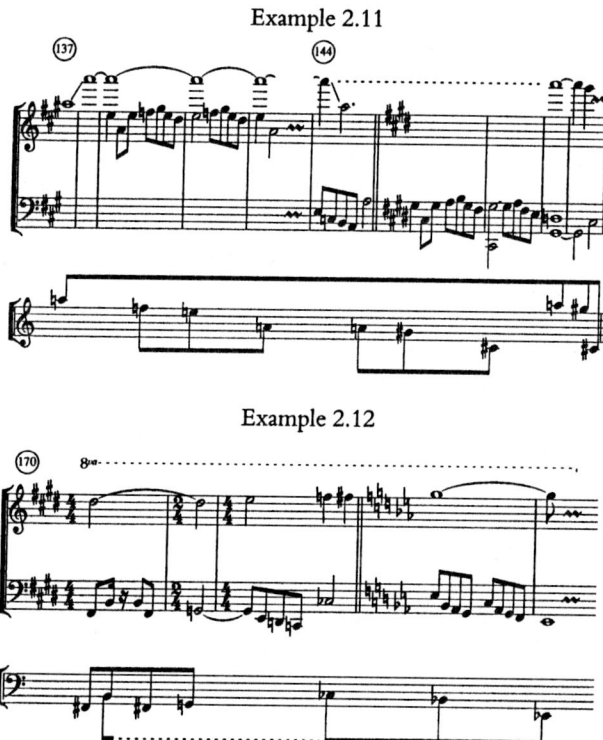

Example 2.11

Example 2.12

What the analysis has suggested so far is that there is a similar shape underlying several equivalent points in the form, and that this shape is motivic, in the sense that it can be identified as part of a paradigm class that is distributed across the corpus of Mahler's works. It is not easy, however, to move from this suggestion to the construction of an interpretant for the motive.

One view might be that this is a typical method by which Mahler approaches boundaries between sections; in other words, it refers to a set of occurrences in the Mahlerian idiolect and carries the seme 'transition' or 'sectional cadence'. On the other hand, a reading which ascribes a somewhat different range of reference to the motive would connect it with its occurrences at foreground levels: the secondary theme of the Andante, for instance, or the examples given as ex. 2.7. One of these interpretants takes the motive as a style-specific feature, whose function is to reinforce the 'Mahler-ness' of crucial points in the form; the other reads these moments in the Andante as part of a specific intertextual web of cross-references. It is not really possible (or desirable) to arbitrate between these alternatives. The first requires a much more complete notion of what constitutes the specifically idiolectic features of Mahler's musical style, and the second requires a code of general scope to make sense of what are otherwise apparently randomly connected moments in different works. It is, in other words, much easier to construct the s-code of the signifier than that of the signified. This is a general problem of musical semiotics; the possibilities of segmentation are virtually infinite for a piece of any complexity.

The fact that the semiotic interpretation of the paradigm table represented by examples 2.7-2.12 is difficult does not, however, mean that it is unrewarding. If the contention that this paradigm has existence as a typically Mahlerian set of signs is accepted, then it suggests that it is only by features such as this that a description of Mahler's style can proceed. John Williamson's idea, that what distinguishes Mahler's harmonic style is largely to do with techniques of prolongation of chromatic degrees (Williamson 1991), gains strength if these prolongations are seen as part of a global motivic vocabulary which extends through different levels of reduction (as in ex. 2.11 above). The relationships between this sort of organisation of whole sections of music and the coding of musical form proper will be addressed in chapter 3 below. The same semiotic process can be seen at work in this middleground as was observed in the patterns of descent in table 2.4. The occurrences of the motive at foreground levels encourage its recognition at middleground levels; and this in turn tends to give significance to the general feature of the treatment of the flattened sixth scale degree in the movement. Ex. 2.12 indicates how the first pitch of the motive in bar 172 (the C♭ in the bass) is anticipated by the B♮ of bar 170, which is itself part of a B♮-F♯-G♮ figure which occurred in table 2.1. Here, this latter group of notes sounds, by virtue of the juxtaposition, to be motivically connected to the middleground shape (it is a sort of retrograde inversion). The adjacency connects two distinct but individually important groups of motives: the bass figure of bars 170-1, as was discussed above, is prominent at the beginning of the first 'B' section (bars 56-9), and then occurs in a major-mode version in the E major section (bars 84-99). The global distribution of the motive manifests the clearest long-range motivic assertion of the major/minor modal alternation that was discussed above, and which is contained in its first occurrence (bars 42-5, units VII-8 and VII-9 of table 2.1). Thus several motivic features are inextricably linked, and the general treatment of the $\hat{6}^\flat$-$\hat{5}$ scale degree in the movement is written into the specific motivic paradigms of the middleground shape and the table 2.1 column VII units. This motivation of the harmonic treatment of the sixth scale degree is particularly relevant to discussion of the E♭ major 'A' sections. The abundance of prominent C♭s in the upper and middle voices of passages such as bars 5-10 are not just typical post-Brahmsian colouring of the harmony; they are a feature which is inscribed within the specific and idiolectical vocabularies of the movement.

The processes of purely motivic semiosis are by now a little clearer. Evidently, this is a rich field, and investigation of the motivic structures discernible in a work is the most obvious starting-point for addressing music of this period. The manner in which features specific to the motivic organisation of the work in hand serve to create a frame of reference for certain more general elements is particularly instructive. Without this process, the general shapes would remain ordinary features of late nineteenth-century common practice; with it, the Mahlerian idiolect sets out to subsume the style which serves as its background. The concept of style in music has always been elusive as an object of analysis, and the concepts of semiotic inquiry are the most likely way forward for its definition. Robert Hatten addresses this issue by an opposition of 'style' and 'strategy', by which he means that the specific context of a work plays with and against the general constraints of the style which makes it intelligible (Hatten 1982). What is observable in the Andante is the transgression of the boundary between the 'stylistic' and 'strategic' in Hatten's terms; the music embodies a deconstruction of its own articulation.

The tendency for motivic connections to proliferate, no matter how strictly paradigmatic criteria are observed, is an indication both of the uses and the limits of this code in creating interpretants for the music. Once a shape has been defined as motivic, its possible paradigmatic associations will be infinite for practical purposes, particularly if the sort of middleground observations of the preceding discussion are allowed into consideration. The only recourse is to a strong concept of sign production, which recognises that not only the signifieds, but the signifiers themselves are created by the listener/analyst. The appeal to a syntagmatic rule (that the middleground shape occurs across almost every significant formal boundary), in constructing the paradigm for the middleground motive sketched above, can only be justified by its results. What started out as the object of inquiry (the general rules governing syntagmatic construction) turns out to be a prerequisite of the segmentation. This deconstructive move also holds true more generally, in that investigation of the motivic code constantly produces connections which require codes of wider referential scope to make sense of them. This is perhaps only to be expected of the motivic code, since motives are by definition created by the connection of non-adjacent features. They function in a 'non-sequential' fashion, to use Barthes' term, and these diffuse, multiple connections cannot fail to invoke codes which also seek to connect the non-adjacent; whether by linking work with work, or work with genre, or work with cultural topos. These sorts of codes are the subjects of the later chapters of this study.

In order to make more general observations about the nature of musical semiosis from the basis of the motivic analysis presented in this chapter, it is necessary to look at the relationships between the motivic features discussed so far and the other codes which take 'purely musical' materials as their signifiers. This chapter will therefore conclude by considering two sorts of 'intramusical' organisation; namely, formal proportion and melodic recurrence.

INTERACTION OF MOTIVE, FORM AND MELODY

The issue of form immediately looks beyond the boundaries of the work in hand. Analysis of form has always proceeded with some concept of formal model or archetype, so that the individual movement gains significance from its relationship to other movements with similar form or function. This complex intertextual field is the concern of chapter 3, which will discuss Mahler's use of sonata form in the Finale and first movement of the Sixth Symphony. At this stage, however, a brief consideration of the formal structure of the Andante, which invokes slightly different issues from that of the outer movements, affords another opportunity to see the interaction of individual impulse, idiolectic placing and general context which is a distinctive feature of Mahler's compositional technique.

There is no problem in assigning a standard archetype to the Andante. As was described at the outset of this chapter, it has a relatively straightforward slow rondo form, whose sections are well-defined to the extent of being separated by double bar lines. The descriptive label, 'rondo', is somewhat compromised, though, by the contrasting lengths of the E♭ sections (55 bars, 15 bars, 28 bars), and by the length of the stretches of music in between them. This somewhat lopsided proportional pattern, considered as an instance of the formal archetype, is balanced, however, by the fact that if the divisions by double bar lines are taken on their own, they display a quite staggering degree of symmetrical patterning. In other words, the consideration of the movement as an instance of symphonic rondo form is relatively unimportant compared with the implications of its proportional scheme as an absolute structure. The conflict between a reading of a set of relations in terms of a pre-existing archetype, and the deduction of its properties from its immanent structure, is a recurrent theme in semiotic theory. It is, of course, particularly relevant to the discussion of music, where considerations of symmetry, proportion, repetition and variation are frequently held to signify simply in virtue of their presence. The most succinct comments on the topic are those by David Lidov, who uses the oppositional pair of terms 'grammar' and 'design': '*Grammar* is order determined by *a priori* abstract rules. Grammar entails a system or language that furnishes abstract rules in advance of the text. *Design* is order determined by concrete symmetries of all kinds, especially, for music, repetition and variation' (1981: 142).

The opposition cannot be sustained rigorously, since the decision as to when a deviation from absolute symmetry implies a pre-existing rule is an entirely arbitrary one. On the other hand, the idea that there is some sense in which prior knowledge of system is subordinated by contact with the specific artefact is one about which much semiotic thought has had little to say. Lidov remarks that 'The point is not that design bypasses grammatical categories, but that when it employs, for example, triads as a category, it is indifferent to their normal grammatical status and to grammatical constraints on their distribution. The power of design is to cause us to abduce categories and rules as a creative act of perception. The text is anterior to language' (1981: 144).

The concept is slippery, for several reasons. Too little variation in symmetry is not sufficient to give meaning to a text: AA form does not really exist in music (since binary form incorporates 'grammatical' expectations as to tonal structure). On the other hand, the simplest pattern to contain contrast and return, ABA form, is also one entirely furnished by *a priori* (i.e., grammatical) assumptions, if one is dealing with minuets and trios. The opposition can also work the other way round; the complex proportional schemes uncovered by recent scholarship in renaissance motets are difficult to dispute, and yet their role in the semiotic process of the music is minimal, being limited to consideration of esoteric precompositional planning. Lidov's point is a pragmatic rather than a theoretical one. His definitions are given in the context of a discussion of the Allegretto from Beethoven's Seventh Symphony, and the concepts are useful in precisely this sort of case, where the expectations furnished by the movement title are relatively weak, but the patterning of the formal sections is readily susceptible to description as a coherent, if unprecedented, structure. Such is also the case with the Andante of Mahler's Sixth Symphony. It is no accident that it is the symphonic slow movement that is under discussion in both cases; the history of slow movement form since the eighteenth century is one in which formal archetypes are much less well-defined than in the case of the other movements of the symphony or sonata. Here, the evident symmetrical patterning of the Andante interacts with motivic and melodic considerations in a complex way which makes several of the observations described earlier in this chapter more clear.

The overall proportions and tonal scheme of the movement are summarized in figure 2.1. The figures at the top refer to bar numbers. At the side, the key structure is indicated, with keys ordered in semitones and the tonic key for the movement, E♭, in the middle. Major mode is indicated by shading above the line, and minor mode by shading below the line. The major sectional divisions of the movement (those used for the tabular description at the beginning of this chapter) are indicated by vertical lines.

On consideration of what Lidov calls the 'design' of this movement, a high degree of symmetry is immediately striking. The movement divides exactly in half at bar 100, the return to E♭ for the second 'A' section (the anacrusis to bar 1 is even balanced by the single crotchet of bar 201). The halves are divided in mirror proportions, 11:9 and 9:11; the outer sections are more or less bisected, whilst the middle two sections again divide in mirror proportions, roughly 2:1 and 1:2. The lengths can be summarized as follows:

Section	Subsection	Subsection length (bars)	Section length (bars)
1			55
	1a	28	
	1b	27	
2			45
	2a	29	
	2b	16	
3			45
	3a	14	
	3b	31	
4			55
	4a	28	
	4b	27	
Total			200

This gives the proportional scheme:

11:9		9:11	
1:1	2:1	1:2	1:1

Proportional schemes of this sort are not as uncommon in Mahler as one might expect. The proportions of sections in the Finale will be discussed in chapter 3, whilst a scheme incorporating bisection and golden section in *Das Lied von der Erde* is discussed in Samuels 1986. It is difficult not to ascribe such patterning to deliberate compositional planning; but whether or not this is the case, the inherent properties of the scheme carry implications for the interpretation of the movement on several different levels. Most obviously, the scheme encourages the view that the central two sections, the E major *Naturlaut* section and the return of the E♭ melody, should be taken together. They provide the pivot of the form, and in some sense balance each other. Similarly, the drive to E♭ via C♯ minor and B (bars 146-73) combines with the final section in the tonic to balance the opening 55 bars (this is borne out by motivic and melodic considerations, since the opening material returns at bar 146). The remaining sections also mirror each other, both being fragmented in texture, exhibiting a number of melodic and motivic parallels, and providing tonal instability and contrast to the 'A' sections.

The remarkable thing about these features is that the prominence that they give to the individual sections of the movement makes idiolectic reference in every case. The juxtaposition of E and E♭ has several precedents in Mahler: on the one hand, in the association of keys a semitone apart, as in the overall schemes of the Fifth Symphony (C♯ to D) and Ninth Symphony (D to D♭); and on the other, in the consistent use of E major to symbolise Utopian escape, most obviously in the Finale of the Fourth Symphony. These two associations actually coincide in the opposition of E and E♭ in the first part of the Eighth Symphony (the '*Accende lumen*' theme and the first subject). E major is also used in opposition to C minor in the first movement of the Second Symphony (which eventually ends in E♭), a connection mentioned above in relation to ex. 2.3. Here, the positioning of E major gestures beyond the work to a use of key relations which is part of the Mahlerian vocabulary. A similar comment can be made concerning the section between bar 115 and bar 145: here the sequence of keys is C major (although inflected towards F major), A major, and A minor. These are, of course, the principal tonal centres of the other movements of the symphony; much of the form of the Finale, indeed, relies on the opposition of C and A, as the next chapter will discuss.

A narrative of key structure and proportion is therefore emerging: the central juxtaposition of E and E♭ is a Utopian image, which is approached via E minor, embodying the major/minor modal opposition evident throughout the Sixth Symphony, and is left via a section which internalises the opposition of the Andante to the rest of the work. This narrative, it should be noted, is similar to those suggested by other aspects of motivic coding in the movement. Indeed, key structure itself is

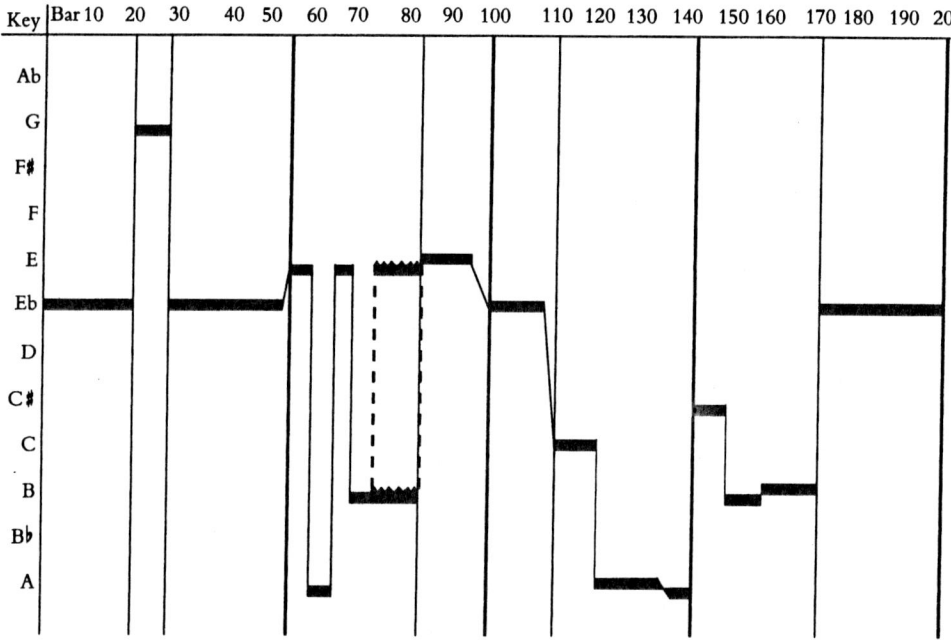

Figure 2.1

acting as a kind of motivic reference. The relative poverty of semiotic reference in the slow movement form is more than compensated by the richness which it gains from its interaction with the motivic code.

The patterns of melodic recurrence within the Andante are fairly well defined by the formal description above. The opening E♭ melody is confined to the 'A' sections, whilst the distribution of the contrasting theme has already been discussed. The only topic remaining for this investigation of signs with a musical material trace is the variation of the opening melody.

There are four statements of the opening theme, at bars 1, 28, 100 and 159; these are brought into juxtaposition in ex. 2.13.

This theme has attracted a fair amount of comment, and indeed disquiet, from analysts. The feature at which most writers have balked is the simple and clear-cut cadence in bar 10, which gives the theme its *volksliedhaft* character, but stands at odds with its use as a symphonic subject. Paul Bekker's remarks, that '. . . One might suspect that Mahler himself found no pure pleasure in this theme', and that it continues 'as if it wished to forget itself' (Bekker 1920: 220), are echoed (though less dismissively) by Adorno, who describes it as standing apart from 'the true

Example 2.13

course of the music, as if this were not [its] own story' (1960: 119/1992:88).[1] Even Schoenberg chose precisely this melody to rebut the charge of 'banality' in Mahler's works, which he does principally by re-writing its five-bar phrases into unequivocally banal four-bar ones (Schoenberg 1975: 460-2). The defence of this movement rests in all these cases on the idea that the specific unfolding of the music dispels or subsumes the elements of banality in the theme. And, if the need to maintain Mahler's aesthetic worth is no longer such a pressing issue, it is still notable that all these interpretations perceive a dialectic between the melodic and the motivic coding of the theme.

There are two principal motivic components recurrent in each statement of the theme. The one which is unvarying is, interestingly, the descending motive of table 2.4. Units from table 2.4 column I appear in the second half of the first bar of each melody, and units from table 2.4 column VII appear just before the dotted line that indicates the mid-point of each. These latter units in fact play an important role in incorporating two-part writing into the three thematic restatements. The other motive which is common to all the melodies is, of course, the table 2.1 motive. This motive, however, is varied (in terms of its interval content) each time that it appears. The table 2.4 motives therefore function as stable, repeated features whilst the table 2.1 motives provide a linear, developmental history. This contrast in function is consonant with the differences in their signifying scope which were discussed above. Modification of motivic detail abounds, such as the re-writing of the second bar in the second melody, introducing the table 2.3 motivic rhythm, and disrupting the balance of first and second bar in the first melody (where the E♭-B♭-E♭ of bar 2 is an inversion and augmentation of the G-E♭-G of bar 1). But what is striking is the manner in which the re-writing and motivic recombination fall into a coherent structure when these statements are placed alongside each other. The initial pitches of the table 2.1 motives describe the arpeggaic ascent G (bar 1) to B♭ (bar 5, repeated at bar 28) to E♭ (bar 32). This ascent is then continued by the counter-melody to the motive at bar 100, which enters on a top B♭. This pattern is not taken up at the beginning of the fourth melodic statement (bar 158), where the melody starts in the bass; but it is noticeable that the final return to E♭ is made by the melodic ascent top D♯ (enharmonic E♭) to top G at bars 170-3. In this way, the motivic connections between the thematic statements are made to serve a linear logic.

This structure is remarkable for its intermittent character, an observation which is reinforced by considering the 'B' sections between the returns of the E♭ melody. Each of these sections contains the prominent melodic interval of a third, a motivic detail which was not tabulated above, although its presence has been remarked. The secondary theme of bar 22 is preceded by the gentle oscillation B♭-G on the flutes. Then, in bar 56, the first 'B' section is introduced by a two-octave portamento on

---

[1] References to Adorno 1992 do not always follow the published translation exactly. Any deviation is the author's own.

Example 2.14

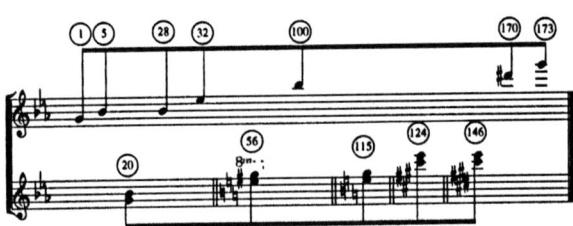

the pitch G, leading to the third G–E♭ as the prelude to the new key of E minor. At the opening of the second 'B' section in bar 115 (see ex. 2.10), this same third introduces the key C major, and then moves to the third E–C♯ in bar 124 (in A major) and bar 146 (in C♯ minor). Thus a completely different set of equally coherent motivic connections, based on this downward chain of minor thirds, is interleaved with the ascending arpeggio of the main theme. Perhaps this is the melodic and motivic correlate of Adorno's comment that the main theme 'stands apart' from the rest of the movement. These connections are summarized in ex. 2.14.

The fact that melodic and formal structures rest on motivic connections in this movement demonstrates both the extent to which the Andante is genuinely autonomous, and the points at which interpretants of more than intratextual scope are required. It is fascinating to compare the partial, interleaving structures of ex. 2.14 with a voice-leading analysis. As was remarked above, a Schenkerian view of the movement would identify G♮ as the *Kopfton*, from its occurrence on the first downbeat, its recurrence in the E minor and C major sections (with a neighbour-note motion to G♯ in the E major section), and the structural descent from the G of bar 173 to the closing E♭ at bar 185 (although G remains prominent in the final fifteen bars of tonic prolongation). In other words, the two motivic/melodic structures fit neatly into the prolongation of the structural tone. This indicates both the cohesion and the fragmentation of the formal and harmonic processes in the Andante; the semiotic status of the voice-leading is inseparable from the interaction of other intramusical codes.

LIMITS OF MOTIVIC CODING

The foregoing discussion has served to demonstrate the primacy of the motivic code in the semiosis of the Andante. It subsumes the organisation of melody and form, furnishes the points of contact between this movement and the rest of the work, and places it within the Mahlerian idiolect. However, it would be wrong to assume that this analysis produces a complete account of signification within this movement. On the contrary: what starts as a motivic analysis constantly finds itself predicated on observations of more general scope. The motivic code acts to require other, non-intramusical, codes. In the end, the claim that it is possible to account for musical meaning entirely by means of 'purely musical' features cannot be sustained. This also serves to indicate what is the genuine fault with the sort of paradigmatic analysis produced by Nattiez and Ruwet: it is not so much the concentration on foreground or surface features as the sole constituents of signs, as the belief that once paradigm classes have been segmented, then their referential function has been established. The huge quantity of data created by Nattiez's *tabula rasa* approach to Varèse's *Density 21.5* is an indication of too little, rather than too much, rigour in segmentation.

This first attempt to deal with the same sort of signifiers as previous semiotic musical analysis demonstrates the necessity for Eco's concept of sign production: it is the nature of the relations between the 's-codes' that is the province of semiotic inquiry. It is this which forms the connection between analysis of musical data and speculation concerning metamusical cerebration; the signified s-codes map onto the signifying s-codes in multiple and unpredictable ways. If it is harder to track down the connections between musical features and extramusical (or intertextual) signifieds than it is to discuss intratextual reference, these connections remain the necessary outcome of the sort of analysis just performed on the Andante. The widening of the inquiry to address these other sorts of signs is the concern of the remaining chapters of this study.

3

CODING OF MUSICAL FORM: THE FINALE

In the previous chapter, the consideration of motivic processes as coded signifying structures demonstrated many of the advantages (and problems) inherent in the definition of music as a semiotic system. Nevertheless, it remains true that the limitation of the analysis to structures of pitch and duration, which are immanent within and unique to the individual work, begs the question of whether the conceptual armoury of code and sign production can address the much hazier issue of how the musical work is to be situated within the contexts and histories of other examples of cultural production. Whilst certain intertextual observations can be made about motivic coding (the establishment of an idiolect, or the latent reference to previous works), and certain extramusical signifieds can tentatively be suggested (the tendency to decay and dissolution, the Utopian breakthrough of the E major passage), other codes are needed to bring the individual work into relationship with specific traditions of composition. The obvious candidate with which to begin this inquiry is the coding of musical form. To the extent to which formal archetypes can be identified in a piece of music, they necessarily invoke some sort of relationship with the previous history of the use of that form. Frequently, in works of the late nineteenth century and early twentieth century, specific earlier composers, or indeed individual works, can be named by formal process alone. For instance, the kinship between Mahler's Second Symphony and Beethoven's Ninth concerns much more than just the use of a chorus. The signifying force of choices concerning form can only be understood within the context of a governing institution of compositional practice. The extent to which writing 'Symphony' at the head of a score becomes a polemic point (as it does by the time of Stravinsky's Symphony in C) is the extent to which the form of any individual work is significant within the institution of symphonic writing.

FORM, ANALYSIS AND RECEPTION HISTORY

There is a further advantage of turning to form as the next subject of semiotic inquiry after motivic coding; namely, that the signifiers involved are constituted solely by musical material. In other words, the scope of reference is only widened slightly by comparison with the motivic code, since the histories constructed as contexts for formal archetypes are made up of musical works. Issues of reference to wider cultural practice will be addressed in chapters 4 and 5; but even the strictly 'intramusical' question of identifying formal types and assessing their signifying potential threatens to become elusive and speculative as soon as any more than the simplest analytical observations are made.

This chapter will focus on the last movement of the Sixth Symphony, in order to approach the question of form via the analytical reception history of the movement. There have been many attempts to analyse the form of the Finale, with the paradoxical result that the coding of form is best seen in discussions of this movement, despite its being the most complex in terms of formal organisation. It is, indeed, not just the most complex of the movements of this symphony, but the most complex by comparison with practically every other movement by Mahler; Otto Klemperer allegedly refused to conduct the work on the grounds that he could not make sense of the form of the Finale. In the Fifth Symphony, Mahler had re-written the convention of a sonata form Allegro opening movement to create a bipartite form which simultaneously engages with the history of symphonic practice and seeks to abolish it. In the Sixth Symphony, the adoption of clear, even Mozartian formal divisions in the first movement (down to an exposition repeat) means that the engagement with formal complexity is displaced to the Finale. Other relationships between the outer movements will be explored in chapter 5; but the contrast in formal organisation makes it hardly controversial to state that they represent alternative models of sonata form procedure, and that this concern with form is in some sense primary in the semiotic process of the Finale. This places Mahler at the beginning of a twentieth-century history of engagement with the tradition of sonata form. As Joseph Straus comments, 'It is no longer possible in this century . . . to write a sonata form that arises organically, spontaneously and seamlessly from the musical relationships . . . Twentieth-century composers inevitably approach the sonata self-consciously and often . . . with malice aforethought' (Straus 1990: 132). Sonata form is invoked in the Finale by both tonal and thematic means. However, any integrative view of its form has to rest on a preferential hearing of certain sorts of musical sign, at the expense of marginalising others. The Finale thus provides a case study in the different potential readings of formal signifiers and formal significance.

The suspicion amongst scholars of the simplistic taxonomy of musical form inaugurated by A. B. Marx, and continued in German (and English) musical education ever since, has made the analytical study of form a controversial topic. The analytical systems of both Schoenberg and Schenker, and more especially their legacies, the Anglo-American institutions of Schoenbergian and Schenkerian analysis, can all be seen as attempts to find a basis for the description of form which avoids the concepts of model and deviation inherent in the terminology of *Hauptsatz* and *Seitensatz*. As a result, a study such as Charles Rosen's *The Classical Style* succeeds precisely to the extent that it proves its central premise, that late eighteenth-century form is better understood in terms of dramatic conflict and resolution, rather than the fulfilment of pre-existing formal moulds (or, in Beethoven's case, the creation of new ones). However, if the *Ursatz* has great advantages, in discussion of tonal coherence, over the terminology of false recapitulations or expanded codas, the shift away from taxonomic categories in analysis of form has obscured at least two important points: firstly, that formal categories assume, and to some extent synthesise, a wide variety of other parameters (from tonal process to melodic development and even programmatic detail); and secondly, that in German music after about 1850 the establishment of *Formenlehre* in conservatoires and textbooks means that the works of composers educated within that system represent a dialectical engagement with a taxonomic view of form. What is a *post hoc* imposition onto the works of Haydn becomes the assumed basis of a work like Brahms' First Piano Sonata. This is a process which can be seen often in the history of composition; it is not unlike the situation created by the publication of popular guides to Wagner's operas, which listed and labelled the leitmotifs. Whilst the relevance of these to Wagner's works may be doubted, they were clearly influential on Richard Strauss' conception of the technique, since he labelled leitmotifs in the sketches of *Salome* and *Elektra*.

If this historical process justifies the use of the terms of the *Formenlehre* tradition in discussing the Finale of the Sixth Symphony, it must be admitted immediately that there are as many different views of how they should be applied as there are analysts who have attempted it. As a result, a survey of the existing literature constitutes a study in the analytical reception history of the work. Adorno's comment, that 'large-scale form is the declared concern in the Finale of the Sixth Symphony' (1960: 131/1992: 97) stands at the head of a long history. The desire to elucidate Mahler's 'declared concern' drives even such a widely-read critic as Bernhard Sponheuer, after reviewing the efforts of his predecessors, to offer his own, slightly different, tabular division of the movement (1978: 314-15). The lack of agreement as to which sections to label as exposition, development or recapitulation accompanies a tacit agreement that these terms are the only ones appropriate to describe the movement's formal organisation. It is true that, in a German- rather than English-speaking context, these terms are much more functional descriptions of sections than they are simple labels. In what follows in this chapter, the history described is one of conflicting conceptions of the systematic organisation of the Finale. What is primary and what is secondary; which elements form oppositions and which form elaborations of each other; these are the recurrent topics of analysis of this sort. The answers produced are therefore illustrative of changing ideology as much as a constant frame of reference.

Clearly, individual sections of the Finale are multivalent within the historical conception of form shared by the composer and German-speaking analysts. From the point of view of a semiotic analysis, what is sought is far from an external arbitration of the points of disagreement. The reasons why any individual analyst should prefer one tabular division over another are interesting, both for what they reveal of the analyst's assumptions about what is important in articulating formal divisions, and for the identification of the sources of multivalence or ambiguity within the musical text. Thus a comparative approach is likely to yield information about both the reception history and the signifying process of the work itself.

The shifts of analytical opinion are described by the terms 'plot' and 'seriation process' in what is perhaps Jean-Jacques Nattiez's most persuasive article to date (Nattiez 1985). He takes another example of analytical multivalence, the 'Tristan chord', which, as he says, 'has the peculiarity of not in itself corresponding to any configuration classified in harmony treatises', and surveys the different harmonic explanations offered by the fifty or more analysts who have attempted to describe its tonal function. Since any classification of the chord necessarily involves altering between one and three of its four notes to achieve a recognisable chordal form, the sort of tonal progression heard in the opening bars of the *Tristan* Prelude has to be justified by each analyst; the contexts to which the differing analyses appeal are termed 'seriation processes' by Nattiez. These contexts in turn arise out of a particular view of the functional coherence of the tonal system, which gives a rationale for the choice of seriation process; and it is this rationale which forms the 'plot' of the analyst. The idea of 'correct' and 'incorrect' analyses is not abandoned, since there may be many reasons for preferring one hearing over another; but the absolute claims of an organicist or essentialist aesthetic are made relative. Nattiez concludes, 'The comparison of different analyses in this way cannot be done in the name of transcendent truth; and when there is agreement among researchers it is not because they have suddenly found *the* truth, but rather because they have *grosso modo* accepted the same outlook and plot' (1985: 117).

Whilst the 'seriation process' required to account for a single chord is relatively easy to identify, the decisions involved in segmenting an 800-bar orchestral score are likely to rest on a wide range of criteria, not always consciously articulated. By contrast, the 'plot' controlling any particular analysis of the Mahler revolves around a few recurrent ideas: the status of Mahler's engagement with tradition (as inheritor, rebel or saviour), the grounds for hearing the work as coherent, and the narrative suggested by the formal process. Shifting conceptions and weighting of these concerns more or less constitute the reception history of this movement. To the extent that all the analyses considered derive from the *Formenlehre* tradition, they may be said to share a 'plot', or at least to exemplify related plots. As a result, comparing tabular analyses of the Finale is not a trivial exercise, although a more thoroughgoing investigation of formal partitioning and progression is needed to assess the results; as Nattiez comments, 'conflicts between analyses are, then, not only conflicts of description, labelling and relevancy, but the result of struggles between plots which inform potential seriation processes' (Nattiez 1985:117). This chapter therefore begins with an overview of the existing analytical literature, before going on to consider what features within the musical text make up the indicators of formal function sought by the analyst.

ANALYSES OF THE FINALE: SECTIONAL DIVISIONS

Some seventy years separate the earliest and latest analyses to be brought together in this chapter. Within that time-span, several phases of Mahlerian scholarship may be identified, and several dynasties have been created. In 1975, John Williamson

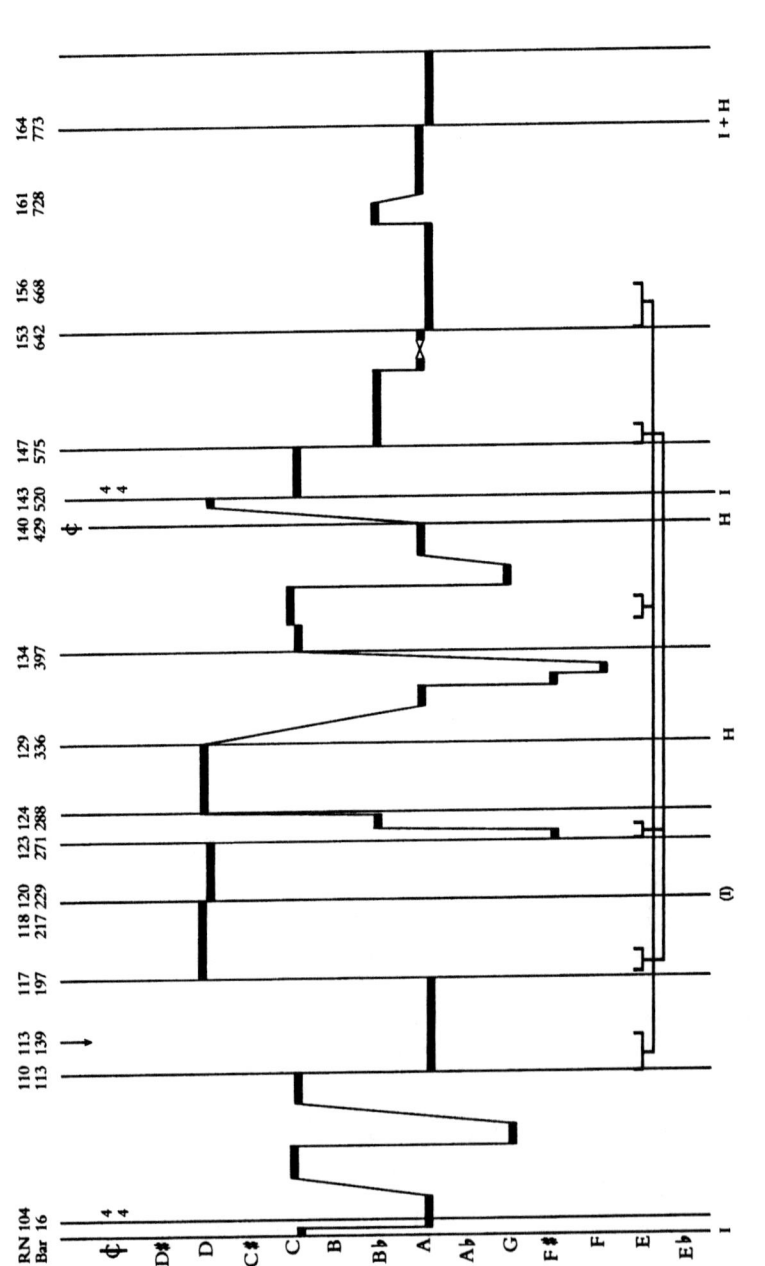

SAMUELS
Mahler's Sixth Symphony

Figure 3.1 [Landscape]

identified three phases of Mahlerian scholarly reception: the initial studies by those who knew the composer, of which Paul Bekker's is the most noteworthy; the works of those who rehabilitated Mahler as a composer of interest in the 1930s, 40s and 50s; and the 'modern' phase of studies inaugurated by Adorno (Williamson 1975: 6-14). Fifteen years after writing this, Williamson still comments, 'the writings of Adorno (1960) have been paramount, and few have escaped their influence; where writers have tried to do so, discussion of Mahler has often hinged on confrontation with, and exorcism of, Adorno's little monograph' (Williamson 1991: 358). It is not entirely coincidental that the six writers who have attempted a detailed partitioning of the Finale represent each of these phases of scholarship. Paul Bekker's own analysis is the earliest, though it extends little further than labelling the main sections. Of Williamson's second phase, Erwin Ratz and Hans Redlich contain a combination of received terminology and idiosyncratic adjustment or description. Both writers attempt to explain Mahler's relation to tradition, rather than simply place him in a context. Adorno's own comments are detailed, especially in the assessment of symbolism and narrative effect. And of the more recent writers, Sponheuer and Constantin Floros can be taken as fairly representing the pro-Adorno and anti-Adorno inheritors respectively.

Before considering the analyses themselves, figure 3.1 attempts to give a rudimentary, 'neutral' formal map of the movement. The shifts of tonal centre are indicated graphically, while sections of undecidable tonality (which are not necessarily transitions as such) are shown by oblique lines. The temporal duration shows $\frac{2}{2}$ bars to be half the duration of the normal $\frac{4}{4}$ bars, as is indicated in the score; however, the numerous changes of tempo (*etwas drängend*, etc.) have been ignored. In addition, two sets of recurring features are indicated: unambiguous repeats of melodic material, and the more theatrical gestures of the introductory chord, with its associated texture of tremolandi strings, woodwind and celesta, and the three hammer-blows (the third of which was deleted by Mahler, although this has not been taken as authoritative by all subsequent conductors, as will be discussed below).

Remaining for the moment with this purely temporal outline of the movement, several points of interest emerge. In terms of proportional divisions, the mid-point of the movement occurs very close to the beginning of the march that develops the first subject (bar 397); more intriguing still, the golden-section division of the movement occurs almost at the return of the introductory chord at bar 520 (this divides the movement at 98.5 per cent of the golden section – the precise division comes at the beginning of the transition back to this double bar, at bar 504, RN 142). Bisection and golden-section division can be found elsewhere in Mahler, as was discussed in relation to the Andante in chapter 2. Whether deliberately calculated or not, there can be no doubt that the architectonic balance of the Finale is influential on its segmentation.

The key structure of the movement is complex, and also the source of much of the undecidability of formal segmentation. The key areas which are placed in opposition by what are, in the view of most analysts, the first and second subjects, are A minor and D major/minor (bars 9-32, then 114-96, as against bars 197-270). However, D occurs only fleetingly after bar 336, and the main dramatic contrast of the movement is the articulation of A major/minor against C major/minor, announced in the opening bars where a C minor melody resolves onto a triad which is simultaneously A minor and A major.

The combination of a subdominant area for a secondary subject group and key areas separated by a third is a frequent plan for Mahler's more extended tonal structures. In the Ninth Symphony, Christopher Lewis (1984) argues for a 'double-tonic' structure which rests for a large part on third-relations (D and B♭ in the first movement). A similar view of the movement in hand would undoubtedly start from the fact that the two sets of recurrent thematic material occur, in A and C on the one hand, and D, F♯ and B♭ on the other (see fig. 3.1). Lewis turns to his elaboration of tonal concepts out of the conviction that 'the analyst must assume that coherence and consistency are essential characteristics of a work of art' (1984: 9); the 'double-tonic' structure is meant to function as an alternative to the Schenkerian *Ursatz*, although the lack of extended passages in the dominant tonality does not mean that a structural dominant cannot be located, or that it has only local effect. The issues surrounding a Schenkerian view of the Sixth Symphony Finale, and the different possible valuations of the tonal scheme of the movement, will be discussed in due course; for the moment, it is sufficient to notice that the key structure is bound to complicate any attempt to map the categories of sonata form onto the thematic and tonal architecture. The fact that the form articulates contrasts of tonal areas, as much as it does contrasts of thematic groups, encourages the view that it is the history of sonata form writing which is engaged by this movement. The eighteenth-century conceptualisation of form as a tonal structure is part of the intertextual reference, as well as the more typically nineteenth-century concern with thematic and motivic working. This again recalls Straus' comments on the twentieth-century preoccupation with 'remaking the past' (see Straus 1990: 96-132).

If these observations on the general organisation of the Finale can be seen as 'neutral', in the sense that they attempt to avoid the use of formal categories, they provide a context for the following consideration of specific analyses. To use Nattiez's terms, whilst sonata form is undoubtedly a concept with 'poietic' pertinence to this work, it should by now be clear that the application of its categories to the Finale is so far from self-evident as to be an analytically 'esthesic' activity.

Ratz, Redlich, Sponheuer and Floros all provide tabular summaries of their formal divisions of the movement. Both Bekker and Adorno refer to specific rehearsal numbers in the course of their discussions, and so tabular divisions can be constructed unambiguously from their texts. These six analyses are placed alongside each other in figure 3.2, to show their points of similarity and divergence. The requirements of space have necessitated some compression of terminology, especially in the case of Sponheuer, whose table is rather more detailed than the others. The German terms *Hauptsatz*, *Seitensatz*, and *Schlußgruppe* have consistently been translated as '1st subject', '2nd subject' and 'closing group'. Similarly, *Einleitung*,

Exposition, *Durchführung* and *Reprise* have been rendered with their standard English equivalents. A cursory survey of these analyses shows that their points of agreement on even the major sections of a sonata form outline are limited to the placing of the coda.

In many ways, the four earlier analyses are the more interesting for present purposes, since they do not rely on the accumulated knowledge of an analytical literature. To consider Ratz's analysis first, he takes the occurrences of the introductory chord as the decisive formal markers, inaugurating development, recapitulation and coda. The concept that this chord acts as a 'formal marker' serves an overtly polemical aim, as his 'brief analysis of one of his most superb symphonic movements is intended to demonstrate an essential feature: Mahler's mastery of form which bears comparison with the greatest composers' (Ratz 1968: 34).

The most important organizational principle for Ratz is that sonata form should present a logic of temporal succession. Thus the two musical features which are sought out by the analysis are firstly sectional delimiters, such as the introductory chord, and secondly motivic connections between themes, which are held to create 'musical logic'. The motivic connection on which Ratz focuses particular attention is the melodic interval of an octave, which unites themes from both first and second subject groups. Ratz is able to demonstrate a variety of intervallic and rhythmic connections between his first and second subjects; but the claim for Mahler's 'mastery of form' still rests on the possibility of assimilating both the sequence of formal sections and their relative proportions to those of 'the classics'. The models Ratz has in mind remain unnamed; perhaps a significant indicator of the extent to which they are a context formed by a pedagogic rather than a compositional tradition. And when he encounters features of the movement which are problematic for this view of form (which Adorno termed an 'onto-theology'), he resorts either to simple unsupported assertion of Mahler's correctness, or to a more contorted justification of Mahler's canonical status. Hence the length of the introduction (113 bars), which is a problem to most of the commentators, is part of the specific plan of the work:

> It is clear that in view of the generously planned introduction the compactness of the exposition must not only have a special meaning but will have its effect on shaping the development. And here, again, we have occasion to admire the almost somnambulistic sureness of formal conception which Mahler possessed to a degree scarcely equalled by another twentieth-century composer. (1968: 41)

On the other hand, the reversal of the second and first subject's appearances in the recapitulation is a deviation from the norm which requires excuse:

> It is not our task to expound what the composer meant by this; such commentaries are only desirable when they shed light on the structure. In this case, however, the transposition of first subject and second subject is easily understandable. In the first place, such transpositions, which aim at symmetry and lead to the form ABCBA, are on occasion found in the classics. Secondly, the material of the second subject group has hardly been touched upon in the development, and is therefore liable to be resumed as early as possible. (1968: 45-6)

bar	Bekker (1920)	Ratz (1956)	Adorno (1960)
1	INTRODUCTION	INTRODUCTION	INTRODUCTION
16			
49			
65			
67			
98			
114	EXPOSITION	EXPOSITION 1st Subject	EXPOSITION
139		Subject 1b	
141			
176			
191		2nd subject	
205			
217		Closing subject	
229		DEVELOPMENT Introduction	Introduction
237			
271			DEVELOPMENT I
288		2nd subject	

Figure 3.2

This makes the hierarchy of decisions quite clear: the formal scheme is primary for Ratz, and functions independently of the processes of motivic development and recurrence which distinguish the movement from its forebears. Hence the second subject's resumption at bar 520 has to be recapitulation rather than development. The formal code at work here operates to obliterate differences between the work in question and a taxonomic set of categories; the simple identification of the correct sequence of categories is sufficient to justify their temporal logic.

This is clearly an analysis created in opposition to assumed criticism of Mahler, answering the charge that he was unable to write coherent forms or respect the

Redlich (1963)	Sponheuer (1978)	Floros (1985)	bar
EXPOSITION *Introduction*	INTRODUCTION Opening gesture; motto	EXPOSITION Introduction	1
I	Genesis of 1st and 2nd subjects; cyclic motive	'Distant music'; exposition motives	16
II	Chorale	Chorale	49
III	Progressive integration	Motto rhythm	65
		'Distant music'	67
IV	lead-up to exposition	Transition	98
1st subject	EXPOSITION 1st subject	1st subject	114
2nd subject	Transition; dissolution		139
		Chorale	141
		1st subject close	176
Subject 3a	2nd subject	2nd subject	191
Subject 3b			205
	Closing group		217
ANTE-RECAPITULATIONS *Introduction*	DEVELOPMENT Introduction	DEVELOPMENT *Introduction*	229
		'Distant music'	237
		I	271
Subject 3b	I	2nd subject	288

Figure 3.2 (*cont.*)

tradition within which he composed. The sense of strain involved in Ratz's manipulation of the musical facts to fit the formal scheme supplies the reason why Hans Redlich reshapes the scheme itself, in the service of much the same apologetic stance. Redlich preserves the *functions* of exposition, development and recapitulation, but distinguishes them from their necessary temporal succession. He relegates the D major group of themes to the status of a third subject group, and describes its reappearance either side of what he takes to be the development as 'ante-recapitulation' and 'post-recapitulation' (the prefixes thus refer to the sections' relation to the development). The ingenuity of the scheme allows Redlich to

bar	Bekker (1920)	Ratz (1956)	Adorno (1960)
336	DEVELOPMENT	Main development 'Negative'	II
364		'Positive'	
385		'Negative'	
397		'Positive'	III
449		'Negative'	
458		'Positive'	
469		'Negative'	
479	RECAPITULATION	Transition	IV
520		RECAPITULATION Introduction & 2nd subject	RECAPITULATION
537			
575			
642		1st subject	
668		Subject 1b	
670			
728		Closing subject	
754			
773	CODA	CODA	CODA
790			
816			
822	END	END	END

Figure 3.2 (*cont.*)

claim a genuine combination of sonata and rondo – taking issue with what he finds to be unclear in Adorno's description of the movement – whilst the 'correct' succession of first and second subject is preserved.

What is fascinating about this (admittedly idiosyncratic) analysis is the displace-

Coding of musical form: the Finale

Redlich (1963)	Sponheuer (1978)	Floros (1985)	bar
DEVELOPMENT I: exposition material	II	II	336
		2nd subject	364
		'Battle scene'	385
	III	III 1st subject	397
			449
		Introductory theme & 2nd subject	458
		Bridge passage	469
II: exposition material	IV	IV Chorale theme	479
POST-RECAPITULATIONS Introduction	RECAPITULATION Introduction	RECAPITULATION Introduction	520
		'Distant music'	537
Subject 3a	2nd subject	2nd subject	575
MAIN RECAPITULATION 1st subject	1st subject	1st subject	642
2nd subject	Altered transition theme		668
		Motivic development of all subjects	670
Subject 3b	Closing group	*Abgesang*	728
		1st & 2nd subjects	754
CODA Introduction	CODA Introduction	CODA Introductory theme	773
Epilogue	Epilogue	Epitaph	790
		Close	816
END	END	END	822

Figure 3.2 (*cont.*)

ment of the compositional virtues which Ratz was at pains to locate, and the points at which a non-traditional formal principle is created to explain Mahler's methods. Redlich's comments are very brief (a single page of description and another of table), but his argument appears to abstract the semes 'repetition' and 'development' from rondo and sonata forms respectively. Precedents for the movement are clearly important, and Redlich suggests Beethoven's Op. 135 String Quartet, Berlioz's *Symphonie Fantastique* and Brahms' First Symphony as possible legitimate father-figures. He hears the process of the movement as the dramatic confrontation of formal principles. In this hybridisation, simultaneously musical and metaphysical, 'the whole Finale oscillates dualistically between two contrasting types of music: one of 'chaotic' germinating character, and one of march-like Allegro sections of a decidedly developmental bent. Both these elements are incompatible, non-integrative, in contrast to the integrative relationship between introduction and Allegro in the Finale of the First Symphony by Brahms' (Redlich 1963: 255).

The function of contrast is thus displaced from *Hauptsatz* and *Seitensatz* to the introduction and thematic complexes. In terms of semiotic process, Redlich views the code of melodic succession to be primary, superseding both motivic development and tonal plan in fulfilling formal expectations. It is particularly noticeable that his table simply numbers the three subject groups, without addressing the fact that the second subject group remains in the same key as the first.

The grounds for taking bars 139ff as the second subject are not hard to find: the repeated quaver triads on the trombones, immediately taken up by woodwind, second violins and violas, contain two signifiers of change: the major/minor triad figure which inaugurated the whole movement, and the new theme on the horns from bar 141 (see ex. 3.1). The treatment of the parallel passage in the recapitulation (bars 668ff) is, however, illuminating. Here the theme from bar 141 is introduced only in inversion, and on the lowest instruments; aural precedence is taken by the theme from the D major complex of bars 191ff, a variant of which is stated *fortissimo* by the B♭ trumpet (see ex. 3.2). Both Ratz and Redlich, however, refer to this as the recapitulation of the theme carried by bass tubas, and low woodwind. Such a clear example of the suppression of one, arguably prior, theme in favour of another confirms that, although each analysis presents its narrative as the uncovering of musical fact, they are both reliant on a formal model fixed in advance, which then dictates the selection of the musical facts which support it and the marginalisation of those which do not. A consequence of this selection is a spatialised, static conception of form as the articulation of symmetry and balance abstracted from the temporal unfolding of the music.

This is not to deny that there are great differences between the two studies: it is striking that the multiple motivic connections between themes noted by Ratz serve only the general idea of 'development' for Redlich, while the form remains 'non-integrative'. Each of his formal sections contains both introductory and thematic material; he comments, 'it can be seen that the dualistic nature of the Movement necessitates dualism in all its ramifications'. This appeal to a philosophical or narrative programme is taken no further, although one might guess that it is in part at least a response to Adorno's unwaveringly dialectical discussion of the work.

Adorno's own analysis is less interested in taxonomic categories than in what he considers to be the philosophical implications of the way in which Mahler presents

Coding of musical form: the Finale

Example 3.1

Example 3.2

each section of the form. Adorno devotes several pages to this movement, which he hears as a successful confrontation of individual impulse – freedom – and coherence or discipline, the 'formal expectations' without which it would become mere solipsism: 'the movement, which traverses immeasurable distances of time, succeeds in squaring the circle: it is dynamic and tectonic in one, without one principle annulling the other' (Adorno 1960: 129/1992: 93). These 'immeasurable distances of time' are part of the listener's perception rather than the literal temporal dimensions of the movement. The philosophical attitude which Adorno perceives to lie behind the formal organisation of this movement is one of 'nominalism'. Nominalism may be described as the critique of general categories through the insistence on the autonomy of individual examples; in other words, the movement 'achieves' its status as a sonata form, rather than sonata form being a given, pre-existing mould (this is what Adorno means by the 'onto-theology' of form). In this way, nominalism attacks the Idealist insistence on taxonomy and categorisation, by emphasising the freedom of the individual impulse. Adorno's view is that the combination of motivic connections between themes, and the use of programmatic techniques to make recurrences as differentiated as possible, constitutes a representation of passing time akin to the techniques of experimental nineteenth-century novels. He notes that 'great novelists like Jacobsen were apt to omit whole periods of the lives of their heroes, lighting up critical phases with abrupt resolve; what Jacobsen selected expressly as a principle of "bad composition" becomes, in Mahler's great formal experiment as well, one of good writing' (1960: 133/1992: 98).

The way in which Adorno's comparison of novel and symphony anticipates the analysis of musical narrative which has become a concern of musicology in the

1990s will be discussed fully in chapter 5. For present purposes, it is important to look at the consequences of this conception, which might be termed a description of the metamusical significance of the movement, for the functions Adorno assigns to the individual formal sections. It is not surprising, in the light of the above quotation, that Adorno terms the development 'the symphony proper' (1960: 133/ 1992: 98). He differs from Ratz in dissociating the introductory chord and the following section of 'musical prose', bars 229–70, from his development section, in order to identify four parallel sections. Each of these begins with 'symphonic' development of thematic material and ends with a 'dissolution-field' (*Auflösungsfeld*), before a formal marker (the hammer-blows at bars 336 and 479, a general pause at bar 397, and the cadence onto the introductory chord at bar 520) recalls the music to its model. In this way, Adorno can argue for a forcefield composed of 'improvisatory freedom', then 'working-out' of material 'in the spirit of sonata form', and finally imposed moments of closure which constrain the freedom granted to the dissolution fields.

Typically, what determines the coding of form for Adorno is not the code of motivic development, as with Ratz, nor the coding of melodic recurrence, as with Redlich, but the extent to which these codes do *not* cohere; the primacy of exposition and recapitulation is replaced by that of development, in a genuine deconstruction, or immanent critique, of sonata form. Adorno is as aware as Derrida of the 'myth of presence': Mahler 'artfully withdraws the recapitulation, which he needs, from the surface of perception. This endows it, in the Finale of the Sixth, with an expression of sketchy ghostliness reminiscent of *Revelge*. The recapitulation becomes an apparition; the character legitimizes the remaining symmetry. Not only here, in Mahler, do sections of emphatic, bodily presence in the music alternate with such spectral episodes. Many movements develop in order to seize or relinquish their own reality; music should be entirely present only as the result of its own enactment' (1960: 126/1992: 93).

And, with a critical incisiveness that is lacking from Derrida's discussion of Rousseau, Adorno locates this myth within the institution of sonata form: 'In the recapitulation, music, as a ritual of bourgeois freedom, remained, like the society in which it is and which is in it, enslaved to mythical unfreedom. It manipulates the natural relationship circling within it as if what recurs, by virtue of its mere recurrence, were more than it is, were metaphysical meaning itself, the "Idea" ' (1960: 128/1992: 94).

This is the value, Adorno argues, of Mahler's technique of constant variation of material, and of the connections, motivic and contrapuntal, which are deployed 'behind the scenes' in the creation of the thematic complexes of the Finale: 'Within the principle of permanent modification the development gains new preponderance, but it no longer functions as a dynamic antithesis to static basic relationships. The sonata principle is thereby changed in its innermost part. The expositions, previously structures with substantial weight of their own, become expositions in the sense of presentations of the *dramatis personae*, whose musical story is then told' (1960: 129/1992: 95).

It has to be admitted that Adorno cannot proffer this interpretation as empirically more justified or methodologically more consistent than those of Ratz or Bekker. In contrast to Redlich's reification of 'non-integration' as a formal signified, Adorno refuses to integrate the significations of the formal indicators. He appeals not to an alternative hierarchy of coding processes, but to an alternative hearing of the results; the constituent criteria that make up his formal code are defined only relatively informally. However, his is an analysis which avoids the privileging and marginalisation of constituent parts that could be seen in Ratz's and Redlich's descriptions of bars 668ff. It remains allegorical in its relation to the text to the very extent that it refuses to symbolise the form reductively.

If these three analyses show a wide variety of interpretation of formal indices, it is perhaps not surprising that there is some measure of consensus in analyses from the 'third phase' of reception history. The most detailed discussions to date are those by Sponheuer and Floros, summarised in figure 3.2. If the declared intention of Ratz and Redlich was to deduce formal organisation from the musical surface, Adorno's discussion can be credited with producing an inversion of this method, so that both Sponheuer and Floros start from an understanding of the 'metamusical' concerns of the movement, and then read these back into the formal scheme. Thus their large divisions of the movement differ only in that Sponheuer retains Ratz's and Adorno's distinction between introduction and exposition; otherwise, their points of difference concern the *function* of the units which they have segmented. Sponheuer's chapter title, 'Breakdown as triumph: the construction of negative immanence of form', indicates his intention to demonstrate analytically a broadly Adornian view of formal significance. His seventy pages of discussion amount to the most thoroughgoing description both of the movement's construction and of the grounds for equating it with a nominalist critique of 'the ontology of form' (Sponheuer's success in working through Adorno's comments can be gauged by the fact that his analysis is more or less adopted wholesale by Hans-Peter Jülg's 1986 monograph on the work). He relies, on the one hand, on a description of the large divisions of the form in terms of the contrast of introductory and sonata sections, much in the way that Redlich does; and on the other, on the 'dramatic curve' (*Verlaufskurve*) traced by the musical 'characters' (borrowing Adorno's concept), which principally refers to the development and motivic recombination of thematic material. Sponheuer considers that the sections following each of the four appearances of the introductory chord constitute introductions to exposition, development, recapitulation and coda respectively; and he comments that the introduction 'is at once an integral part, in altered form, of each of the formal sections that it inaugurates; but also does not end up in a merely static, demonstrative role' (Sponheuer 1978: 312).

The roughly equal lengths of the first three main sections are held to be an important symmetry, with the coda 'standing as the *Abgesang* of the whole' (1978: 313). Again, the importance of this is in its function: 'such symmetries are too frequently encountered in the architecture of the Finale to be chance happenings: in them is seen the penetration of the structural conception of the whole (which may also be termed the dynamically balanced conception of the formal sections) by every individual element' (1978: 313).

Sponheuer is at pains to achieve a 'best solution' to the problems of formal description posed by the movement, drawing on Ratz, Adorno and Eberhardt Klemm to produce the outline shown in figure 3.2. Each section, however, is placed within a narrative of inevitable closure, in which the formal aims of the movement are achieved through the movement's own destruction. Sponheuer ends by commenting that 'the coda then gives the final, negative answer: that no fulfilment is possible' (1978: 319). Sponheuer bases this hearing, on the one hand, on the code of motivic development; and on the other, on the relationship of the Finale to the opening movement of the symphony. He describes the first movement as

... the negative image of the Finale, in the sense both of a close relationship – the movements have in common sonata form, their tonality, the expressive character of their theme complexes and indeed the same characteristics of musical process – and also of opposition – in that the Finale, in handling the same elements, does not just 'evoke' the first movement, but also 'revokes' it.
(1978: 321)

This interpretative armature enables Sponheuer to assign Adornian characters to the detail of the motivic and tonal workings of the movement, and to take to task Ratz and Redlich for seeking some sense of fulfilment or autobiographical catharsis in the course of the movement ('Neither has any basis in the musical reality of this A minor symphony'). He closes by linking this view directly to the form: 'In his Finale ... Mahler bids farewell to two forms of musical – and not only musical – falsehood, to the affirmative immanence of closed artworks and to the illusion of the *Durchbruch*, that Utopia can be attained' (1978: 352). As with Adorno, the form succeeds to the extent that it undoes itself: the symmetrical proportions and exhaustive working-through of motivic material lead to the negation of the ideal of transformation and Utopia that the development and recapitulation of sonata form necessarily contains.

Floros' analysis is much less detailed than Sponheuer's, and resists the Adornian impulse to negativity by stressing the richness of the diversity of materials; the implication seems to be that since all human life is here, there is no need to see the negative episodes as having the last word. In this, Floros returns to Ratz's reliance on motivic connections, now as a genuinely 'non-sequential' code: 'The sombre theme of the introduction (which also appears in inversion) takes on hymn-like traits towards the end of the recapitulation (bars 728-753) through its transposition to the major; but soon after possesses an even gloomier form than at the beginning in the requiem-like trombone lines of the coda (bars 790-808)' (Floros 1977: 181). The religious imagery of the analysis is clearly intended to suggest a more positive narrative for the movement than that of Sponheuer. Floros has two grounds for this line of argument: firstly, he invents a new formal category, that of 'music of the far distance', in order to describe the movement's dramatic balance; secondly, he appeals to an intertextual formal meaning by comparing the movement with Strauss's *Tod und Verklärung*. The category of 'distant music' replaces that of Adorno's and Sponheuer's 'dissolution fields', suggesting that the 'norm of sonata form' has become a containing mould for the playing-out of specifically Mahlerian musical characters. Floros quotes all the preceding analysts, as if to suggest that the eclectic form of his own analysis mirrors the process of the music. He comments that if the 'distant music' of the introduction is 'compared with the genuine exposition, development and recapitulation, then what an initial hearing suggests is confirmed, that if the musical events play themselves out on two fundamentally different planes: one unreal, dreamlike and as if from the distance; the other real and present [*vordergründig*]. This gives a better understanding of what Mahler had in mind when he said concerning the sections with the cowbells, that they made it seem "as if he stood on the highest peak in sight of eternity"' (1985: 178).

This is a startling reversal of the reading of formal function preferred by the Adorno/Redlich line of interpretation. It is supported by two observations striking for their reliance on extramusical criteria. First, Floros quotes Ratz's comment on Mahler's deletion of the third hammer-stroke in the Finale, which the composer once described as 'felling the hero' of the work. Mahler removed it for the publication of the score in 1906, at which time he also placed the Andante second and the Scherzo third in the sequence of movements. Redlich is quite certain that he wished to reinstate it but never had the opportunity of doing so in print, since the symphony was not republished (see Redlich 1968: xxiv-xxv). Ratz, however, suggests that Mahler had 'overstressed the impression of an absolute end which, in truth, is no end' (Ratz 1968: 48; Floros 1985: 182). Floros does not elaborate the claim, but for Ratz it forms a specific metaphysical narrative, where 'That which Mahler took, in 1903, to be total extinction ... now shows itself in a new light; Man has fulfilled his task ... Thus, death is not the end, but the ascent to higher spheres' (Ratz 1968: 48).

The other observation made by Floros is the description of the Finale as the 'antithesis' [*Gegenpol*] of Strauss's *Ein Heldenleben*. Whilst this comparison initially seems rather random, it does at least place Mahler in an intertextual network of specific pieces in which formal schemes and metaphysical meanings can be equated. The two works are not compared in any detail (neither were the Finale and *Tod und Verklärung* slightly earlier); rather, Strauss' incomprehension of Mahler's treatment of the hammer-strokes (related by Alma), is adduced as evidence of the worth of the opposition.

However one judges the methodology or results of Floros' or Sponheuer's discussions, the reliance on criteria of wider referential scope at precisely the moments at which the coding of form becomes 'unreadable' is instructive. Time and again the discussion turns away from the musical substance to account for the privileging of one set of formal divisions over another, or the preference for one hierarchy of formal function over another.

If the reception history, analytically speaking, of this work shows a continuing tradition of alternative interpretations rather than overall agreement, it is reasonable to assume that there are aspects of the musical text which give rise to the conflicting critical views. It is clear from the above that the objects taken up by the interpretants of the formal code are frequently not specified by the analysis, and are in any case of diverse sorts. The next section of this discussion will therefore attempt a slightly more detailed consideration of the musical text in order to identify the working of formal signifiers.

INDICES OF FORMAL FUNCTION

An appropriate place to start a discussion of musical polysemy in this movement is the section between bars 229 and 270, which begins with a repetition of the introductory chord of bar 1, and ends with an abrupt modulation into F♯ major for what most analyses take to be the second subject group. For Ratz, Sponheuer and Floros, this section is the opening of the development, although their descriptions of its function vary widely; for Adorno it is a transitional section before the development begins; for Redlich it is an 'ante-recapitulation' of the closing group (the themes at bars 270ff). The final formal possibility is given by Bekker, who regards this as the end of the exposition, and does not locate the development's beginning until bar 336. The model for this section is the passage of 'musical prose' that immediately follows the opening C minor/A minor gestures of the introduction (bars 16-48). This earlier section is in itself enigmatic as far as formal function is concerned; some of its materials are taken up later in the exposition, others not; its status as introduction is far from clear.

A voice-leading analysis suggests itself as a suitable first approach to the definition of signs in this passage. Few have attempted a thoroughgoing Schenkerian view of Mahler's compositional procedures, and this section provides ample evidence for this reluctance. Ex. 3.3 gives the outlines of the voice-leading in this section. Whilst any reduction of harmony as elusive and chromatically inflected as this must be open to challenge, for present purposes this graph will be taken to be uncontroversial in its representation of the part-movement.

The most immediately striking feature of this graph is its harmonic stasis, particularly in view of the weakness (and hence, in normal tonal circumstances, instability) of the harmony which is prolonged through these 42 bars. This is predominantly a $\frac{4}{3}$ sonority in which a B♭ is maintained over a D pedal; the apparent resolution onto a D minor triad around bar 255 is immediately undermined by the

Example 3.3

B♭ and B♮ neighbour-notes, which reintroduce the B♭ as part of a ⁴₂ preparation for the slide into F♯ at bar 271.

Harmonic stasis is evidently one of the features of 'musical prose', which complicates any reading of formal function in these bars. They appear to embody not so much a harmonic transition as a delay of contrapuntal motion: the progress of the structural lines is held in abeyance. The consistency with which the D♯ of the upper voice and the G-A-B♭ middle-voice line are maintained not only provides the aural coherence of the section, but ensures that it presents itself as a distinct formal unit. At the same time, the moment of movement, when the upper D♯ falls to a C♯ at bar 271, is still a relatively weak choice for such an important boundary as the beginning of the development section, which is the reading favoured by Adorno. The texture by and large consists of contrapuntal lines in the upper registers over very low pedal Ds, and the abandonment of the bass line at bar 271 encourages the new section to be heard as a subsidiary contrapuntal motion, although the consequent lightening of the texture (and the arpeggiated chord on the harp) also acts as a signal of some sort of formal change. This interplay of texture and voice-leading is part of a general conflict between signs, what might be called a 'semiotic polyphony' in these bars; it is the relative weight given to the features that compete for primacy that will determine the reading of formal function.

If the peculiarities of the voice-leading are taken as the primary indicator of formal function, then this gives grounds for returning to Bekker's reading of these bars as a codetta to the exposition: the tonal structure does not provide significant change, and acts as a prolongation of the contrapuntal lines that eventually shift back to the tonic at bar 364. This is indeed the reading provided by John Williamson, who makes a convincing case for the unlikely project of a graph of the entire movement, complete with *Urlinie* (1991: 367; his graph is given here as ex. 3.4). He reduces the 173 bars between the establishment of D major and the return of A to a neighbour-note motion, which also explains the linking of D major and B♭ major/G minor as alternative tonal regions to the main A major/ C minor mixture.

If the voice-leading is compared with melodic or motivic codes, however, then the grounds for the majority of the readings compared above become clear. To take first the features that are 'sequential', in the sense of Barthes' *S/Z*, there are three

Example 3.4 (from Williamson 1991)

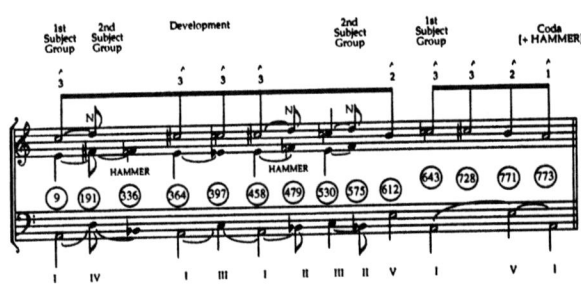

fragments of melodic material clearly related to earlier parts of the movement. Firstly, the melody of the introduction (bars 3-8) appears in bars 231-7, in inversion and with three entries in canon (first violins, bar 231; cellos and basses, bar 233; second violins, bar 234). Secondly, the melody from the D major section (bars 191-5) appears at bars 250-7, on trumpet and trombone; it contains only its beginning, however, and is terminated by a characteristic second-plus-arpeggio falling figure which is repeated in augmentation in the rest of the orchestra (the theme is taken up again, in a similarly truncated form, after the double bar line at bar 270). Finally, the basses in bars 258-69 have a phrase which first appears in bars 97-9, and is incorporated into the march theme at bar 116. It is hardly necessary to point out that these melodic fragments are taken from introduction, second subject and first subject respectively, according to the labelling of most analysts; for Redlich, for whom the melodic code is primary, this section is part of a larger span, bars 229 to 335, which has a recapitulatory function; though the only element he believes to be truly recapitulated by it (in the sense that the melody then requires no later reappearance) is the theme at bar 288.

The 'non-sequential' features of these bars are altogether more interesting. Motivic redeployment of earlier material, apart from the constituents of the melodies just described, comprises three groups of material: first, the demisemiquaver flourishes in bars 239-40 (first heard in bars 25ff); second, the five-note motive on tuba in bars 236-9 and (in diminution) 240-2 (an augmentation of the figure at bars 97-9); and third, the falling second-plus-arpeggio noted above, which appears by itself in bars 244 and 248. This last motive is a good example of the Mahlerian idiolect, having a prominent role in the second subject of the first movement, and connecting it, as Floros remarks, with the melody at bars 205ff in the Finale (and also with the introductory melody: it appears in bar 6). As in the Andante, typical patterns of descent are an important indicator of idiolectic style. The voice-leading and texture make all of these motives prominent. They tend to occur in the middle register, between ostinati or pedals at the extremes; and the overall stasis of the harmony encourages the multiple connections (such as the transformation of the five-note figure in bars 236-9 through diminution in bars 240-2 to triple diminution in bars

258-69), to assume semiotic importance. All of which makes it unsurprising that Ratz, Sponheuer and Floros view the section as development.

The remaining 'non-sequential' features, however, do not fit neatly into either hierarchy of formal signifiers. There are (again) three of these features: the introductory chord, which establishes itself as a paradigm class of its own through repetition; the celesta and harp ostinati; and the cowbells and deep bells. All of these features are non-developmental, by comparison with the motives just discussed; they can be repeated, but they cannot be varied. At the same time, they are non-linear; unlike melodic material, they do not imply a necessary continuation (this is the sense in which they are 'non-sequential'). Furthermore, they are unusual in the context of symphonic writing, and so can be accommodated within a description of the form only by assuming a specific semiotic importance.

To take first the case of the celesta, cowbells and deep bells, the semiotic interpretation of their function requires a code of much more generalised scope than those of motivic process or formal structure. Since the sounds are, more or less, unprecedented in symphonies before Mahler, they require more recuperative effort. The intertextual nexus which suggests itself is that of programme music, or Wagnerian opera, or possibly ballet (in the case of the celesta, first used by Tchaikovsky). In other words, some sort of musical narrative, bringing this 'extra-symphonic' material into the formal discourse of the symphony, is required to 'produce the text' from these features: they are, for instance, crucial in Eggebrecht's general discussion of Mahler's depiction of 'the other' in symphonic music (Eggebrecht 1982: 22ff). Where analysts comment on them at all, it is to contrast them with the 'real' business of the movement: Sponheuer, for example, describes the section as having an 'unreal, dreamlike character', making a connection with the first movement's similar episode (bars 201ff). The implication is that a code of wider referential scope than that of form is required. The different methods by which a musical narrative might be produced from these features is the concern of chapter 5 below; but the important point here is the way in which any attempt to produce signifiers of formal function inevitably finds limiting points which necessitate the intervention of a new code. This state of affairs is intertextual; form can be approached only by implicit comparison of the Symphony with pre-existing works, but this comparison ends by identifying points of the formal organisation for which the code cannot account.

The introductory chord is an altogether different case. All of the analyses tabulated above, except Bekker's, locate an important boundary at bar 229, simply because of the occurrence of this chord and texture, and in defiance of voice-leading and melodic considerations (after all, if bar 191 is taken as the opening of the second subject group, then quitting it after only thirty-eight bars is somewhat abrupt given the proportions of the movement as a whole). Although this colouristic wash of sound does, like the celesta and harp figures, recall programmatic (indeed, impressionistic) technique, this chord is embedded not so much intertextually as 'intratextually': its recurrences within this work narrow its 'signifying range' to suggest that it acts as a marker of formal boundaries. Such markers, 'signposts' to the form, are a common Mahlerian idea: one has only to think of the cello and bass scalic flourishes that open the first movement of the Second Symphony, or the eight horns in unison that announce the exposition and recapitulation in the first movement of the Third Symphony. What is different here is that the formal outline delineated by the appearances of this chord is far from obvious; rather than clarifying the model to which the musical surface is related, however obliquely, it simultaneously raises the prospect of an identifiable formal archetype, and frustrates any reading of what that archetype might be. This is true even of the chord's appearance at bars 520ff, which nearly all analysts take to be the recapitulation. Here the chord introduces a repeat of the opening melody and resolves it to the major/minor triad motif, as it did at the opening. However, as in bar 229, the voice-leading does not support this natural formal reading. The bass is a strangely persistent D♮ beneath the C-E♭-F♯-A♭ harmony, and the 'resolution' onto a C major/minor triad at bar 530 is a delay of the tonal return to A major/minor, which occurs (as Williamson points out), after the lengthy preparation of a structural dominant, at bar 642 with the recapitulation of the march theme.

There are, obviously, several ways in which these facts can be accommodated within a sonata form description of the movement. Perhaps the most satisfying interpretation is to say that similar formal dynamics are being played out asynchronously, on different levels, with the result that here, the thematic recapitulation occurs before the tonal resolution. This 'double-archetype' approach to form is identifiable elsewhere in Mahler (a simple example is the recapitulation of the Fourth Symphony's first movement, discussed in Samuels 1994); it is really the equivalent, for the analysis of form, of Lewis' 'double-tonic' interpretation of tonal process (an idea credited originally to Robert Bailey). But, from the point of view of the semiotics of form, the introductory chord actually renders undecidable the status of the section that it introduces. The chord is 'unreadable' except as a formal marker, an indicator of a major sectional division; but any reading of it must wilfully and arbitrarily privilege one sort of sign over others identifiable at this point. This state of affairs, in which the semiotic profile of the text simultaneously insists on and denies a reading, is familiar in contemporary theory and philosophy as the conclusion of any deconstructive analysis: it is a state of aporia, a situation in which the structuring of experience, upon which any construction of meaning relies, exposes itself as arbitrary. Here, there is an aporia inevitable in any attempt to fix the temporal unfolding of the movement in a formal scheme; and it is this aporia, generated by the expectations that it frustrates, which indicates the extent to which the Finale does act to confront the institution within which it situates itself. As the foregoing discussion has amply demonstrated, any reductive analysis of the form is likely to founder on the complexity of the movement; but it is not merely because the music is complex that the form remains polyvalent through and

Coding of musical form: the Finale

Example 3.5

through. It is only by means of the relativism inherent in the approach of a semiotic analysis that the deconstruction of form embodied in this movement can be brought to light. Adorno's comments come closest to describing this effect of the music; but even in his discussion, the informality of the musical observation leads to a reliance on metaphor and metanarrative which beg the question of their relationship to the musical text.

The question of formal division can also be approached from the opposite side: rather than beginning with the musical features located in these bars and trying to assign value to them, it is worth beginning with the stretch of music between what is definitely exposition and what is definitely development, and considering the alternative possibilities for the location of the formal boundary from this perspective.

Since the march melody at bar 114 is considered by all analysts to be the first subject, the obvious point from which to begin to identify formal motion away from the exposition is the shift to D major (via a typically Mahlerian whole-tone chord) at bar 191. Because of the necessity of including a second subject, the earliest candidate for the development's beginning is bar 229. The music returns to A major/minor at bar 364, which is identified by all analysts as development. These are, therefore, the extreme points of the section to be considered in looking for the beginning of the development.

The problems, for a conventional analysis, of placing a formal boundary within this section begin with questions of voice-leading, which is summarised in ex. 3.5. The harmonic stasis of bars 229–71, remarked above, is shown to be part of a more general harmonic condition in the larger section. The D-B♭-G-F♯ middleground formation between bars 229 and 336, to which the C♯ in bar 271 is a neighbour-note, is itself part of a larger prolongation of chord IV, with the top D more or less a neighbour-note to the $\hat{3}$ of bars 114 and 364. Williamson's graph of the top voice corresponds with this reading, as is seen in ex. 3.4. This illustrates once again Mahler's predilection for intensifying an effect (in this case, a large-scale harmonic motion) by 'doubling' it, or applying it to itself; here, the recursive voice-leading procedure creates functional uncertainty for a stretch of seventy-three bars.

In terms of voice-leading alone, ex. 3.5 shows that each of the candidates for the sectional division is unsatisfactory in some respect or another. Williamson, indeed, chooses bar 364 as the opening of the development for precisely this reason, although the return of the tonic is brief, and the motivic continuity either side of the bar line makes this an odd decision on syntactic grounds. Adorno's choice, bar 271, is, as remarked above, the most unstable area within the whole section. Bar 288, to which Sponheuer allots importance as the start of the development proper after an introductory section, is founded on a fifth degree of an implied local D tonic, which is never established; it has the paradoxical status of being the most stable passage, harmonically, in this section, whilst being clearly subordinate, tonally and contrapuntally, to the remaining two candidates for the formal boundary, bars 229 and 336.

These latter two moments parallel each other in more than one way. A fortissimo unison D followed by a momentary pause at the double bar, a sustained woodwind or brass chord, busy string writing, and melodic material introduced by an octave leap, are common to both. The chordal aggregate in each case is similar not only in pitch collection but also in function, as ex. 3.5 indicates. The B♭ neighbour-note, contained within a G minor triad (which in bar 229 has an added F♮), in both cases turns its chord into a structural weak beat: bar 229 appears as a neighbour to the D triad of bar 191, and bar 336 is a more straightforward upbeat to bar 364. The B♭, sustained throughout the section (it reappears in the B♭ triad of bar 278), is the long-range voice-leading feature which most lends coherence to these bars. There is, of course, no reason why a formal section should not be inaugurated by a harmonically unstable pitch-structure; but in both these cases, by the time that the voice-leading has arrived at a point of relative repose, this hardly serves to support the reading of formal boundaries. Simply because of the length of the passages involved (bars 229-88, and 336-64), other factors have intervened in the meantime.

If the effect of these parallel pitch-structures is to make the formal reading of this section undecidable, a consequence of this semiotic aporia is the difficulty of accommodating to a formal description the deployment, at bar 336, of the first hammer-stroke and the major/minor triad motif. In effect, the 'non-sequential' gestures established as potential formal indices are shared out between the double bar lines at bar 229 and bar 336, as if deliberately to complicate or frustrate the reading of the form; Mahler's own formal procedure of creating indexical gestures within large movements that engage with formal tradition is in this manner rewritten as an artifice, a product of this movement rather than a premise. This is the ground of Adorno's perceived 'nominalism' in Mahlerian form; the nominalistic denial of formal assumption is extended even to those aspects of form which lie within the Mahlerian idiolect. When Adorno writes of 'the rhythm of necessity and freedom' in the development section of this movement, he is responding to this procedure, one which both necessitates a narrative to articulate the form, and ensures the dialectic of individual impulse and constraining negativity which are marks of any such narrativising attempt.

THE LIMITS OF FORM

At this point, discussions of the form of the Finale as a single topic tend to break down. Faced with the limit points of the application of existing formal categories to the musical text, the analyst is faced with a choice: either to invent new categories, or to turn to alternative codes to justify a preferred hearing. There has been no lack of the former alternative. One line of inheritance is represented by Adorno's taxonomy of Mahlerian form via the categories of breakthrough, suspension and fulfilment; this is taken over by Sponheuer and Jülg to provide a complete descriptive vocabulary for the formal process, particularly in their discussions of the development. Non-Adornians, such as Ratz and Redlich, also invent categories to describe the 'dualism' of the musical characters. For Ratz (1968: 43ff), this involves describing the whole development (which he locates as bars 336 to 478) in terms of alternating 'positive' and 'negative' sections, predominantly on the basis of whether they develop previous melodic material (the 'positive' sections), or present a prose-like motivic dissolution (the 'negative' sections). Curiously, this is almost the exact opposite, in narrative terms, of Adorno's 'strict' and 'free' characterisations, although the sectional divisions are also different, since Ratz considers only the passage between the two hammer-blows in this way. This combination of specific formal types (such as the 'breakthrough') and general formal orientation (that of 'dualism') is what Jülg hopes to synthesise when he describes the form as a sonata whose 'dynamic' sections are interrupted by 'static' material first heard in the introduction (Jülg 1986: 118).

Since there is a limit to the justifiability of inventing new general categories on the basis of an individual work, it is the second option mentioned above, that of turning to a new code to supersede that of form, which is the conclusion of most of the analyses mentioned in this chapter. Just as choices within the code were seen earlier to rely on codes of more limited referential scope (melodic succession, motivic process and so forth), so the conclusions of formal investigation invoke codes of wider reference. A musical narrative, of some sort or another, is the inescapable conclusion of most of the analyses discussed above; it also enables the work to be sited intertextually, in relation to traditions of composition and individual works of music, or to other forms of cultural production. This reliance on the narrative code is not quite inevitable; among more recent discussions of the movement, Mathias Hansen's stands out as an analysis which so transforms any sonata form model for the movement as to render it redundant (Hansen 1980). His solution is to argue for the primacy of the generic code, both in the first movement and Finale; he terms the movements 'original' and 'negative image'. Generally, this reference is to the march, which acts to subvert the 'high cultural' symphonic genre; specifically, the reference is to the Andante of Schubert's Ninth Symphony, which he argues to be an explicit model for this semiotic interpenetration of genre and form (Hansen 1980: 12). This inventive idea is chiefly relevant to the current discussion in that it, too, rests on an intertextual range of reference; it is much more grounded in musical observation than Floros' sudden invocation of *Tod und Verklärung*, but it responds to the same sense of difficulty in 'producing the text' in formal terms.

It is not surprising that an analytical inquiry that began by considering structures immanent to the work in hand should end by demonstrating the inevitability of reference outside the work, and indeed outside the cultural medium of musical artworks. In this way, a semiotic investigation of the work proves deconstructive; analysis of motive and form turn out to depend on codes which were excluded by the definition of the inquiry. The specific codes which the foregoing discussion has suggested are those of genre, on the one hand, and narrative, on the other. Genre is clearly of great importance to the issue of form, since it too relies on a musical text and an intertextual nexus. Narrative, to go further, threatens to take leave altogether of the musical trace, linking the work more generally with other art forms, philosophical concerns or socio-economic history. Before the second half of this study goes on to consider these codes, however, it is worth emphasising the importance of the way in which they arise directly from the consideration of motive, form and tonal process, despite being less reliant on structures of pitch and metre. It is precisely because of the simultaneous necessity and impossibility of disentangling Mahler's compositional procedure in narrow musical detail from issues of general philosophical scope that his works have established and maintained their stature within postmodern culture. A remark of Donald Mitchell's, that Mahler's works are 'at once deeply personal, and completely public' (Mitchell 1961: 95), stems from this interdependence of signifying strategies. A semiotic approach is the only method which can demonstrate analytically the link between the compositional and the extramusical, both so characteristic of Mahler.

4

GENRE AND PRESUPPOSITION IN THE MAHLERIAN SCHERZO

'Scherzo' was by no means an automatic inscription for Mahler at the head of a symphonic movmement, as Constantin Floros observes (1977-85, vol. 2: 165). If in the Sixth Symphony this invocation of convention has a polemical edge, the nature of this polemic must be sought on several different levels. Firstly, the movement title underlines the decision to embrace the four-movement symphonic schema of allegro, scherzo, slow movement and finale. More importantly, the etymology of 'scherzo' suggests a distortion of generic type (in its original speeding up of a minuet); a latent expectation which is always the occasion for irony and parody in Mahler's denoted scherzos. Finally, a scherzo involves dance forms, which in this symphony (and generally in Mahler) enlarge the scope of the music beyond those dance genres normally associated with symphonic practice – minuet and so forth – to those from outside the realm of 'art music', specifically the waltz, ländler, and Bohemian folk-dances.

This is not to say very much; but in order to investigate the semiotic specificity of this movement, and to try to bring some analytical justification to slippery signifieds such as irony or parody, the concept of the code must be broadened beyond the consideration of structures immanent to the music and identifiable as patterns within the graphic text which is the work's transmitted material form.

The question of genre is one which introduces the social and cultural context of the composition to the analysis. Carl Dahlhaus argued (somewhat one-sidedly) that there is a gradual change from the eighteenth-century reliance on generic expectations to the state of affairs in the early twentieth century, where an individual work is no longer necessarily related to a general category (1983: 149). Dahlhaus locates this transition in the general trend of a decay of 'social function' for music, so that the autonomy of the artwork proclaimed by the Romantic aesthetic came to militate against the mediation of individual and social experience (seen in a 'nexus of "external" social function and "internal" musical technique') which had been an artistic aim of the previous century (Dahlhaus 1983: 149). Mahler's music is situated at the end of this process, when genre can signify only through an act of force, as it were, on the part of the composer. This aesthetic nominalism (to use Adorno's term) does not, however, mean that genre is unimportant or divorced from social realities; indeed, Mahler's engagement with his social context can best be approached by attempting to identify the role of generic typology in the work.

GENRE AS A SEMIOTIC CATEGORY

As a topic of interest for theorists, questions of genre in nineteenth-century music have recently received a fair deal of attention, especially in studies of Chopin. Jeffrey Kallberg notes that genre as an aesthetic concept has had a variable history: Benedetto Croce, for instance, denied its significance altogether (Kallberg 1988: 239). Kallberg's own approach is to take issue with Dahlhaus in order to develop the idea of a 'generic contract' between the composer and listener (the concept of genre as a contract is one which has been elaborated by literary theorists; it is discussed, for instance, in Dubrow 1982). This avoids what he perceives to be the main difficulty of Dahlhaus' discussion, namely that genre is considered only from the point of view of the composer, as 'a monotonal backdrop against which the more colourful play of individual genius might take place' (Kallberg 1988: 242). Kallberg wishes to establish the 'communicative properties' of genre, and stresses that this involves more than the classification of shared characteristics between pieces:

> [Shared characteristics] provide factual information about a term; they classify it. But they do not explain its meaning. The meaning of a term instead is connected to the willingness of a particular community to use that word and not another ... Research into the effects of genre should involve the reconstruction of contexts and traditions, and the perceptions of composers and their audiences, both historical and modern.
> (Kallberg 1988: 243)

This is, of course, effectively a description of a code in the semiotic sense: a shared body of knowledge through which a community can create meaning from a text. Kallberg emphasises the 'reconstruction of contexts' in a historiographical sense; but a consideration of genre rests equally on intertextual investigation, appealing to the history of the use of generic forms rather than hypothesising the expectations of a real or constructed 'historical audience'.

This recognition of the intertextual character of generic typology suggests a way round some of the difficulties that recur in recent writing on the topic. For instance, it can be very difficult to distinguish between the effect of genres imported from a 'foreign' musical source (such as the incorporation of fugue within a sonata structure), and those which have an extramusical source (such as the waltz). There are many examples of situations somewhere between these two, as in the conversion of dance form into salon genres in Chopin's shorter piano works. Also, generic definitions cannot be exclusive: Kallberg takes Dahlhaus to task over his vagueness in defining piano genres, especially the treatment of the 'lyric piano piece' as a single phenomenon, which is obviously inappropriate in the case of Chopin (Kallberg 1988: 242 and note 18). Chopin consistently uses generic reference to link a piece with an alternative type to that of its title; Jim Samson describes the result as 'collusion' between the composer and listener in aesthetic pluralism, as genre is used both to impose order and destabilise any finality of meaning. Significantly, he points out that this is linked to the question of 'popular' and 'high' musical expression:

> It is a commonplace of criticism that 'popular' and 'significant' music became increasingly incompatible in nineteenth-century bourgeois-capitalist society, establishing an opposition between conventional language and an avant-garde. It is less often remarked that in a substantial body of nineteenth-century music this opposition was actually embodied within the individual work, as popular genres increasingly took on a parenthetical, as distinct from supportive or enabling, role in art music.
> (Samson 1989: 225)

The difficulty in specifying the effects of genres, rather than just asserting their importance, is a recurring feature of the recent interest in the topic. To take another example, Leo Treitler agrees with Charles Rosen that the Finale of Beethoven's Ninth Symphony represents a combination of formal genres which give an image of integration and unity, in an attempt to resolve the conflicts of the earlier movements of the work (Treitler 1989: 25-8; Rosen 1975: 440-1). But Treitler has problems in defining the significative value of the sequence of genres that he identifies. He hears the overall form of the Finale to be determined by the genres of both symphony and concerto. Further, he hears specific reference to the formal process of the opening movement in the construction of the Finale. The sequence of genres continues. Firstly he identifies a set of variations that appears to arise solely out of the thematic material ('If the statement of such a melody is to be stretched out . . . it can be only through repetition'). Secondly, come recitative and operatic finale which signify because of social expectation as 'dénouement'. Finally, there is a fugue which curiously exists only as a signifier of another genre, in its capacity as 'development' ('the fugue functions as a sign of sonata form'). Treitler undoubtedly has some persuasive points to make in his discussion of the musical effect of the movement; but his question, 'How seamless is the synthesis of genres in the Finale, and does it all resolve as a new total form into which the individual components are assimilated?' remains unanswered, because he cannot define the specificity of the signifying role of each genre. He ends by concluding that Beethoven 'contributed to a reduction in the distinctness of genres'; but an equally valid comment might be that Beethoven was amongst the first to recognise the potential of genre as a means of expression.

These different effects of genre in fact derive from different ranges of intertextual reference. In concept, a code of 'generic typology' is situated midway between those codes which refer entirely 'intramusically', such as motivic working or harmonic process, and those – such as musical narrative or programme – which refer entirely 'extramusically', requiring interpretants that are wholly cultural. The generic code unites musical features – principally rhythmic units and melodic shapes – with coded knowledge of conventions which lie within or outside the tradition of art music. This is also true of the coding of formal archetype; but the difference with the identification of genre is that a social practice as well as an artistic convention is invoked. A form such as ländler, march, minuet or waltz carries some inheritance from its origin as a social activity, no matter how much it may also have a history within the practice of 'high art' composition.

THE SCHERZO OF THE SIXTH SYMPHONY

The combination of a complex interplay of generic types and relative simplicity in other respects is perhaps responsible for the fact that the Scherzo has remained the least discussed of the movements of the Sixth Symphony. It is made up of a fairly clear ABABA form; its motivic materials are not only limited (melodic and rhythmic motives recur between sections and saturate the textures), but audibly linked to those of the outer movements; and the A minor tonality dominates the harmony, time and again dissolving onto repeated quaver As, which are either unaccompanied or function as pedal notes. The simplicity of the Trio sections offended one of the first critics to apply the epithet 'Tragic' to the symphony, Alois Weigl (Istel n.d.: 103ff), and the contrast between the Trio section and the 'A' sections is described as 'nightmarish' by Adorno (1960: 140/1992: 103). Adorno locates the 'asphyxiating effect' of the movement in the constellation of limited material, symphonic formal intention and profusion of *Charakteren*, which here refers to generic types. He comments that the Scherzo, 'which is motivically and harmonically bracketed by the outer movements, poses the question of distilling a maximum of changing characters [*Charakteren*] from a minimum of starting material' (1960: 140/1992: 103). Adorno is concerned to defend Mahler from the charge of melodic monotony, whilst also displacing the signification of the ländler and Trio sections away from their folk origins and towards the larger symphonic intention. This places the compositional technique in the context of the symphony as a whole, in which compulsion and tragic closure recur as the latent content of the music: 'The unity [of the Scherzo], which omits nothing [in using the first section's motives in the Trio], is itself intended to form a character, to establish that tormenting insistence which precedes the stiff, intentionally *drängend* Scherzo theme' (1960: 140/1992: 103). This for Adorno distinguishes the movement from the scherzos of the Fifth and Seventh Symphonies, which he describes as 'development-scherzos' that present a suite of *Charakteren*. It is notable that the leap to a comment on unity, which hears its insistent presence as a problem rather than a virtue, is founded on a dissatisfaction with the paucity of motivic material. This is close to a semiotic exegesis: where one code fails, another, of wider referential scope, is invoked. Adorno's comments as they stand remain suggestive, but cannot, however, be substantiated; they appeal to an intuitive assessment of the outline of the movement. In order to investigate the semiotic state of affairs more closely, then, the different genres underlying the material of the movement need to be identified, and their employment within the specific Mahlerian schema of the symphony needs to be traced with some care.

The three generic types principally in play in the movement are the march, the ländler, and the folk dance of the Trio section, labelled '*altväterisch*' (I am indebted to Paul Banks for the information that this word may refer to a specific Bohemian dance that features the asymmetrical combination of ⅜ and ⅘ metres). The identification of generic types is not easy, especially when distinguishing between different triple-metre dances such as Viennese waltz, Parisian valse, and Bohemian ländler. For the purposes of this analysis, the typology developed by Floros (1977-85, vol. II: 165-78) will be taken as authoritative.

It is remarkable that the Scherzo of the Sixth Symphony is not used by Floros to provide examples of dance genres in Mahler's output. He refers to the incorporation of 'ländler' elements into the Scherzo sections as 'A grisly metamorphosis of the ländler genre', and contrasts this with the way that 'the whole Scherzo is taken over by the ländler' in the Fifth Symphony (1977-85, vol. II: 165-6). His descriptions embody the same contrast as Adorno's comments: the two movements serve as companion studies in the use of generic materials, the Fifth Symphony deploying a succession of types which are eventually contrapuntally combined, and the Sixth Symphony recombining similar motivic materials to create the illusion of succession. The contrast is, as much as anything, one of the representation of diachronic and synchronic progression; the respects in which these two movements resemble each other in their symbolic imagery will be explored below. First of all, however, the use of the generic code must be defined in some detail. The easiest way to begin is to see how the material of the opening sections (up to the appearance of the Trio) is defined and used.

RHYTHMIC SEGMENTATION

A paradigmatic rhythmic analysis provides a convenient starting-point for the investigation of this code, since rhythm is the parameter via which different dance forms may most readily be distinguished. Floros identifies several rhythmic features which in his view define the Mahlerian ländler, which he places in turn in the context of previous symphonic composition as well as popular music. In fact, he distinguishes between the *gemächlich* ländler of main sections and the slow ländler of trio sections. Although his definitions are fairly informal, they provide a starting-point for the difficult business of identifying generic indices:

> Mahler's *gemächlichen* ländlers adhere to the profile of Bavarian dances. Their important distinguishing feature is the accented rhythm: not only the first beat will be emphasised, but – correspondingly weaker – the second too. (Different marcato signs frequently appear in the score directions). The melody favours small intervals; arpeggios come seldom if at all. The ornamentation is again noteworthy: trills and mordents proliferate.
>
> (1977-85, vol. II: 173)

Example 4.1   (from Floros 1985)

Bruckner, Fourth Symphony, second movement

Mahler, Second Symphony, third movement

Mahler, 'Rheinlegendchen'

Ländler from Zillertal (Tyrol)

Two-part ländler themes:

Bruckner, Third Symphony, second movement

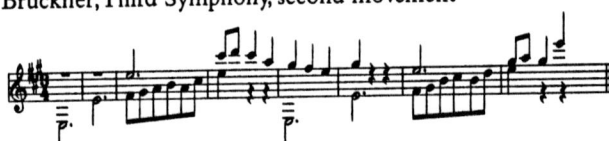

Mahler, First Symphony, second movement

The 'slow ländler' type is in explicit contrast to that described above: only the first beat is stressed, and arpeggios feature in the melody ('larger intervals are articulated to exploit their expressive potential': 1977–85, vol. II: 174). Obviously, there are features common to the two types, and these are illustrated by examples from Schubert, Bruckner and a collection of folk-dances (Floros 1977-85, vol. II: 380; these examples are given here as ex. 4.1).

The features which can be derived from these examples, and thus taken to define the ländler genre, are principally rhythmic. They consist of a regular ¾ pulse (or a diminution of ⅜) with continuous crotchet movement; frequent division into

	I	II	III	IV
1	♩.	♫ ♪	♫♫	♫♫♫♫
2	♫♩.	♫♫ ♪	♪♫♫	♫♫♫
3	♫♫♫ | ♩	♫ ♫	♪|♫♫|♩	♫♫♫
4	♩ tr ♫	♫♫ ♫	[♪|♩]	♫♫♫
5		♪ ♪ ♫	♪ ♪ ♪ ♪ ♪	
6		♪ ♪ ♪ ♪	[♫]	
7		[♪ ♪]		

Table 4.1

quavers, especially in the patterns ♩ ♫♫♫, ♩ ♫ ♩, or ♫ ♩♫, or ♫♫♫♫; and two- or three-quaver anacruses. These features are sufficient to distinguish the ländler from waltz types. Floros has much more difficulty separating French *Valse* from Austro-German *Walzer*; but for the purposes of the present analysis, the identification of rhythmic units which act as semiotic indices is, fortunately, uncontroversial. In addition to these rhythmic features, typical melodic shapes tend to outline triads, with the quavers supplying passing notes and ornaments such as turns.

Whole-bar patterns are the largest repeating unit which can be rigorously segmented, and so these form the basis of the analysis of bars 1-32 summarised in table 4.1. For purposes of comparison, a score reduction of these bars is given as ex. 4.2. Only twenty-one distinct patterns are identified, which account for every note in the score. The following adjustments have had to be made:

1 Some instrumental lines have been ignored, where they consist of a partial doubling of a unit in another voice (such as the flutes and piccolos in bar 20).

2 Similar considerations have led to the inclusion of the rhythm in horns 2, 4, 6, 8 in bars 11-13 as II-6 (♪♪\|♫ ♪♪\|♫ becomes 2 × ♫ ♪). The rhythm is in any case completed by the entry of the other horns in bar 13.

3 Some anacruses have been ignored. These are all single-quaver figures, either identical with the following bar (as with the first instance of II-1 and IV-1) or conflating two patterns (as with the ♫♫ which precedes the first instance of I-4). This exclusion is necessary at this stage of the analysis, in order to identify the whole-bar patterns which have been taken as paradigmatic; a second analysis, based on single-quaver patterns, would reveal a degree of recombination of units which might result either from syntagmatic rules within the generic code, or from generic transformation within this section. This issue, however, will be discussed below (pp. 100-1, 108-9).

98 Mahler's Sixth Symphony

Example 4.2

Example 4.2 (*cont.*)

The number of occurrences of each pattern is given in table 4.2. Rhythmic unison and part-doubling have been ignored, so that the analysis is for the moment concerned with a purely rhythmic profile of these bars. Between one and four (and usually two or three) rhythmic strands are present at any given point.

The arrangement of paradigmatic columns in these two tables is relatively informal: the columns arrange rhythms according to increasing numbers of stressed beats. Thus column I contains rhythms which stress the first beat of the bar, column II those which stress the first two (through the shortening of the second quaver and the slur), column III those which stress all three, and column IV those which divide two or more beats into semiquavers. The rows represent a judgment of increasing complexity, with the simplest units in each class at the top and the most complex at the bottom. Square brackets contain units which are held to be incomplete versions of paradigmatic units. Whilst II-7 and III-6 are straightforward cases, III-4 is more important, and really deserves a place in column I, or a column to itself. It occurs at the cadence (bars 30-2, full brass), where it sounds as an elided form of III-3, which it follows. This is the only instance in these opening bars of true rhythmic development (in Schoenberg's sense of the term); the occurrence of the unit weakens the generic typology at the sectional division, and deflects

	I	II	III	IV
1	3	6	16	13
2	2	1	7	2
3	6	1	2	2
4	2	1	[2]	1
5	-	1	8	-
6	-	4	[1]	-
7	-	[1]	-	-
Totals	13	14	33	18

Table 4.2

attention away from the generic code, back towards the more standard code of symphonic form.

Although these tables provide only limited data, and ignore for the moment the whole issue of temporal succession, several observations still emerge. First of all, the rhythms which act as uncontroversial indices of the ländler genre are those in columns II and IV; these columns contain 32 of the 78 units in the graph (41 per cent). Column II shows the stress of the first two beats with the second 'correspondingly weaker' described by Floros above; the rhythms of column IV abound in all his examples (ex. 4.1). Indeed, the similarity of II-3 and IV-2 demonstrates the intersection of these paradigms within the genre. The remaining three columns are more problematic, and it is by tracing the levels of generic reference involved in these units that the complexity of the operation of the generic code in these bars can be brought to light.

I-1 and I-3 consist of a complete bar without smaller division. These might almost be called 'null units', since they provide no characteristic rhythm and so escape the generic code. However, since four of the five occurrences mark sectional divisions (the melodic ascent to E in bar 10 and the return to A in bar 31), the paradigm as a whole becomes associated with the ländler type. In the case of I-3 and I-4, this association causes semiotic confusion: these rhythms are clear (and Mahlerian) march rhythms which have featured in the first movement and will return in the Finale (e.g. first movement, bar 134; Finale, bar 19 and bar 131). This identity is not obscured by the triple metre of the Scherzo.

This analysis contends that these bars utilise the generic code to effect a transformation between ländler and march types. To this end, it is important that whilst the 'signifying scope' of the dominating ländler units remains wide, that of the subsidiary march units invokes not just the march as a type, but the Mahlerian idiolectical march, and, narrower still, the piece in hand. It is in this context of a tension between the two genres (which is not a state of balance or ambiguity, but a semiotic dynamic) that the units of column III become important. The three equal quavers are less specific in terms of genre than the rhythms of columns II and IV: as a rhythm, they fit in with ländler-type melodies; but as a pulse, they again constitute a sign of the march typology. This fact is exploited by the opening bars of the Scherzo, where the overlapping III-1 and III-2 rhythms suggest the ⁴⁄₄ crotchets of the first movement:

First movement:	⁴⁄₄ ♪♪♪♪| ♪♪♪♪	[strings]
Scherzo:	⅜ ♪| ♫♫| ♫♫	[timpani]
	⅜ | ♫♫| ♫♫	[strings]
i.e.:	⁴⁄₄ ♫♫♫| ♫♫♫	

The sforzandi on the timpani's anacrusis and the strings' downbeat in the Scherzo create a momentary ambiguity of metre which combines with the entry of the melody, which is in both movements a dotted-rhythm anacrusis at the end of the second bar. This brings us back to the importance of anacruses within the generic code, which was mentioned above. Anacruses are an index of the ländler-type melody, as Floros points out; they do not have prominence within the march-type. But here they enlarge the predominant three-beat units into four-beat units, a process which serves in the opening bars to confound the ländler and march types, and specifically the march genre indices of the first movement. If the function of anacrusis is taken as a seme in its own right, it may further be observed that these bars constitute a structural anacrusis to the whole movement; a function emphasised by the entry of the violins, with the rhythm III-5, in bar 2. This is the topmost voice, and yet its melodic importance is undercut by the fact that it remains a single-pitch figure for three bars, serving as a long upbeat to the melody proper in bar 5. All this is taken up again quite explicitly at the beginning of the first Trio, where the off-beat metre of the *altväterisch* melody arises from this combination of generic types as march becomes pulse and thence the new genre. It is this 'hallucinatory' effect which is at the root of both Adorno's comment and Alma's anecdote of her children playing on the beach.

MELODIC STRUCTURES

Whilst a purely rhythmic analysis serves as an illuminating provisional definition of this code's operation, it is obvious that temporal succession and melodic content cannot be ignored in establishing the signifying force of these units. Indeed, it is the contention of a semiotic analysis that musical signs only arise as the interaction of different parameters, rather than as the function of any one sort of structure. If the rhythmic analysis is taken as a viable provisional segmentation, then the next step ought to be to adduce the temporal order and pitch content to the profile given in tables 4.1 and 4.2. This is done in table 4.3.

Here each column contains one of the rhythmic units from table 4.1, with bar numbers given at the side and exact repetitions indicated by arrows. Anacruses extra to the criteria of the column are bracketed with an 'A', and also indicated if they form part of a preceding unit.

It can be seen from this exercise that there is a very high degree of correlation between rhythmic and intervallic units; in other words, each rhythm tends to have its own distinctive melodic shape. Some are completely constant, such as I-3 and III-5; all have a limited number of intervallic features. Conversely, shapes do not recur between columns, except in the sense that each large column (i.e. each table 4.1 column) has intervallic features distinctive of it. These now deserve detailed consideration.

1. I- rhythms all emphasise a single note, which is always either the tonic or dominant scale degree, and generally reinforced by an octave doubling. The apparent exceptions of the I-4 units substitute F♮ for the octave E expected in I-4/16.

Table 4.3

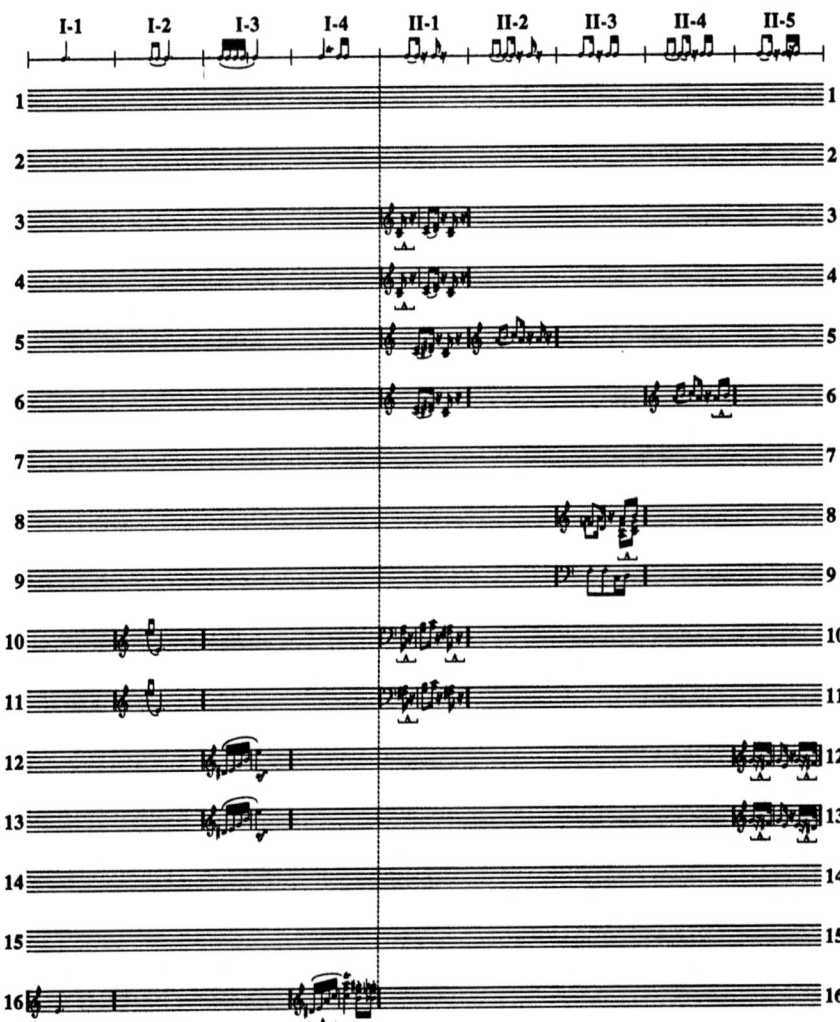

Genre and presupposition in the Mahlerian scherzo

Table 4.3 (cont.)

Table 4.3 (cont.)

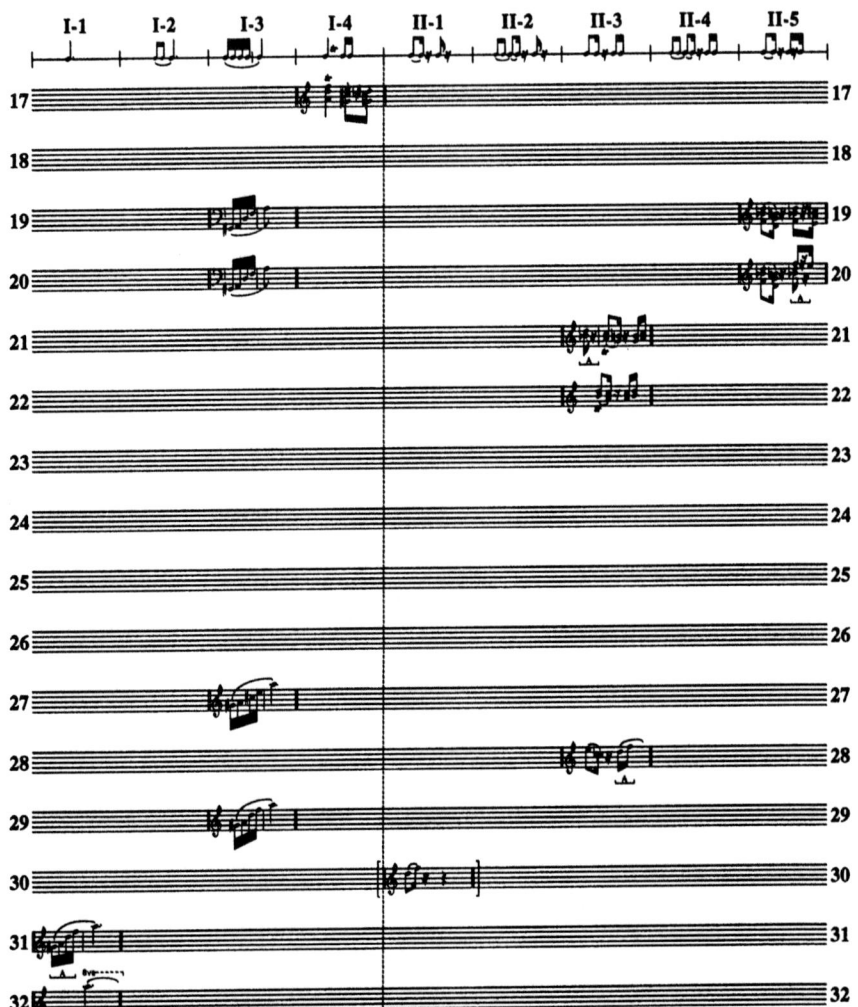

Genre and presupposition in the Mahlerian scherzo

Table 4.3 (cont.)

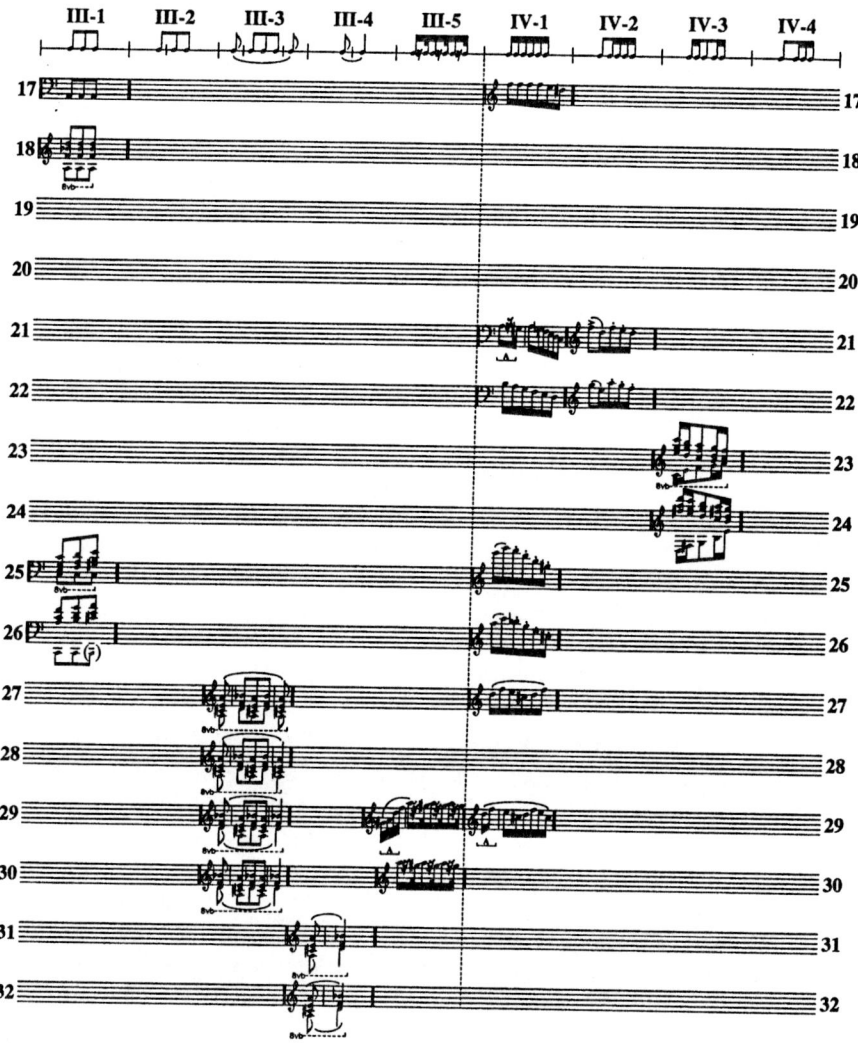

2   II- rhythms tend to involve the melodic interval of a third, and to be presented in parallel thirds. The apparent exceptions are II-1, where a harmonic third is prolonged by neighbour-notes which themselves form a melodic third; and II-3/9, 21, and 22. The latter two both exhibit the prolongation of a harmonic third by lower auxiliaries, leaving the only true exception to be II-3/9, which is a bass figure associated with rhythms from column IV when it recurs later in the movement.

3   All the units in III- columns involve single-pitch features. Many consist of a repeated pitch, embellished by chromatic neighbour-note motion in the case of III-3 and III-4. Even the units which consist of a scalic ascent all occur as inner parts in rhythmic unison with a pedal pitch in the bass.

4   Only the IV- units provide linear melodic movement. They consist almost entirely of scalic motion, broken by steps of a third in IV-1/25 and 26. The destination pitch of each unit is always different from the starting pitch; in other words, these units provide the dynamic element in this section.

To expand on this summary, it is remarkable how much of the melodic material is static in pitch contour: more or less all of the units under I-III above present a succession of static pitch levels rather than linear progression. The exceptions are the most unequivocally ländler-type units, found in the IV- columns. This provides a measure of the confusion of the 'generic contract' in these bars. The ländler is a repeating dance form, whereas the march as a type has to do with progression (in both the musical and the metaphorical sense); yet here it is the march that remains static, whilst the ländler provides forward movement. The voice-leading makes the process clear (it is given in ex. 4.3). The first ten bars outline an ascent to E2, in which the structural movement is provided entirely by means of the IV-1 units: the movement from A to C, from C to E, the F/E neighbour-note figure in the inner part, and the unfolding of D to F in the bass. This gives an additional reason for including unit II-3/9, which leads the bass from the F to the E, in a IV-5 column, as was suggested in the discussion of table 4.3. The structural ascent concludes powerfully on octave Es in bar 10, with the inner and top voices presented by octave grace notes on violins and horns, in I- units (discussed above). Instead of a melody and accompaniment (the importance of which will be discussed below), moments of contrapuntal structural movement are identified with ländler units, whilst the initial and final pitch levels of the ascent are prolonged via non-ländler generic units. A slippage of harmonic background and generic foreground occurs.

Returning to the paradigmatic rhythmic segmentation, the very ease of its operation deserves comment. The units are clearly distinguished, virtually isolated from each other. The seventy-eight units of table 4.1 give only twenty-one different rhythmic types (and seventy-two of the units, 92 per cent, use only thirteen of the rhythms), a remarkable economy of means which becomes more evident as the Scherzo progresses: the only new units to appear before the Trio at bar 98 are

Genre and presupposition in the Mahlerian scherzo

Example 4.3

additions to table 4.1 column IV (♪♪♪, ♪♪♪, and one instance of ♪♪). Neither are there many new melodic figures; the oscillation of two notes in the rhythm ♪♪♪♪♪♪, the chromatic descending ♪♪♪♪♪♪♪♪ figure at the final cadence, and the triad in the new rhythm ♪♪♪ more or less account for them all. This 'sealing off' of the rhythmic and melodic units at the level of the bar is a powerful ground for asserting the primacy of the generic code. The codes discussed in relation to the other movements produced paradigms where a single rhythm or pitch contour was frequently common to several extracts otherwise quite different. Here, the semiotic foregrounding of a generic typology of pitch and rhythm marks a complexity of 'generic contract' which this analysis contends to be primary to the listening experience of these bars.

LIMITS OF THE ANALYSIS

There are limits to this form of analysis. Firstly, the distribution of the segmented units is problematic. They permeate the whole texture, to the extent that table 4.3 accounts for every note in the section; a fact that would still be true of an analysis of the whole ninety-seven bars up to the Trio. Indeed, each column furnishes examples of top, inner and bass voices in an almost systematic fashion, whilst on the other hand rhythmic unison of separate voices (as opposed to part doubling) only occurs once (in bar 18). In this way the whole texture becomes melodic; melody and accompaniment do not form opposed categories, as each becomes the other. The importance of a melody-and-accompaniment texture as a signal of the generic code can be indicated by comparing these bars to such other Mahlerian symphonic ländler movements as the second movement of the Second Symphony, or the Wunderhorn song 'Rheinlegendchen'. Nor is the textural change due just to a shift in compositional technique. The scherzos of the Fifth and Seventh Symphonies are also much simpler in texture by comparison with the Sixth (despite the proliferation of contrapuntal voices in the former, which will be discussed below). Only the Rondo-Burleske of the Ninth Symphony follows a comparable process to the present movement.

Example 4.4

This melodic saturation of the texture is a corollary of a feature that was remarked above, namely the closure of the units from one another. Genres invoke expectations relating not only to melodic and rhythmic shapes, but also to typical middleground shapes and formal outlines. Whilst middleground shapes can indeed be constructed, here the signifying process that leads from surface features to generically recognisable larger structures is halted at the level of the surface units. There is a slippage between harmonic outline and generic foreground, which is exploited in two ways. The first is the use of typically Mahlerian neighbour-note figures in the middleground to provide prolongational coherence. This process begins with the E/F neighbour-note pair: F is maintained as a neighbour to E, via the column IV units, in bars 1-10. The pair are then presented as a simultaneity (between fourth horn and strings plus woodwind) in bar 16. The eventual movement away from this E/F figure is again by IV-units, in bars 21-5. The voice-leading of bars 13-27 is summarised in ex. 4.4.

The E/F pair gives way to the A/B♭ pair, to which it becomes a triadic thickening, in bars 27-33. Here the neighbour-note motion is taken up by the III-3 and III-4 units, whilst the I- units again maintain the semitone as a simultaneity (now inverted to form a major seventh). The fact that this neighbour-note alternation escapes the generic code is reflected in its use as a focal point throughout each section, culminating in the Neapolitan harmony and whole-tone descent that disintegrates into the brief coda after bar 400.

The second feature of these bars which exploits the tension of generic and symphonic expectations is the linkage or development of the melodic motives that make up the table 4.3 units. This once again invokes the issue of the use of anacruses, for it is these single-quaver figures which are used in motivic development. The shapes in question are the upward semitone-plus-arpeggio in four demisemiquavers (I-1, I-3, I-4, III-5 and IV-4), and the various terminations of II-units used as anacruses (♪⁊, ♫, ♪⁊♪). These two groups differ in developmental scope. The ♫♫ rhythm does not occur except as an anacrucial third beat, and unites extracts over several columns. Noteworthy is the fact that it cannot be taken as a ländler-type feature (i.e., it does not occur in any of Floros' examples, or in any definitely ländler-based movement by Mahler; it is, of course, typical of Mahlerian marches); in other words, semantic links are created by the subsidiary genre within the code. Equally, the II- rhythm which has the most similar distribution is ♪⁊♪ (it occurs in III-4 and – exceptionally – once in IV-1), which is also not a ländler feature. All the II- figures which occur as anacruses also occur as terminations of units; they link units whilst preserving their rhythmic profiles. It is this technique which preserves the distinctness of the single-bar units whilst linking together ländler-type units (in columns II and IV) to create melodic lines, or marking particular bars as having melodic or harmonic importance. In this way Mahler's melodic process, which frequently recombines relatively long stretches of melodic material (a fact remarked on ever since the première of the First Symphony), is adapted to the specific intention of generic play in this movement. The other feature with developmental scope in these bars is the chord sequence of columns III-3 and III-4, where alternation of two chords (an A triad and a B♭ triad) is repeated with rhythmic elision. This serves to mark the A/B♭ neighbour-note alternation discussed above as 'non-generic' in the sense that it escapes the code.

Thus the semiotic state of affairs when the trio section begins in bar 98 is more complex than the naivety of the simple arpeggios and root-position triadic harmony would suggest. The equivocation between three-quaver and four-quaver (including anacrusis) rhythms is turned into an alternation of $\frac{3}{8}$ and $\frac{4}{8}$, and then an alternation of each of these with $\frac{2}{4}$, allowing the ♫♫ and ♫♪ rhythms to be transformed into ♫♫ and ♫♪ figures. This is disconcerting, not especially because of the asymmetry of the rhythms (which can be accommodated, following Paul Banks' suggestion above, as a new form of generic reference), but because the new genre is composed entirely of fragments from the previous, generically complex, section. Moreover, the asymmetry of the Trio is created by presenting as successions precisely those fragments of rhythm which previously created the generic uncertainty when they occurred as simultaneities. It is no accident that the literal point of connection between the two sections is the repetition of a single note, as ♪|♫♫ in the scherzo and as ♪|♫♫ or ♪♩|♪♩♪♩♪♩ in the trio.

This analysis has been detailed, in order to establish several features both of the code under discussion and the particular form of signification displayed by this piece. In particular, the use of a code as the organising term in the analysis emphasises the extent to which the structuration of no single parameter suffices to describe the effect of the intertextual reference. Rhythmic, melodic and harmonic indices interact with formal divisions, middleground voice-leading and archetypal background shapes which refer to a symphonic scherzo coding, in a complex play of forces which makes generic reference neither Dahlhaus' 'monotonal backdrop', nor part of Kallberg's 'contexts and traditions', but rather a foreground component of the work's process.

However, up to this point the analysis has done little more than investigate the method by which the generic code is brought into play by this movement; it has not got as far as attempting to describe the signifying effect of this code, although Adorno's asphyxiation may perhaps by now be more clearly understood. And indeed, taking the matter any further is fraught with problems. On the one hand, if it is claimed that a semiotic analysis offers powerful descriptive possibilities for the investigation of signifying structures, then it is hardly possible to stop short of making claims concerning the significance of each coded structure. On the other hand, it is all too easy to fall back at this point into statements regarding 'the meaning of the music' which are not the more substantiated for being couched in technical terms.

The theoretical position is that so far the generic code constitutes one of Eco's 's-codes'. The embedding of the code in the text has been identified, and this reading justified. This analysis has suggested in turn some ways in which the s-code can be mapped 'extroversively': within Mahler's oeuvre (via ländler types, etc.), and, more broadly, within the institution of writing symphonies. What has not been addressed is the nature of the *signified* s-code required to complete a semiotic chain. It is the difficulty of suggesting the specific nature of a structured code lying *outside* the work in question which dooms most attempts to specify musical significance to generalisation or over-simplification.

It is clear that to identify genre is not to describe significance. The rhythmic and melodic motives in the Scherzo do not 'signify' the ländler; they use reference to the ländler genre in order to signify something else. In order to specify what this something else might be, the rest of this chapter will widen the scope of the discussion slightly by considering its 'companion' movement, the Scherzo of the Fifth Symphony.

THE SCHERZO OF THE FIFTH SYMPHONY

Adorno's description of the Scherzo of the Fifth Symphony as a 'development-scherzo', in opposition to that of the Sixth Symphony, is a telling one. However, there are also resemblances between the two movements which concern more than mere form. The mode of generic reference in the earlier work is, at least at first sight, easier to establish. Certainly Floros thinks so, since this movement furnishes his prime examples of both sorts of waltz type in Mahler (1977-85, vol. II: 381, 384). Floros distinguishes between the Austro-German *Walzer* and the Franco-European *Valse*, and further divides the former into two sorts ('one distinguished more by rhythm, the other more by melody'). According to this categorisation, the first section of the Fifth Symphony Scherzo is an Austro-German *Walzer* (first type), with insistent crotchets on weak beats in the accompaniment, and the Trio is a French *Valse*, characterised more loosely as 'cantabile, delicate, even song-like' (its exemplars are Berlioz's *Symphonie Fantastique* and Tchaikovsky's Fifth Symphony: Floros 1985: 176-7). Floros gestures towards the contrasting signification of the two genres in a comparison which underlines the potency of generic nuance to his Austro-German ears, even if this is mixed with an engaging cultural prejudice: 'Compared with the élan, the elemental force, indeed "*Wildheit*" of the Austrian *Walzer* of Mahlerian practice, both *Valses* [i.e. the Berlioz and the Tchaikovsky] appear nothing short of domesticated' (Floros 1985: 177).

The concentrated counterpoint built of generically coded motivic fragments at

Genre and presupposition in the Mahlerian scherzo 111

Example 4.5

the opening of the Fifth Symphony Scherzo is in many ways very similar to the process in the Sixth Symphony. The effect, however, is different: rather than the transformation between genres and a general ambiguity of expressive function that was found in the Sixth Symphony, in the Fifth some notable generic characteristics of the waltz are emphasised in order to articulate a melodic structure which has simultaneously to fulfil the needs of a character piece and a symphonic movement of vast proportions. The scale of the movement has often occasioned comment: at 802 bars, it constitutes the largest single formal component of the symphony. This is the only work in which Mahler places this weight on the scherzo.

Thus in the opening fifteen bars (summarised in ex. 4.5), an opening two-bar statement from four horns leads to a thirteen-bar melody made up of rhythmic counterpoint, first with solo horn against clarinets and bassoons, then with the latter instruments against flutes and oboes. As with the Scherzo of the Sixth Symphony, a paradigmatic rhythmic analysis would show a propensity for one-bar rhythmic shapes, with typical melodic lines associated with each: for instance, the upward scale in the rhythm ♩♪♪♪♪♪ in bars 5, 11 and 14; or the turn in the rhythm ♩ ♪♪♪♪ in bars 7, 11 and 13. Each melodic line combines shapes such as these, which, whilst generically specific, are detachable and can pass between rhythmic strands, with at least one rhythmic type distinctive to the line in question. These distinctive rhythmic units are also strongly characteristic of the waltz genre (for instance, the ♪ ♩. ♪ of the solo horn in bars 4–5 and the ♩ ♪ ♩|♪♪♩. ♪ of the clarinets and bassoons in bars 6–7). This process fulfils the need for developmental motifs whilst creating the impression of seamless melody. The recombination of units to provide the sense of sectional (eight- or sixteen-bar) cadence within asymmetrical numbers of bars is crucial: to this end the flutes and oboes in bars 13–15 redeploy rhythms from the horn in bars 3–4 and the clarinets in bar 5. If the

Example 4.6

opening two bars from the four horns are taken as a structural upbeat, these figures in bars 13-15 can be said to conclude a thirteen-bar phrase which acts as an iconic sign of the sixteen-bar period of the symphonic waltz. A similar function is performed by the pizzicato strings; their line is too sparse to be a functional harmonic accompaniment, but it nevertheless cannot be understood except as the generically conventional string accompaniment to the waltz. This reification of generic units continues in the proliferation of contrapuntal lines, so that from bar 18 there are three melodic strands, plus an intermittent pizzicato accompaniment, all constructed from the motives of the opening bars.

It is no great hermeneutic leap from these observations to the statement that Mahler is exploiting the 'generic contract' with the listener in order simultaneously to invoke and to subvert the genre of the waltz and its relation to the scherzo of symphonic practice. The fluent progress of the dance is re-written as a convention by the general compositional process in this movement, which culminates in the memorable combination of four melodic lines simultaneously in bars 782ff; indeed the coda presents virtually all the previously defined motivic material in the space of only twenty bars.

This tendency is anticipated by Adorno's comment on Mahler's use of earlier musical forms, that 'the character, to the very extent that it characterizes, is no longer simply itself; it has, as its name indicates, the value of a sign' (1960: 69/ 1992: 48). One of the most notable specific techniques used in the service of this characterisation is the use of generic 'fingerprints' to construct the middleground voice-leading necessary to the coherence of the symphonic form. The movement opens with Mahler's favourite device for creating an unresolved top line, a $\hat{6}$–$\hat{5}$ equivocation (B–A) which reappears in bars 18 and 20, in both cases establishing a $\hat{5}$ which is maintained until the sectional cadences on D♯ in bars 15 and 39. In every new melodic line, the rhythmic unit which defines that line features a motivic descending second: these intervals are used to outline a diatonic scalic descent in the first violin line of bars 15 to 25 (and again in bars 26 to 31), and then re-used as a chromatic descent in the same ♩ ♫ rhythm in bars 47 to 60. It is correspond-

Example 4.7

Example 4.8

ences such as these which a Schoenbergian view would take up as instances of Adorno's 'development-scherzo' process. The new key area (B minor) is introduced with another $\hat{6}$-$\hat{5}$ appoggiatura, and the 'ungeneric' chromaticism of the line is to be understood by analogy with the preceding melody. A code of symphonic development can also find a relationship between the obsessive descending semitones of the violins and the overall semitonal slide from B minor to B♭ major in which they are embedded. The notable feature of this organisation is not that middleground structures are required to sustain the form, but that these structures are consistently articulated by the same units that provide generic reference.

Interaction of genre and form is seen clearly in the melody of the Trio, the French *Valse* described above. The opening four bars present pairs of rhythmic motives, the second pair including glissandi, which combine with the pizzicato string accompaniment (more regular this time) to convince Floros of its non-Austrian domesticity (ex. 4.6).

The generic reference is so clear that bars 137 and 138 are retrograde inversions of bars 135 and 136. But from this point, the melody is less generically conventional. The fifth bar lacks a pair, and the extension to an eight-bar phrase creates a curious hiatus, as if a bar were missing; indeed, the repeat that follows immediately avoids this sense only by finishing after seven bars. The motivic descent of a second between the first and third beats of the bar (marked in ex. 4.6 as x) is first heard as the ubiquitous $\hat{6}$-$\hat{5}$ appoggiatura, and is combined with embedded three-note descents (y) to create repeated $\hat{5}$-$\hat{1}$ falls. This obsession with motive x extends to other themes in the Trio sections. The counterpoint to the immediate repetition of the theme (ex. 4.7) introduces a five-note figure, which is contracted to two bars in the following 'A' section (bars 236–7, woodwind) and then emerges as a new theme at bar 237 (ex. 4.8). This theme, which by the end of the process represents a synthesis of all the waltz melodies heard so far, is the one which is reiterated and further developed in the 'suspension' sections (to use Adorno's term) that mark moments of collapse at bars 269 to 306 and just before the coda, at bars 683 to 727.

Example 4.9

At its first statement, it is a ten-bar melody from which almost any pair of bars could be removed to leave a balanced, eight-bar phrase. This generic playfulness continues into the second Trio section, where the melodic line spells out its motivic antecedents with patient clarity (ex. 4.9a and ex. 4.9b).

Although this has been a somewhat lengthy analysis, it serves to demonstrate that generic reference and symphonic design are not as separable in this movement as most discussions have tended to imply. In the scherzos of both symphonies, Mahler employs dance elements which, through the reification of their constituent signs, carry a multiplicity of meanings; these meanings are of much more extensive scope than the cliché of aristocratic diversion. The asymmetry and middleground construction identified above are the analytical corollary of the aesthetic confrontation of 'high' and 'low' cultural genres which is central both to the defenders and detractors of Mahler's works. Mahler's use of socially coded material is a perennial topic of debate in the critical literature. Dahlhaus comments that 'one of the ineradicable clichés of Mahler criticism, his juxtaposition of 'sublimity' and 'banality' has been interpreted by polemicists to mean that Mahler was unable to realise his intentions properly, and by apologists to mean that he was indifferent to his thematic material as opposed to the function it serves within the form; it has even been taken to mean that he "rescued inferior music" and represents an "aesthetic prefiguration" of the future reconciliation of society' (1983: 163). In the Fifth Symphony, the curious dialectic of art-music and popular-music genres goes unnoticed by a critic such as David B. Greene, who hears only a symbolic negation of the first part of the symphony: 'The Scherzo turns its back on death, heroism and the quest for peace. A horn call that summons itself from nowhere moves us into the glittering world of the Ländler and the Viennese waltz, an infectiously cheerful whirl in which the future and the self are sometimes forgotten, sometimes suppressed and sometimes affirmed' (Greene 1984: 74). By contrast, Adorno considers the nominalism of a form built out of reified fragments of 'inferior' genre music to be capable of restoring what the 'superior' symphonic genre had lost. He comments, 'Music's appeal against its split into an upper and a lower sphere, which has left its mark on each, is pursued by Mahler in such a way that the ferment induced in the lower sphere is to restore by force what correctness in the upper has forfeited' (1960: 86/1992: 62). The introduction of elements of culture-industry commodity music acts as a critique of the 'ontology of form', for 'if the Mahlerian thematic nuclei have something fixed, derived about them, this non-spontaneous element on the other hand defies the reifications of formal theory' (1960: 120/1992: 89).

In this view, the 'fixity' of the generic units described in the foregoing analyses is essential to the 'unfinishing' of the form. This is a considerably more complex semiosis than the 'direct' hearing of Greene, in which the waltz is heard as forgetful of its 'upper sphere' function. If Adorno could only regard such escapism as inexcusable inauthenticity, it is nevertheless true that his own discussion affirms rather than denies the importance of generic reference as the force which motivates both of the scherzos under discussion.

The extent to which the scherzos of the Fifth and Sixth Symphonies share a common compositional technique makes the generic play of the former, which can be identified with relative ease, the key to disentangling the complex semiosis of the latter. In both, there is a dialectic of generic and symphonic-formal codes, which has been identified in the analyses above. This dialectic can only be described in semiotic terms.

From the basis of the comparison of these works, it is now possible to take the discussion of generic reference a little further. For if the generic code has a complex referential scope within the institution of symphonic writing, this does not imply that its reference within 'lower sphere' music, and hence its potential for extra-musical interpretants, is irrelevant to the sort of investigation that a semiotic analysis proposes.

At this point, then, the difficult task of attempting to specify reference outside the musical work enters this study for the first time. There are several advantages of approaching it in this way; not least, the tendency towards unsubstantiated metaphorical interpretation founded on anecdote or solipsistic hearing is avoided. However, it has to be conceded that any attempt to link non-musical, or extroversive, interpretants to symphonic composition is more likely to be guilty of partiality or arbitrariness than analyses based on the introversive investigation of motivic working or formal construction. For this reason, the next step in this chapter will be to consider three modes of reference which are both consistently used in relation to Mahler's scherzos and which are applicable to artworks and cultural artefacts other than music. These are the interlinked rhetorical figures of irony and parody, which both derive from the identification of cliché and which act to engender an artistic mode that is particularly threatening to the artwork of the cultural 'upper sphere', that of kitsch.

IRONY, PARODY, CLICHÉ

It was remarked at the outset of this chapter that one of the fundamental marks of a scherzo is that it is a distortion of a minuet. Indeed, the three interlinked processes of cliché, irony and parody are in this way involved in the convention of the form itself. If they are frequently invoked in writing on Mahler, their working is extremely elusive. They are, in fact, all functions of generic coding. It is the context given to a component part of the music by its genre that enables it to be recognised as a cliché, or alternatively allows irony or parody to be heard in its deployment.

A semiotic definition of the three terms is the best way towards distinguishing their effects. Irony and parody both derive from a contradiction between the contexts of the signifying and signified s-codes. In other words, the code identifies a signifying unit, and furnishes expectations of its use; but it also identifies a signifying context which is not that of these expectations. In the case of irony, the specific meaning of an utterance is in literal opposition to its context: thus the use of a dance form or song form, within the context of a scherzo or sonata form, can be heard as ironic. Parody is of wider scope; here the specific utterance is simply not in accord with its context; in other words, it is a distortion of the genre from which it derives. Some concept of genre is necessary for the operation of parody, and is almost always present in cases of musical or visual (as opposed to linguistic) irony. Cliché is slightly different; here it is not the broadening of semiotic scope which defines it, but the narrowing of that scope, so that a unit is read directly as an instance of a specific genre, with no possibility of other reference. Normally, this kind of semiotic short-circuit denies a cliché any signifying power; it is too readily subsumed into the general code to have any specific charge. Maybe because the accusation of cliché has been a censure of artistic works throughout the history of criticism, its effects have not been sufficiently studied. There are at least two ways in which cliché can play an important role in works which are not themselves trivial. On the one hand, a cliché can often provide a powerful image which the text that relies upon it must simultaneously exploit and conceal; whilst it may be suggested or invoked, it must not be explicitly stated. For instance, the difference in the treatment of the cliché that 'murder requires vengeance' goes a fair way to explaining the relative merits of *The Spanish Tragedy* and *Hamlet*. On the other hand, the opposite strategy is to use a cliché in an explicit context where its status as cliché becomes the signifying factor; as in most of the speeches made by Polonius, to remain with a Shakespearian example. It is this latter case which articulates much parody and irony.

All of these possibilities are present in the two scherzos under discussion. It is no accident that the only times in the Fifth Symphony Scherzo that Mahler employs the cliché of string pizzicato accompaniment as an upbeat to the *Valse* melody of the Trio sections is when returning to these sections after the 'suspension-field' or 'dissolution-field' climaxes, in bars 307–8 and bars 428–9. It is suggested again in bars 728–34, but here the approach to the coda necessitates a different combination of materials. In these passages there is irony, both in the fact that a cliché can stand as the 'correct' continuation of the most 'symphonic' or 'unprecedented' passages of the movement, and also in the persistence of the *Valse* as the opposing genre to the *Walzer*. These moments are part of the more general tendency to cliché which is

Genre and presupposition in the Mahlerian scherzo

the result of the reification of generic units analysed above. In this way, the animation of the symphonic argument by the clichés of dance genres turns the whole movement into a parody of the traditional scherzo of earlier symphonies.

If this state of affairs is easier to identify in the Fifth Symphony, it is no less present in the Sixth. The interpenetration of genres identified by the analysis above constantly displaces denotative signification of generic units from connotative signification; although Mahler does not place the score indication '*mit Ironie*' or '*mit Parodie*' above the march rhythms in bars 11-19, this is a technique which is ironic through and through. Mahler does in fact repeatedly indicate the non-ironic, 'natural' or 'direct' profile of the Trio sections as '*natürlich drängend*'. Here a complex situation obtains: the surface irony (and straightforward parody) of the march/ländler combination gives way to irony on a more formal level when they are subsumed in the *altväterisch* country dance.

For the purposes of teasing out referential meaning from these movements, one of the most notable consequences of this generic play is the tendency towards collapse and dissolution at sectional cadences. Such moments are of course not rare in Mahlerian movements other than scherzos; but in the works discussed in this chapter they appear a direct outcome of the supervenience of the symphonic formal scheme over the generic. In both works, the elements combined at these moments are pedals on the tonic note of the movement (without clear tonic harmony), chromatic downward-moving melodic lines, and a use of whole-tone scale and augmented-triad harmony in the approach to a final tonic triad. In the Fifth Symphony, the longest section constructed in this way is the passage leading to the second group of Trio sections, bars 269-306. This acts as a cadence to a restatement of the secondary melody of the 'A' section (bars 40ff), here in a curious Lydian D minor (bars 250ff). A whole-tone bass descent (C-D-B♭) with an upper-voice A♭ pedal is halted on a D pedal in strings and woodwind, *fff > pp* (bar 269), and contradicted by the four horns in turn with F♮s, *ff > pp*. The D♮ is maintained as a pedal throughout the following section, accompanied by solo horn lines falling chromatically from G to D. The only gesture towards harmonic closure is an augmented triad on F♮ which only just touches an A triad before the double bar line and the new section in D minor (bar 307). Robert Hopkins describes this passage as an example of 'abatement' (not dissimilar to Adorno's 'suspension'), creating a sectional close by non-harmonic means (Hopkins 1990: 66-7); but if these bars do indeed embody closure, it is with a significance which advances greatly beyond a 'very fresh use of tonality' (Hopkins 1990: 65, drawing on comments by Donald Mitchell, Dika Newlin and Robert Bailey). The equivalent moments in the Sixth Symphony are also the passages preceding the Trio sections (bars 79-97 and bars 259-72). In the first of these, chromatic neighbour-notes to A major and A minor triads in bars 79-86 lead to pedal A♮s at registral extremes, the major/minor triad motive on trumpets, chromatic lines on violins and woodwind which have strong whole-tone associations (the on-beat notes in bars 89-90 give a

Example 4.10

complete whole-tone scale), and the *ff* > *pp* dynamic noted in the Fifth Symphony passage. Here the cadential section subsides onto A♭s repeated as a quaver pulse: another example of abatement.

What is important in these passages for the purposes of this study is the direct relationship between this sort of cadencing, which acts as an immanent critique of its own formal function, and the generic coding of the sections closed and introduced by the passages. It is no accident that the abatement of secondary parameters goes along with motivic dissolution in each case: the solo horn melodies and their echoes in the Fifth Symphony become shorter and shorter; the chromatic oscillation in the Sixth Symphony becomes a single-pitch pulse. This dissolution, particularly in the Sixth Symphony passages, serves little by little to denude the units of their generic reference. In other words, the process of closing the section gradually obliterates the generic code, as this code serves the needs of formal function. This process in itself becomes characteristic: the play of genres leads inevitably to 'negative fulfilment', a signifier of destruction, at its end. In contrasting ways, the final sections of each movement reinforce this hearing. The sections just discussed are used as preludes to the final coda of each movement, and both codas extend the closural crisis to the final double bar. This appears at first sight not to be the case in the Fifth Symphony, since the coda consists of the bravura combination of melodic lines noted earlier. But there are evident cracks in this mirror of positivity: the frenetic score indication, '*sehr wild*', and the use of whole-tone scales. These are heard in bars 763-6 and then to great effect in bars 778-81, where the final settling onto a D triad is approached by a strange combination of chromatic voice-leading and augmented triads (ex. 4.10). In the case of the Sixth Symphony, the Trio section is re-written as if it were a textbook example of motivic dissolution: fragmentary forms of motives are combined in sparse counterpoint within the Trio's shifting time-signatures, and even the major/minor triad is dissolved as a minor/diminished triad in bar 427. The use of dissolution as an alternative to cadence is so persuasive that both movements end with a statement of their opening melodic motives. Even more striking is the way in which both codas constitute fairly clear prolongations of their respective tonic triads, albeit with chromatic inflection. In other words, the substitution of generic destruction for harmonic cadence is taken as authoritative: the passages of crisis described above form the structural approach to the composing-out of the final chord.

What is seen here, then, is a forcefield of generic and symphonic codes in which clichés derived from dance genres are put to ironic and parodic service. The use of cliché is particularly charged: it is always in danger of appearing to be kitsch, the mass-produced, reified image of high art expression. This is a general state of affairs in Mahler's scherzos, and to some extent in all of his music: the invocation of ländler and waltz inevitably threatens to undermine the symphonic frame in which it is presented.

In order to give some greater specificity to this mode of reference, however, it is necessary to find a way of describing this use of cliché, which is simultaneously the subject of desire and aversion within the music. And there is, indeed, a topos of nineteenth-century culture which gives allegorical embodiment to this fencing with kitsch. To some extent present in descriptions of Mahler's music from the start (indeed, even within the composer's own statements), it is a topos which typically lurks outside many texts in visual arts, music and literature; a spectral, threatening Other which must be suppressed and denied by the narratives which gain most force from it. This is the topos of the Dance of Death, whose incorporation of cliché, the image of the dance, and a dominating impulse towards the most literal 'negative fulfilment' makes it a seductive analogue to the typical musical process of the Mahlerian scherzo.

THE DANCE OF DEATH

The Dance of Death has a long history in Western culture, enjoying two periods of widespread popular dissemination, in the fifteenth and nineteenth centuries. Whilst its many manifestations have been the subject of various iconographical studies, there have been few attempts to assess its importance as a cultural referent of remarkable constancy. Tilman Seebass comments that 'the study of the Dance of Death is of necessity an interdisciplinary undertaking, and the main reason for unsatisfactory results, where they occur, is a scope too narrow on the part of the scholar' (1981: 329). The medieval origins of the motif are not irrelevant to its nineteenth-century popularity, although the differences between the typical earlier form and its romanticised version are telling.

The earliest examples of the motif date from the fourteenth century, but the most famous example was the set of murals in the cloister of the Church of the Holy Innocents in Paris, executed before 1424, and possibly earlier than 1380 (Warren 1931: x-xii). Although the paintings were destroyed in the eighteenth century, they apparently showed a procession of the degrees of mankind, starting with the Emperor and proceeding through Pope, King, Archbishop and so forth down to commoner. Each figure was led by a skeletal figure towards the grave; the common mortality of every rank was the clear message of the frieze, made yet more explicit by the verses beneath each painting, which were published by Guy Marchant in 1486 accompanied by a set of woodcuts. It has been suggested that the decimation of the Black Death led to the sudden and extraordinary uprise in the

Figure 4.1 Holbein, *A Cemetery*

popularity of the motif during the following century: examples, typically wall paintings or sets of panels in the choirs of churches, are found from Norway to Spain and from Britain to Hungary. Significantly, perhaps, there are numerous extant examples in the mountainous rural areas of Bohemia, Austria and Italy where Mahler grew up and where he returned each summer (a survey of those which survived into the twentieth century is found in Clark 1950; the history of the motif in German literature is given by Koller 1980); the Tyrol in particular has a long-established cult of death. An important element of the motif in its medieval version is the social basis of the procession; this is a corporate dance, in which Death shows no individual fear nor favour.

As the motif was developed, particularly in literary forms (the earliest reference in a poem is from Jean le Fèvre in 1376), the need to include female equivalents of the male characters – Empress, Abbess, and so forth – led to a shift from rank to age as the ordering principle of the succession, since Virgin, Beloved and Bride were needed to make up the numbers. Thus a gradual evolution from social organisation to personal history began (this is described by J. Huizinga, 1924: 129–35). What is important here is the obliteration of social difference: young and old, great and small are called to the great round-dance (the *Reigen*) in the realm of the Other; it is this group dance that is the image which gives rise to the motif.

The *locus classicus* of the Dance of Death, and the source for its nineteenth-century revival, is of course Holbein's series of woodcuts, first printed in 1538 and in more or less constant circulation since then; they were the subject of numerous nineteenth-century editions. Holbein's figures combine the procession of the ranks of mankind with the destiny of the individual, as Death leads each of his figures in a manner appropriate to them, by turns tender, humorous and sardonic. With Holbein, too, the connection between the motif and music-making becomes stronger. The earlier Dance of Death was much more a procession than a dance (at least in the earthly realm), although the figure of Death may well have been depicted dancing. However, several of Holbein's skeletons are playing instruments: organ, bugle, pipes, drum and xylophone amongst others (see for example figure 4.1; the involvement of musical instruments with the medieval iconography is studied in Hammerstein 1980).

The idea of a dance towards the grave became irresistible to the Romantic imagination of the late eighteenth and nineteenth centuries. The motif was the subject of poems by poets as different as Baudelaire and Walter Scott. The term 'macabre', so crucial to the description of much nineteenth-century art, significantly derives from the fourteenth-century French poem in which the Dance of Death is entitled 'dance maccabre'. Interestingly (given Mahler's reverence for his works), Goethe used the motif at least twice. In his poem *Der Totentanz* (1813), the horror of the dance is reversed: a watchman comes upon the dance of skeletons in the graveyard, and steals a winding-sheet, condemning its owner to crumble to dust at the stroke of one o'clock. And in the last Act of *Faust*, Sarah Webster Goodwin identifies a dance of death, or at least an imitation of one of Holbein's vignettes, in the song of the skeletal *lemures* digging Faust's grave:

> In youth when I did live and love
> Methought 'twas very sweet,
> To go where song and frolic was,
> And thither ran my feet.
> But age, with his stealing steps,
> Has clawed me with his crutch;
> There the grave's door: I stumbled in,
> 'Twas open overmuch.
> (Goethe 1959 [1831]: 286)

There is, then, hardly any need to argue for the currency of the image in Mahler's intellectual environment; indeed, the story of his recurrent nightmare, in which he would dance with Death, who appeared dressed as a *bon vivant*, is more a testimony to a common cultural obsession rather than an idiosyncratic neurosis. Schnitzler's *La Ronde* and Strindberg's *Dance of Death* are only the most explicit uses of the figure in drama roughly contemporary with Mahler; for a hundred years or more, the figure was widespread in popular, reproducible forms which developed into a

Figure 4.2 Langlois, *Essai historique* . . .

potent combination of morbidity and eroticism; this history, indeed, might justifiably be seen as the origin of kitsch itself (it is described by Webster Goodwin, 1988: 3-6). It became more and more common for the figure of Death to be shown leading a young woman to the grave: a typical example is figure 4.2, an illustration to Eustache Langlois' *Essai historique, philosophique et pittoresque sur les danses des morts* (reproduced here from Webster Goodwin 1988: 220). The naked breasts of the young woman, the attitude of her arms in a partner dance with Death, the shroud which also suggests a bridal veil, the devil grinning from Death's genitals, the shadowy figure piping and drumming in the background; all these elements combine in a figure of extremity and transgression.

Without embarking here on a discussion of the musical *Danse Macabre*, the next stage of this inquiry is to identify the musical images which became strongly attached to the figure in its nineteenth-century manifestation. There are two linked images which deserve comment: the masked ball and the waltz.

The links between the ball, sexual danger, and death are exemplified at some length by Webster Goodwin. Whatever the social realities may have been, the cultural perception of the ball changed greatly from the middle-class entertainment of Jane Austen to the vertiginous whirl of *The Great Gatsby* (let alone the dance scene in *Wozzeck*). The ball is a liminal occasion in several ways: it takes place outside the normal settings for social interaction; it is the scene for sexual transaction, often the interface of the world of social mores and the underworld of adulterous affairs; it allows the interaction of young people of the age between childhood and the social definition of adulthood; it allows the meeting of different social classes, such as soldiers and aristocratic ladies; and it treads the outermost borders of social respectability, whilst remaining bound by complex social conventions. The masked ball heightens this liminality by making literal the theoretical interchangeability of the participants. The contrast between the conventional appearance of members of society outside the ballroom and the behaviour revealed within is the social analogue of the dissimulation represented by the mask. Apparent social respectability masks immoral sexual appetite; with it, nubile desirability masks a lewd lack of innocence. The possibility for dangerous deception, and the arbitrariness of couplings in the dance, could not fail to acquire metaphorical significance in literary works, even without their grounding in social fact. The popular perception of the ball may be judged from the following advertisement for a masked ball in Rouen in 1837, which sounds both inviting and warning tones:

Long live the masked ball! Here's to the sparkling light of the candles, to the glitter of the gaslight, to the enticing strains of the orchestra, that thunderous harmony set loose by waltzes, galops, quadrilles, bright spangles lifted by Musard or Julien from the glorious mantle of Mozart, Meyerbeer or Halévy; long live the masked ball! In a great ballroom, where they mingle and rub shoulders, passing by in all directions, the motley, joyful crowd of dominos dressed in every shape, style and colour of costume. There is no etiquette, no ceremony, all are equal; women and young men greet each other familiarly; the woman has gained her freedom, she has escaped from male guardianship; she is emancipated. But not all masked women know how to stop at the freedom afforded by the mask; how many carry on to licentiousness? How many go as far as throwing aside the mask? and how many take off the mask to show only a tired, lined face when you had imagined them to possess all the grace and freshness of youth?

(from the *Colibri*, 29 January 1837; quoted in Webster Goodwin 1988: 130)

Associated with this double-edged image of the masked ball, whose motley cavalcade of costumes betrays a true Bakhtinian carnival, is the new dance of the early nineteenth century, the waltz. Warnings abound of the danger of the waltz, the

Figure 4.3   Rowlandson, *The Masquerade*

ultimate experience of socially licensed sexual pleasure, from sermons to dance tutors; one version of it was even banned from court by the Emperor Franz Josef. Webster Goodwin finds its most extreme manifestation in an American monograph of 1877 published under the pseudonym William Herman, which asserts quite baldly that,

> The modern waltz is not merely 'suggestive' as its opponents have hitherto charitably styled it, but an open and shameless gratification of sexual desire and a cooler of burning lust ... It is an actual realisation of a certain physical ecstasy which should *at least*, be indulged in private and no pure person should experience the same except under the sanctity of matrimony.
> (quoted in Webster Goodwin 1988: 143)

What Webster Goodwin calls the 'transparent prurience' of the author does not stop short of quoting from one society lady what must be one of the earlier descriptions of female orgasm to be publicly circulated:

> the climax of my confusion was reached when, folded in his warm embrace, and giddy with the whirl, a strange, sweet thrill would shake me from head to foot, leaving me weak and almost powerless and really almost obliged to depend for support upon the arm which encircled me. If my partner failed from ignorance, lack of skill, or innocence, to arouse these, to me, most pleasurable sensations, I did not dance with him a second time.
> (Webster Goodwin 1988: 143-4)

The monograph relies on the themes of deception, licence and excess to provide its voyeurism; it should come as little surprise that its title is *The Dance of Death*.

One of the best-known successors to Holbein in the nineteenth century, Charles

Genre and presupposition in the Mahlerian scherzo

Figure 4.4 Rowlandson, *The Waltz*

Rowlandson's *The English Dance of Death* (1814-16), contains both a masked ball and 'the waltz' as scenes in its sequence of engravings (see figure 4.3 and figure 4.4). Death here is male, coming to seduce and violate; there is an intersection here between the Dance of Death motif and that of Death and the Maiden. The inexorable course of the music compels the woman to dance to her destruction, whether the downfall be sexual or mortal (the image of the devilish fiddler is yet another folk-tale figure which becomes incorporated into the motif). There is a political edge to Rowlandson's engravings, which is true of other occurrences of the motif: again and again he shows death overturning social hierarchies, whether revealed in the masquerade, cuckolding the aged husband or carrying off the treasure of the jealous father: the old order is set to pass.

This brief description serves to establish the social and cultural context of the Dance of Death in the nineteenth century, and its participation in the motif of the ball and the waltz. In order to bring this context into play with the scherzos of Mahler symphonies, several comparable situations in other musical and literary works need to be examined. Quite apart from the works entitled *Danse Macabre* or something similar, the depiction of the dance towards extinction in musical works has a long history, and one which deserves a full study in its own right, stretching at least from the Scherzo of the *Eroica* to *La Valse*, and including the *Symphonie Fantastique*, *La Traviata* and, inevitably, the *Rite of Spring* along the way. Within this history, Mahler occupies a relatively complex place, and one in which the relation of the motif to the musical and signifying processes of his compositions has to be approached carefully and through comparison with more straightforward examples. But it is the incorporation of allusion to the history of the motif, combined with resistance to its consumable version as kitsch, which ultimately makes the Scherzo of Mahler's Second Symphony the ideal choice for the postmodernist parody of Berio's *Sinfonia*.

Equally, there is a history of allusion to the popular version of the motif in literary works, especially in the depiction of ballroom scenes as crucial moments of narratives. The ball is often the setting for a fatal encounter for the heroine of nineteenth-century novels; *War and Peace* includes more than one such episode, and the seduction of Anna by Vronsky in *Anna Karenina* follows her reckless participation in a waltz. The comparison to be drawn between such moments and the process of signification in the Mahler movements is best approached through an understanding of the role of cliché and kitsch. For if the dangerous, liminal state induced by the intoxication of the waltz derives its power in the novels from the cliché of the Dance of Death motif, this is a symbolic meaning which must be suppressed or remain latent within the text in order to avoid a descent into kitsch, which would disempower the work by removing its status as 'significant art'. Alternatively, if the motif appears within the narrative, it must be handled in such a way as to avoid the reification of cliché. In *S/Z*, Roland Barthes skilfully identifies several ways in which Balzac's story *Sarrasine* does this: here, the motif is written into an antithesis which not only distances it from the narrative, but makes possible a symbolic reading crucial to the opening of the story. The passage in question reads:

The trees, imperfectly covered in snow, stood out faintly from the grey background of a cloudy sky barely lit by the moon. Seen in this fantastic setting, they seemed vaguely like spectres half-clothed in their shrouds, the gigantic image of the famous Dance of Death. Then, turning to my other side, I could admire the Dance of Life!

(Quoted in Barthes 1970: 30-1)

Barthes comments of the first half that it is not so much the cold as the lack of coverage and lack of light that creates a reference to the lack involved in the figure of Sarrasine, a castrato disguised as a woman:

The moon is the *negation* of light, warmth reduced to its own lack: it gives light only by reflection, without itself originating it; thus it becomes the luminous emblem of the castrato, a lack manifested by the empty glamour borrowed from femininity in his youth (Adonis), and which becomes only leprous greyness in his old age (the old man, the garden). (Barthes 1970: 31)

Barthes goes on to comment on the neatness of the antithesis 'Dance of Death / Dance of Life', which makes the narrator himself the boundary between the two opposed syntagms, and thus the supplement which is the locus of the symbolic reading: 'It is through this *excess*, which arrives in the discourse after the rhetorical figure has been saturated, that something can be told and the narrative can begin' (Barthes 1971: 35). The Dance of Death motif is subordinated to a complex figure which inaugurates the story: significantly, it is applied to objects *outside* the ballroom which is the scene of the action. Balzac suggests the kitsch image in order to make possible a symbolic reading: but like the trees themselves, this image must remain outside the fully-lit narrative, a shadowy presence which cannot be fully revealed. It is not only the dancer who flirts with death in the motif; the author must also tread a fine line between the thrill of the dance and the danger of kitsch.

Perhaps the greatest example of the waltz as a liminal moment comes in the novel which above all represents the immanent critique of the system of cultural production which makes it possible, and which actually contains many points of contact with Mahler's own attitudes, although there is no evidence that he ever read it: this is *Madame Bovary*. Adorno (once again) comments in passing on the parallel between Mahler's works and this novel (1960: 85/1992: 61). The structural similarities between it and the Sixth Symphony will be explored in chapter 5 below; but for the moment, the concern is with the process of signification.

Webster Goodwin once again gives an instructive discussion of the role of the Dance of Death motif in the novel (1986, re-used in a slightly shorter version as chapter 5 of Webster Goodwin 1988). Emma Bovary participates in two balls during the novel, and it is the first, at La Vaubyessard, in which, as Webster Goodwin comments, 'she glimpses a world at the chateau which will make it impossible for her ever again to be satisfied with her simple and limited existence' (1986: 199). It is this experience, in which she dances with the Viscount, which sets in train the events which lead ineluctably to her suicide at the end of the novel; the second ball is a parodistic parallel of the first, and is, inevitably, a masked ball. The passage is worth quoting at length for the subtle combination of details which allude to the popular, kitsch version of the motif:

At three o'clock in the morning, the cotillion began. Emma had never learned how to waltz. Everyone in the room was waltzing, even Mademoiselle d'Andervilliers and the Marquise. No one was left except the guests who were staying in the house, about twelve persons in all.

In spite of her ignorance of the steps, one of the waltzers, whom the others called familiarly 'Vicomte', and whose very low-cut waistcoat seemed as though moulded on his torso, twice asked her to dance, saying that he would guide her, and that she would manage very well.

They began slowly, then started to move more swiftly. They turned and twisted, and everything about them turned and twisted too, the lamps, the furniture, the panelled walls, the floor — like objects on a pivoted disk. As they passed close to the doors, the lower edge of Emma's dress blew against her partner's trousers: their legs became intertwined. He lowered his glance and looked at her. She raised her eyes to his. A languorous dizziness came over her. She stopped. They started again, and, quickening his pace, the Vicomte swung her away to the far end of the gallery, where, quite out of breath, she all but fell and rested her hand for a moment on his breast. Then, still twirling, but more soberly, he led her back to her place. She stumbled against the wall and put her hand over her eyes.

When she opened them again, a lady was sitting on a stool in the middle of the floor with three dancers on their knees before her. She chose the Vicomte, and the music struck up once more. Everybody looked at them. Up and down the room they went, she, keeping her body motionless and her chin lowered, he, in the same posture as before, with back straight, elbow rounded and lips protruded. She certainly knew how to waltz!

(Flaubert 1981 [1857]: 49-50)

The similarities between this passage and those quoted above are clear enough, down to details such as Emma's 'languorous dizziness' or the intertwining of the dancers' legs. Webster Goodwin draws out the specific connections between this scene and Emma's death, principally elaborating the Freudian scene of a choice between three fates represented in the final paragraph. In terms of the technique used to present the motif, the shifting of narrative viewpoint is an important effect which is as dizzying for the reader as the waltz is for Emma (Webster Goodwin 1986: 213-14); the writing itself becomes infected by the motif, a narrative stance which complicates the status of the narrating voice. This effect is not far from the similarly giddying influence of the waltz genre on the symphonic form of the Fifth Symphony Scherzo.

The clichés incorporated into the passage just quoted are symptomatic of the greater cliché – the Dance of Death – which cannot be named within the text. The role of cliché in Flaubert generally is explored at length by Michael Riffaterre in an article quoted by Webster Goodwin (Riffaterre 1984). He describes the process more broadly, in terms of 'presuppositions', defined as 'the implicit and requisite preceding conditions of an explicit statement'. This level of signification is intertextual, yet it does not invoke the reference directly in the surface of the text. Riffaterre comments, 'these figures refer to sign complexes that they substitute for and repress, as it were, pushing them back into intertextual latency' (1984: 178). Riffaterre discusses complexes of allusion around ideas such as classical quotation or the depiction of the adulteress. The role of generic reference in music is very close to this metonymic process in literary presuppositions. Riffaterre distinguishes carefully between the metonymy of the presupposition's textual marker, and the metaphorical or symbolic relation that it may have with the other elements within the text, rather than outside it. Within the scherzos, too, there is a distinction to be drawn between the harmonic and formal function of the units of the generic code, and their relationship as clichés – marked units – to the genre which they presuppose.

How, then, does the identification of this complex of metonymic associations within the nineteenth-century sociolect illuminate the hearing of the Mahler scherzos? Not in a direct fashion, certainly; Mahler is not attempting to depict the Dance of Death in the fashion of Saint-Saëns, nor even deriving a musical image from it in the slightly more oblique manner of *Giselle*. Rather, the motif is an instance of a cultural presupposition which enables the generic code to signify intertextually. The Dance of Death remains outside the text, in the sense that it is not the subject of direct reference; but it animates the treatment of generic materials and its presence is signalled by the presence of clichés within the music. The waltz themes of the Fifth Symphony flirt with the motif in a dangerous invocation of the banal which threatens to drag the symphony down to the level of kitsch; the banal is the dreadful Other which is figured by the motif itself, and which must be resisted – whether by 'learned' counterpoint or 'significant' formal design – at the moment that it appears most seductive. The perpetual possibility of repeat which is the necessary corollary of a dance genre – the tune can always be played one more time – threatens to undermine the 'teleological' demands of symphonic form, in which each movement must justify its progress towards a conclusion in order to have a coherent place within the whole work. In the same way, the Dance of Death figures the ultimate repeatability of Death: the Dance will always continue with another partner, and the motif renders the narrative of the individual life meaningless, at the very moment that its representation becomes standardised as a cliché.

In this sense, Mahler's scherzos derive power both from the image of the individual flirtation with erotic and fatal power in the waltz, and from the *Reigen* in which all mankind, great and small alike, appear insignificant in the great dance of the Other. In the Fifth Symphony, this topos gives a powerful hermeneutic ground for explaining the effect of using the waltz genre in both scherzo and trio sections of the movement. The Dance ceases, only to be replaced by an image of itself; the generic reference is unceasing, and this signals the presence of the cultural presupposition. The inevitable confusion of the motif with the musical genre via the conventional representations of the ball and the waltz goes a long way towards explaining the Viennese *Wildheit* of Mahler's waltzes so prized by Floros.

An obvious objection to this comparison is that the Scherzo of the Sixth Symphony does not appear to contain reference to the waltz in the manner of the Fifth Symphony. Closer examination of the movement and the motif, however, reveals two levels of reference in which the motif can participate. First of all, the ländler genre which is the primary referent of the code is not as innocent as it seems. Despite the fact that ländler themes are persistently interpreted by commentators on Mahler to be an image of country life, a reference to the folk music of his childhood and an antithesis to the acculturated world of the conventional symphony, this is at odds both with the history of the genre and the biography of the composer. Mosco Carner has a rather different history of the dance:

The Austrian court traditionally staged popular feasts called 'Wirtschaften', 'Königreiche', and 'Bauernhochzeiten' – dramatic representations of scenes of peasant life in which members of the imperial family appeared in costumes of peasants or hunters. These entertainments were in the nature of *bals champêtres* . . . Composers such as J. H. Schmelzer wrote ballet suites containing ländlers for these festive occasions, and later neither Haydn nor Mozart considered it beneath his dignity to write *Teutsche* or German Dances for the masked balls given by the court during Carnival at the Redoutensaal in the Hofburg.

(Carner 1981: 435)

There is extremely scant evidence for the idea that Mahler was familiar with the ländler as a folk-dance of his childhood; both Paul Banks and Vladimir Karbusicky emphasise the cultural filtering of the *volkstümlich* elements in his mature works. Banks comments that in Mahler's mature works, 'the intention is not to create an imitation of folk music but a highly romanticised vision of it . . . The feature common to these poetic techniques [in 'Wo die schönen Trompeten bläsern'] and Mahler's handling of *volkstümlich* elements is the consistent sacrifice of folkloristic accuracy in favour of a romantic evocation of *Das Volk*' (1982: 28-9).

The peculiar background of Mahler's childhood, in a German-speaking *Inseln* within Bohemia, must certainly have had a large part in creating his affinity for German folk stories; but this affinity was always mediated through literature or art music (see Karbusicky 1986). In the case of his scherzo melodies, the obvious musical antecedents are in the ländler of Schubert and Mozart (see the illustrations used by Floros given here as ex. 4.1 above). It is the acculturated, distinctively Viennese version of the ländler which makes its appearance in the symphonies. This is not to deny that the ländler contains an image of the natural, pastoral world outside city and society; but the dance is precisely an image of this idyll, not a part of it. This is a striking example of Riffaterre's 'presuppositions': like quotation in a literary work, the ländler in art music does more than refer to the country dance. A quotation 'presupposes a particular use of the quotation, a context-bound quoting behaviour' (Riffaterre 1984: 178); pastoral is a well-defined literary genre in its own right, and the recognition of the idyll as a fantasy is an integral part of the ländler's portrayal of the natural world. There is more to this observation than a concern for scholarly rectitude. It is difficult to view as accidental the association of the seventeenth-century ländler with dissimulation and carnival when, as Carner points out, the waltz was a direct historical development of the earlier dance: Joseph Lanner's first waltzes were published as 'Ländler' and 'Deutsche' (Carner 1981: 436). There is an almost exact parallel between the musical and social developments of the dance: the minuet was speeded up to become the scherzo, and the ländler was speeded up to become the waltz; thus both the distortion of the scherzo through the adoption of the waltz, and the retreat to the eighteenth-century pastoral image of the ländler in Mahler are dissimulating moves: different constellations within the same signifying complex. In this context there is new significance to the fact that the Trio sections of the Sixth Symphony Scherzo give another pastoral contrast to the concatenation of march and ländler in the 'A' sections. As the analysis earlier in this chapter demonstrated, the *altväterisch* dance theme is literally constructed from the signifying units of the ländler and march.

What appears 'natural' is based on the cultural: the mode of signification presupposed by the ländler is made explicit by the musical process.

If the use of ländler rhythms and melodies does not escape the referential complex associated with the Dance of Death, then the second level of reference within the Sixth Symphony Scherzo is much more directly involved with it. This level concerns the use of the march genre, and the status of cliché within its use. The most immediately striking moment of generic reference in the movement, and thus the most clichéd gesture, is the passage of trills on woodwind including piccolo, first heard in bars 16-17, which are a clear reference to military marches. When a closely related motive occurs in the Finale (bar 124), Adorno comments that 'one seems to have heard the passage . . . innumerable times' (1960: 73/ 1992: 50). Again there is a flirtation with kitsch, a heightening of the generic reference which almost amounts to a distortion. This is even more true of the return of this figure in bars 73-4, where Mahler again doubles it on xylophone, the one use of this instrument in the symphony. The associations of the xylophone used in this way and the macabre are hard to resist: indeed, trills similar to these are heard accompanying the march of the skeletal army in the *Wunderhorn* setting *Revelge*. The association of the military march with the Dance of Death has as long a history as the waltz: when Holbein's skeletons are seen playing musical instruments, these are often the drums and pipes of military bands, and one of them does indeed play a xylophone. Again, it is the association of cliché and the motif which makes it so potent as a presupposition of the music.

The contention of this discussion, then, is that the two scherzos represent different constellations of forces, both of which involve the Dance of Death as a motif in play with the teleological requirements of symphonic form. The place of the motif in possible narrative analyses of the symphonies is an issue which will be discussed in relation to the Sixth Symphony in chapter 5 below. For present purposes, the implications of these contentions for the use of genre as an analytical code need to be considered with some care.

THE STATUS OF THE ANALYSIS

There are many potential objections to this sort of analytical enterprise. The methodology can seem speculative in the extreme, and the likelihood of contradictory evidence alarmingly high. For this reason, what needs to be emphasised is that the analysis does not claim to have discovered Mahler's intended programme for the symphony, nor even an unconscious programme latent within the musical text and waiting to be discovered. Such a fixed meaning would indeed not stand up to empirical justification. What a comparison of the effects of the motif in literature and in the symphonies does do is open up a range of intertextual significance which both lends some weight to the otherwise solipsistic and impressionistic comments of critics like Greene, and tends to undo accounts of the effect of the movements in terms of formal function and voice-leading coherence. In this way, it works allegorically, resisting closure of meaning since it identifies a range of reference whose effects are unpredictable and which the musical text cannot master. The analysis is deconstructive to the extent that it demonstrates how little prescription can be made for the effects of generic play once this play is identified.

This approach has virtues, too. Genre is a notoriously difficult topic precisely because its existence as a partially social construct suggests that its interpretants should also be socially constructed and culturally determined. The foregoing discussion moves beyond the contention that waltz genres refer to other musical waltzes (such as Chopin's piano pieces), or to the social occasions of balls and concerts; the reference is to the history of reference of this sort, a complex of associations and contexts of quotations. If irony and cliché are to be studied in any detail beyond asserting that they occur, then the distinction of modes of semiotic coding seems the only methodology which offers a model of their function within complex works of art.

The task of investigating musical signification which reaches outside the bounds of musical intertextuality leads on to the even more complex task of asking whether there are semiotic codes whose interpretants are entirely extramusical. The place of the sort of reference uncovered in the scherzos within an overall narrative scheme for these movements and for their symphonies as wholes is a topic which has remained largely untouched in this chapter; obviously, to the extent that the motif of the Dance of Death becomes associated with each movement, it asks to be joined with other significant motifs within a narrative scheme; and in the Sixth Symphony, the association of ending with destruction and negation is hardly a controversial assertion. The semiotics of such narratives is the focus of the last part of this study.

5

MUSICAL NARRATIVE AND THE SUICIDE OF THE SYMPHONY

One of the areas of contemporary literary theory which has provoked most comment from scholars outside its original field is 'narrativity'. This interest may perhaps be dated to Roland Barthes' comment, that 'the narratives of the world are numberless' (Barthes 1977: 79), which directs attention to broader concerns than the mandarin inspection of literary texts. On the face of it, however, narrative is an unlikely topic for music theory, since music appears to lack the linguistic basis essential to the concept of narrative. Nevertheless, several recent attempts to adopt the terms of narrativity have demonstrated that the musical work is more susceptible to this sort of inquiry than one might at first think.

In terms of the semiotic theory presented here, the possibility of a code of musical narration represents the most abstract, or extroversive, mode of reference to be considered. It must be defined as a form of musical sign which has a signified without any immanent existence in the structures of the work. The analyses which follow are therefore in some ways more speculative than those in the preceding chapters; they attempt to identify respects in which narrative is the appropriate model for the discussion of Mahler's semiotic strategy, or in other words to bring theoretical consistency to that totem of Germanic Mahler scholarship, *Musiksprache* (Williamson 1991: 371-2).

At the head of this enterprise, once again, stands Adorno's now often-quoted aphorism, 'It is not that music wants to narrate, but that the composer [Mahler] wants to make music in the way others make narratives' (1960: 85/1992: 62). Whatever else this dictum involves, it identifies in Mahler's technique a level of organisation analogous to narrative, but not reducible to simple extramusical reference. In other words, this is a semiotic code, supplying the signifiers of an act of narration, but not necessarily signifiers of narrated acts. At once, as so often, Adorno's gnomic style encapsulates the problematic of Mahler's attitude to programme music in its grammatical form: commentators have always both insisted on the close relation of programmatic techniques to the symphonic style, and balked at the poverty of Mahler's own programmes (or those of other commentators) as explanatory texts.

THEORIES OF MUSICAL NARRATION

A code relating to the narrative act was the addition proposed by Jonathan Culler to Barthes' five codes in *S/Z* to remedy a 'fatal flaw' in the typology (Culler 1975: 203). The recognition that there are moments in the 'classic text' where the voice can belong neither to an omniscient author, nor a participating character, but only to a *narrating* presence, effectively the voice of the reader, was the crack into which Barthes had already inserted his deconstructive lever, in discussing the phrase 'Zambinella, *as if* terror-stricken'; he describes what is heard in this phrase as 'the *displaced* voice which the reader grants, by proxy, to the narrative ... specifically the voice of reading' (Barthes 1970: 157, quoted in Culler 1975: 196).

It is attractive to consider this phenomenon as a semiotic category susceptible to analysis, although at the beginning, Barthes' treatment of it as a liminal point, undercutting the five 'readerly' codes and affirming the distance between story and event-sequence, is worth bearing in mind. There are several ways in which this code of narration might be transferred into the realm of music theory. First of all, there may be aspects of the musical text which invoke the metaphor of narration, in the manner of programme music; here one might legitimately ask what sort of a narrator is presenting the image of the programme, and whether such a thing as a 'point of view' is constituted by the musical gestures. This is indeed an area of aesthetic hermeneutics which has been little investigated, since the mere establishment of a programme for a work such as a Mahler symphony is fraught with complications, let alone the question of defining the nature of the dialectical engagement of listener and musical narration.

The recent research devoted to widening the concept of narrativity to include the texts of music theory has attracted the attention of Jean-Jacques Nattiez himself (Nattiez 1990). His discussion effectively focuses on two distinct features of literary narrative which are essential to the theoretical definition of narrative coding. In both cases, their possible application to music is far from obvious. Firstly, there is the well-established opposition between 'story' and 'discourse'; that is, between the sequence of events occurring in objective time, and the sequence of signifiers which embodies them in a narrative. Nattiez takes as his point of departure Seymour Chatman's *Story and Discourse*, which carefully defines these terms (Chatman 1978: 19-21). The terms differ from theorist to theorist (they derive from the Russian Formalists' *sjuzhet* and *fabula*), but the constant idea is the distance, the 'narrative gap' between the text and the world which is the necessary condition of narrative, and yet which the narrative often attempts to conceal. Certain forms of plot play self-consciously with the distinction (detective fiction, for example, in which the event that occurs first in the 'story' – that is, the murder, theft, or whatever – occurs only near the end of the 'discourse', at the *dénouement*); others deny it. Its trace in the text is the past tense: 'A Saturday afternoon in November was approaching the time of twilight', for instance, already posits a narrator who knows more about a certain temporal location than the reader. This distinction, to Nattiez's mind, can never be more than a metaphor in its application to music, since the literary text just 'is' a narrative in a way that a musical work can only be made to be by a special effort of interpretive listening. He comments that 'if music could, of itself, be a narrative to the extent that human language can, it would speak directly to us and there would be no difference between language and music' (Nattiez 1990: 242). What we are left with, he concludes, is 'a narrative frame of mind', a willingness to map the 'discourse' of the music onto an imagined event-sequence, normally under the encouragement of a title such as *L'Apprenti sorcier*.

Whilst this insistence on the fact that music and literature are not the same art form is very proper, one might object that the gap which is so obvious in the case of musical interpretation is nevertheless still there in the case of written narrative; it is, of course, the feature of all writing which Jacques Derrida foregrounds in order to deconstruct the claims to 'presence' of such 'non-narrative' forms as philosophy or history. Nattiez states, 'When I read the sentence: "the duchess left at five o'clock", I do not need a title in order to realize that I am dealing with a narrative' (1990: 242). However, even here there are a number of items of information necessary for a narrative reading of the sentence (is it a novel? a press release? a telegram? Who is the duchess? A racehorse? An ocean liner?), none of which is supplied by the text itself. A 'narrative frame of mind' is necessary in literature too; the question is rather whether any other sort of 'frame of mind' is equally viable in approaching music. Nattiez uncovers a level of difficulty in 'producing the narrative' for musical works with suggestive titles or programmes which, far from keeping the art forms separate, serves to illuminate the situation in literature.

One thing which emerges from this discussion, however, is the necessity for the listener or reader to *construct* a narrative. And this leads to the second feature of narrative which is of relevance to the present study: the definition of narrative as more than a mere sequence of events or states. Nattiez employs Chatman's terms, according to which 'story' is constituted by the relationships between 'existents' and 'events'. Causality is indispensable to a narrative reading of a linguistic sequence: indeed, it is the hypothesis of causality between historical events which defines the historical narrative, in opposition to the annal or chronicle (a topic debated in Hayden White's influential essay 'The Value of Narrativity in the Representation of Reality', White 1987: 1-25). If causality creates narrative, coherence is the desired gain from it. Nattiez quotes Paul Ricoeur's description of the similarities between human action and text: 'Without leaving everyday experience, are we not inclined to see in a given sequence of episodes in our lives "(as yet) untold" stories, stories that demand to be told?' (Ricoeur 1983: 74). This ability to 'narrativise' (White's term), in order to give coherence to event-sequences, is the cause of narrative's allure: it gives meaning to life, brings understanding out of history. It also accounts in a large part for the popularity of literary programmes for nineteenth-century pieces of music: as tonal convention was increasingly taxed to provide coherence in the art-work, a literary analogue was sought as an alternative or additional source of the desired unity. This resulting coherence was then taken, paradoxically, to confirm the superiority of the musical form over the literary.

Nattiez concludes that it is this definition of narrative as connected event-sequence that provides a point of comparison with music. Musical events, like linguistic sequences, may be organised by listeners into coherent narrative image-sequences. This is, of course, only a rough equivalent to literary narrative activity: its arbitrariness is of a different order from that involved in reading a book. And whether it be a group of French schoolchildren making up stories to go with *L'Apprenti sorcier*, or a professional American musicologist comparing Beethoven symphonies with contemporary novels, the activity remains a hermeneutic metaphor: there can never be a 'real' content to music upon which agreement could be as unanimous as over the plot of *The Return of the Native*. Nattiez declares that

> music is not narrative and any description of its formal structures in terms of narrativity is nothing but superfluous metaphor. But if one is tempted to do it, it is because music shares with literary narrative the fact that, within it, objects succeed one another: this linearity is thus an incitement to a narrative thread which *narrativises* music. Since it possesses a certain capacity for imitative evocation, it is possible for it to imitate the semblance of narration without our ever knowing the content of the discourse. (Nattiez 1990: 257)

Again, one suspects that all of the defining characteristics of musical discourse which permit this categorical opposition of music and literary text will be found to reappear as features of literature as well: the necessity for the listener's decoding activity, the arbitrariness of narrative causality, coherence as a desired construct rather than a given feature of the work. But Nattiez has defined the two most important respects in which the adoption of narratological theory has to prove its relevance to music: the deconstruction of the opposition between music and literature suggests the ultimate end of the inquiry, and the force of the comparison suggests that music demands to be taken as text rather than temporal immediacy. But before the whole issue of textuality in music is addressed, it is necessary to expand on the issues highlighted by Nattiez. We now have two possible ways in which a 'musical narrative' might be constructed, without falling back on the outdated concepts of programme music: on the one hand, as the semiotic state of intermittent 'moments of narration' within a work; and on the other, as a hermeneutic strategy covering the formal and thematic outlines of an entire work.

Related to the first category is the concept of musical narration put forward by Carolyn Abbate (1991). Starting from Mikhail Bakhtin, she develops the idea of 'voices' in the musical work, above all in opera, where the fiction of spoken dialogue represented in sung recitative or aria is the occasion of 'moments of narration' where the music itself directs the listener's experience of the fictional narrative. This is particularly true of moments where characters in opera really do sing (for the other characters), as in *Lakmé*; or where a programme contains direct speech, as in *L'Apprenti sorcier*. Abbate also suggests that 'moments of narration' are constituted by the points in the *Todtenfeier* movement of Mahler's Second Symphony where music disruptive to the work's harmonic or formal coding as symphony enters. Her discussion of the Mahler is instructive. The passages which interest her are the interruptions by what is labelled in the manuscript the 'Gesang' theme (incidentally given as ex. 2.3 on p. 35, above): entering first in E major, it has often been described as a polar contrast to the opening C minor death march material. Abbate makes this ordinary analytical observation extreme by claiming that the disjuncture between the two 'subject groups' overruns any attempt to impose a formal category:

> What seems significant is not the [formal] pattern itself, but these various sites of hyperbolic musical disjunction. Cracks fissure the music at the entry of the 'Gesang' and at certain reentries of the Funeral March. They mark the boundaries of a membrane laid down by an outside 'voice'. They mark the entry of a song suddenly performed. (1991: 151)

In this view, musical narration consists of 'rending the fabric of music' (Abbate 1991: 152); moments of narration are isolated, liminal points which reveal the artificiality of the musical discourse.

It should be pointed out at this stage that this view of a narrative code is not the only one possible. Indeed, what Abbate identifies is much more the absence or failure of coding than any properly semiotic category. Her idea of moments of excess is at times close to Adorno's *Durchbruch* and *Suspension*; but where Adorno conceives of these as specifically Mahlerian formal types, repeated gestures which constitute an immanent critique of the economy of symphonic writing, Abbate's 'moments of narration' result from a more general view of the state of musical discourse in the nineteenth century. She defines narrative, following Ricoeur, as the mode which signals distance between the story and the events of which the story tells. Since music presents events directly, inasmuch as the stuff of most musical analysis is the structures represented by the notes on the page, and not a fictional or actual 'out there', musical narrative has to be an extreme and extraordinary case: 'music seems not to "have a past tense"' (Abbate 1991: 52).

If, as in Culler's view, a genuine code of narration is indispensable for the semiotic understanding of literary texts, then it would seem reasonable to look for something more prevalent than a typology of isolated, liminal gestures as its musical equivalent. This second view of musical narrative, which seeks both a more direct comparison with literature and a more stringent insistence on 'purely musical' features, forms the other main line of recent inquiry.

In one sense, the concept of musical narrative is a direct consequence of the increased length and surface complexity of nineteenth-century artworks. The idea of the work of music as an autonomous, self-regulating and abstract structure seems inadequate in the face of pieces frequently inspired explicitly by literary texts, and whose reception history has always sought to model the musical experience on literary forms. It is this sense of music's 'telling a story' that has led Anthony Newcomb to seek paradigms from nineteenth-century novel plots in the analysis of Schumann (Newcomb 1984 and 1987) and latterly Mahler himself (Newcomb 1992). Effectively, Newcomb invokes a 'code of narration' to account for (and in the case of Schumann, to rehabilitate critical regard for) points of formal organisation which are problematic in a formalist account of musical coherence. This makes a great deal of intuitive sense, particularly when Newcomb adduces copious examples of near-contemporary discussions of Schumann's Second Symphony which do not share the embarrassment felt by twentieth-century commentators faced with what even Carl Dahlhaus has to term 'formal incoherence' in the Finale (Newcomb 1984: 240, quoting Dahlhaus 1972). Newcomb's idea is that the Finale embodies a transition between two traditional models – that it begins as a *lieto fine* rondo, and is transformed into a 'weighty, reflective summary' in sonata form (Newcomb 1984: 246). This transitional form involves various references to earlier works, especially Beethoven's Fifth Symphony, and represents a 'plot archetype' of struggle (in the first movement) turned to affirmation, victory and resolution of conflict (in the Finale), which is shared not only by the Beethoven Symphony but also by various forms of the Romantic *Bildungsroman*. Schumann's love of Jean Paul, something shared by Mahler, is suggestive in this context.

From a theoretical point of view, there is a problem with this version of musical narrativity. It can easily seem to be more the establishment of a programme for the piece in question (albeit a more sophisticated and historically grounded programme than those of old-fashioned 'guides to the classics') than an investigation of its signifying structures. This is particularly true of Newcomb's more recent essay on Mahler's Ninth Symphony (1992), where the phases of the typical *Bildungsroman* are mapped onto the gestural outlines of each of the four movements. Newcomb argues against the hitherto near-universal acceptance of the idea that this work is preoccupied with death, an elegy either for Mahler's own life or for the Austro-Germanic symphony, whose history it draws to a close. Newcomb's reading involves a combination of general observation and fairly precise (if informal) analysis: for instance, he makes much of the motivic turn figure which inaugurates the secondary sections of the Finale, and indeed closes the whole work. Its original (and conventional) context as an anacrusis, and therefore as a signal of beginning, is, Newcomb argues, the key to understanding the close of the work: it indicates a point of possible departure, rather than inevitable surcease. As the hero of the *Bildungsroman* achieves maturity and adult social status, so the Symphony has achieved some sort of musical equivalent, closing its narrative on the threshold of new experience. Newcomb comments that 'it seems not so much that Mahler's movement (and symphony) ends, as that its formative energy, always ready to be stirred again into life, passes out of hearing' (Newcomb 1992: 136).

What is involved here is a particular understanding of symphonic writing, the authority for which derives from Mahler himself and from other contemporary thinkers, especially Freud (in his comments on transformed repetition as the attempt to master and control past experience). Whatever the merits of this style of commentary (and these are considerable), it is hard to avoid Abbate's criticism that it hides 'a nostalgia for historical security ... a belief that reduplicating the story-telling analyses of the nineteenth-century in new (rather more abstract) guises recovers nineteenth-century repertories in a perceptual form close to some historical original ... Programme music ... is thus recuperated in many twentieth-century narrative interpretations' (1991: 25). The great merit of Newcomb's approach (for the purposes of this study) is that it defines narrative strategies that cover the entire work. In other words, it envisages a semiotic code by which the listener engages with the musical text. This forms 'narrative activity' – Paul Ricoeur's phrase that is analogous, in semiotic terms, to Eco's 'sign production' (from Ricoeur 1980 and 1983). However, the working of this code remains essentially the subject of hypothesis and informed guesswork.

One feature of Newcomb's analysis is its reliance on intertextual aspects of the musical work. Not only previous musical models, but literary narrative paradigms and aesthetic categories are essential to decoding the work's significance. It is in the intersection of these intertextual categories that narrative takes place and meaning is produced (Newcomb 1992: 119). Thus any consideration of what may qualify as a 'narrative code' in Mahler's Sixth Symphony rests on the concepts of intertextuality and thus (inevitably enough) textuality in music. The conflict between Newcomb's and Abbate's conceptions of narrativity in music may therefore be to some extent resolved by a consideration of the ways in which musical works deserve to be described as texts, in the sense of the term defined by recent critical theory.

When Jacques Derrida asserted that 'there is nothing outside the text', he produced a rallying-cry that has since had profound consequences in the human sciences. In a sense, this claim is one made by the semiotic thought that Derrida might seem to oppose: all human communication is effected by means of systems of signs, articulated in groups of occurrences that can be called texts. Indeed, it is by extending this understanding of sign system from manufactured artefacts such as books, clothes or television programmes to all aspects of human activity whatever that the texts studied by structuralist theory are displaced and decentred. If I am merely the confluence of texts without origins and without comfortingly reliable referents, then the text is simply where I find myself.

This concept of text leads to a much loftier self-image for theorists than that of the Muse's handmaid: far from the solitary inspection of esoteric examples of artistic creation, the engagement with texts, the study of textuality itself, is, if not the essence of life, at least that which must now replace essentialist thinking. The concept of ontological essence is replaced by that of intertextual difference; and as John Frow has pointed out, it is in this specific sense of the differences between texts, the identification of what is 'outside' a given text, therefore 'non-textual', that Derrida develops the notion of the 'general text':

A 'text' that is henceforth no longer a finished corpus of writing, some content enclosed in a book or its margins, but a differential network, a fabric of traces referring endlessly to something other than itself, to other differential traces. Thus the text overruns all the limits assigned to it so far ... everything that was to be set up in opposition to writing (speech, life, the world, the real, history, and what not ...). (Frow 1990: 49, from Derrida 1979: 83-4)

This assertion does not, as some seem to have thought, mean that everything is text and there are no longer any boundaries or differences in our experience. The text is precisely that which designates things as outside itself; simply, these margins and boundaries turn out ceaselessly to be complex and problematic. Frow quotes Rodolphe Gasché's description of this 'general text' as the 'border itself, from which the assignment of insides and outsides takes place, as well as where this distinction ultimately collapses' (Gasché 1986: 279-80 in Frow 1990: 50).

If the text is to be generalised, then, Derrida wishes to avoid its being totalised: the text, it turns out, is not where I find myself, but where I am lost, unable to discover an 'out there' which is not another text, and unable to construct a text except by positing an 'out there'.

Turning now to the nature of musical texts, this concept of textuality forms a context that allows us to locate music within all other discourses, whilst insisting on its self-demarcation. In other words, there is an attractive prospect in being able to introduce musical discourse into other realms, and maybe elucidate it with new theoretical techniques; but at the same time, the apparent autonomy of the musical artwork, its methods of designating other music and indeed other forms of articulation as 'outside', as 'non-textual', must be interrogated. It is in this sense that Derrida makes an opposition between the concept of 'general text', of unclosure, and that of 'ideology' which is the attempt to close off the text (Frow 1990: 48).

This brings us a fair way from the starting-point of the consideration of a code of musical narrative. But before the question leads to the collapse of the concept of narrativity altogether, and the dismissal of any form of analysis as just one more ideological closure, it is worth attempting to consider some musical outworkings of this theoretical tangle.

A FIRST NARRATIVE (BOUNDARIES OF FORMAL SECTIONS)

To approach the main subject of this study by a roundabout route, and to allow Adorno to guide the beginning of this discussion, there is a passage of Mahler's Fourth Symphony that might justifiably be taken to represent one of Abbate's 'moments of narration'. This is (typically enough) a gap: in fact, the boundary between the first and second subject groups (ex. 5.1).

Adorno, in contradiction of Abbate, hears the whole of this first movement as 'in the past tense', and ascribes to it the narrative 'Once upon a time, there was a sonata' (1960: 129/1992: 96). And it is clear that this textual gesture, this 'composing within quotation marks', leaves as its trace the boundary between first and second subject. Adorno's disquiet stems from what he describes as the 'far too self-contained' second subject. It is, he claims, a theme from an instrumental song unable to be assimilated into the sonata form. These brief comments can be elaborated by focusing on the general pause before the double bar line. The preparation of the dominant is pedantically emphatic: the imitative texture contains semiquaver scales that are quite unusual for Mahler, and which perhaps invoke the end of a first subject group in Mozart. In fact, the scalic rush to the dominant degree clearly signals a 'bifocal close' to the first subject (the eighteenth-century history of this gesture is discussed by Robert Winter, 1989). What makes the

Musical narrative and the suicide of the symphony

Example 5.1

passage different from Haydn or Mozart is the imitation: what would be a unison emphasis of the tonal structure in a classical period form is here divided between violins and cellos and basses. The result emphasises not so much the tonal function, as the fact that it *is* tonally functional. The music has brought us to what must be the threshold of the second subject, and the hesitation is a mark of a genuine aporia, a slippage: no theme whatsoever can satisfy the stylistic demands that such a preparation lays on it. It would not be enough to continue either the Mahlerian 'modernism' of features such as the sleigh-bells, or the 'archaism' of the tonal structure.

Now it has to be admitted that Adorno can manage this narrative reading only by mapping the dialectic of the historical development of musical form onto the social realities of Mahler's own time. But it is noticeable that this reading is both analytical (in the narrow sense) and critical (also in the narrow sense). It attempts to account for the presence of notes on the page, and its justification is in the history of sonata form and tonal process: not so far from the sort of assertion represented by a Schenkerian reduction of these bars. But where a Schenkerian reduction would find no problem at all, Adorno hears an intertextual problem: in fact, the problem of the unproblematic nature of this transition. Narrative is the only possible description of the claims made for this sort of signification.

It is worth further expanding on Adorno's comments by considering the most enigmatic and magical episode of this movement, which comes at the end of the development (ex. 5.2). Again, traditional forms of analysis would have no problems here. The motivic material has almost all been derived from the first subject group in step-by-step fashion during the development, and the dissonant

Example 5.2

climax over a tonic G pedal is resolved by a detour to F# minor, and, via some aurally explicit voice-leading (generally altering one note of each triad at a time by semitone step), to the tonic cadence after the double bar. But once more, disquiet is signalled by a pause, this time a pause not even within the bounds of metre, but simply introduced at the double bar-line. The recapitulation begins in the middle of a phrase, with the developmental outcome of first and second subjects.

Harmonically, this is a perfectly understandable completion of the passage before the double bar; motivically, its credentials are impeccable. One way of accounting for this moment is to say that thematic and harmonic schemes have got out of synchronisation here (a favourite Mahlerian device), since the first subject begins before the double bar line (disguised by the pause, the voice-leading, and changes of instrumentation and texture). But formally, and at the level of textual discourse, this moment is the outcome of aporia, presenting the continuity of formal units as a fiction. Mahler simultaneously meets the needs of presented continuity – in the thematic recapitulation and voice-leading – and presents this formal return as disjunction, the harmonic grammaticality as an alienating, 'quotation-mark' device. In semiotic terms, several codes of listening are required at this point; codes of

Musical narrative and the suicide of the symphony 143

Example 5.3

thematic continuity, motivic development and formal scheme conflict in a way which leaves the only way of 'making sense', or of 'producing the text', to use Michael Riffaterre's phrase, to be the resort to a code of musical narration. This code refers in an exclusively intertextual fashion within the institution of symphonic composition. Two further features reinforce this reading of the semiotic situation. Firstly, Adorno notes that the coda, after a deliberately perfunctory recapitulation, gives us what had been missed out at this general pause, following on the soulful and enigmatic lament by the solo horn (ex. 5.3). To use Barthes' terms from S/Z (1974: 28-30) here a sequential code, that of thematic development, is deliberately made non-sequential, as if it were a form of motivic reference.

Furthermore, the most blindingly obvious feature of these bars is that they contain the opening motive, at pitch, of Mahler's Fifth Symphony on the trumpets. No motivic analysis can account for this interruption except as a gesture beyond the work, and, most remarkably, forward to the as yet unwritten work. It makes the myth of compositional succession part of the textuality of Mahler's symphonies. No matter whether this trumpet-call was inserted in a revision or not; here we have not only music in the past tense, but in the future tense too.

This example from the Fourth Symphony is instructive because of the way a highly complex narrative situation is created out of relatively simple harmonic and formal moments. The Sixth Symphony, however, presents a considerably more difficult task: its scale and engagement with formal models are on a different level from that of the earlier work.

The first movement makes an interesting comparison with the Fourth Symphony because it is the only subsequent symphonic movement to display comparably clear formal outlines in a sonata form model. Indeed, the 'archaic' feature of an exposition repeat (whose existence Adorno could present as a discov-

Bar	Section	Thematic material	Key
1	Introduction		A minor
6	EXPOSITION First subject group	March theme (1a) and secondary theme (1b, first heard on trumpet, bars 29ff)	A minor
57	Bridge passage	Major/minor triad motif and chorale theme	A minor
77	Second subject group	Theme 2	F major
123	Exposition repeat		
130	DEVELOPMENT	First subject material	A minor, E minor, D major
202		Second subject and chorale	C major, G major, E♭ major
256		Theme 1b material and chorale	B major, B minor, G minor
291	RECAPITULATION	First subject	A major, A minor
339		Major/minor triad motif and chorale	A minor
357		Second subject	D major, E minor, E♭ minor, C major
449	CODA	Second subject	A major
486	END		

Figure 5.1

ery in 1960, so unfashionable was it for fifty years after the work's composition) is a symptom of the similar dialectic between formal process and musical material in the two works. The situation in the first movement of the Sixth Symphony is the reverse of that in the Finale: far from being the subject of ideological choice, the formal function of the sections of the movement leaves practically no room for discussion, certainly at least in the exposition, as the components of a *Formenlehre* typology are presented with schoolmasterly insistence. And for this reason, the coding of formal archetypes is paradoxically insufficient in 'producing the text' of this movement; again, a narrative is involved.

Despite its drastic simplifications and misleading categorisation, a straightforward tabular analysis may for once be the appropriate preface for the discussion (figure 5.1). To follow Abbate's idea of 'narrative moments', a suitable point of departure is the passage parallel to that considered in the Fourth Symphony, the transition to the second subject group. Here the later symphony displays a disjuncture

Musical narrative and the suicide of the symphony

Example 5.4

equally surprising as that in the earlier work. The march rhythms of the first subject subside in bars 51-5, and the first statement of the 'fate' rhythm and A major/minor triad on the trumpets follows in bars 57-60. There follow sixteen bars of woodwind chorale, accompanied by pizzicato versions of the first subject on the strings, before full orchestra launches into the second subject on the upbeat to bar 77 (ex. 5.4).

From the point of view of creating our *Formenlehre* tabular analysis, these bars are fairly clear: we have a cadence, a bridge theme (the chorale), and the second subject in a new key (F major). But just as the ease with which the listener can follow the progress of the form disturbed Adorno in the Fourth Symphony, these bars are disquieting for their apparent lucidity. For a start, each of these sections is radically differentiated in texture, dynamics and orchestration. There is a conventional requirement for contrast between first and second subjects; but the use of a clearly non-symphonic genre (the chorale) precisely at this moment, which is so crucial to the symphonic process, foregrounds the artificiality of the choice. This is the sort of moment that lies at the root of Adorno's description of Mahler's form as 'nominalist': again, the myth of formal succession is rewritten as fiction, narrated by the music.

The harmonic and voice-leading profile of these bars is fascinating. The secondary key area of F major has been prepared, after a fashion, by the occurrence of B♭s in the melodic line earlier on (first at bar 36, as a sort of neighbour to the A in bar 38 (violins), and then in bars 47-55, where the resolution to A is left in the air). In this context, the B♭ major triad at bar 75 would be a perfectly good transitional chord; but the chorale tries to slip instead onto another E major triad in bar 76, a somewhat tautologous half-close in parallel with bar 68, which in any case gets no further than an augmented triad (a good instance of Mahler's predilection for whole-tone chords at moments of swift transition). The three-quaver anacrusis that follows is disjunct in terms of the harmony, the high D creating a neighbour-note figure with the C of the augmented triad, and the F♮ in the bass creating a parallel neighbour-note feel with the E♮. Not that the voice-leading here is disjunct in some Stravinskian, deliberately incoherent sense; far from it. Ex. 5.5 shows how the E-D-C line lies over all three of the sections under discussion, setting up the C♮ as the obsessively repeated pole of the second subject very much in the way that A♮ is the constant point of return for the first subject group. But the moment of

Example 5.5

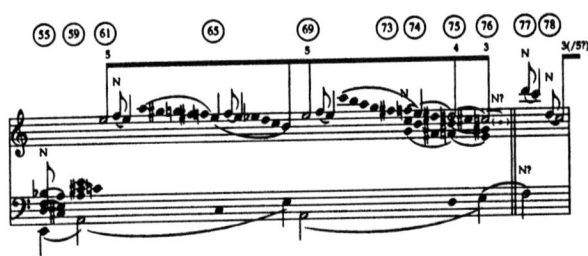

crossing the boundary is baffling just as it is delicious: it is clear that the D and C form a neighbour-note figure, but for a moment it cannot be heard which depends on which; the same goes for the bass movement. The chromatic line which in bars 63-4 was a graceful elaboration of the E-F-E figure turns bars 73-6 into a collapsing, heterophonous image of uncertainty. Not harmonic uncertainty, surely, but a narrative uncertainty, a gesture signalling the artifice of the sonata model at this point.

The equivalent passage in the recapitulation is also worthy of attention (bars 338-60). Here, however, the process is one of smoothing over the boundaries between the blocks of material, rather than counterpoising textural dissimilarity with local voice-leading progression. The oboes, flutes and horns join the trumpets for the major/minor triad motive, in a softening of the orchestration (aided by simultaneous *ff > pp* and *pp < molto* dynamics on oboes and flutes) which removes the sense of abrupt disjuncture. The motivic material is also overlapped at both this section boundary and at that between bridge and second subject. The strings then double the harmonic movement of the chorale in the woodwind, in diminution, so that the harmonic pulse is preserved over the whole passage. However, the chromatic, collapsing slide into the second subject is made more extreme in this second passage than the first, finishing with a curious enharmonic shift based on a half-diminished seventh chord in which the only clear feature is the prominence of A♮ rather than C♮ as the goal of the melody, its heterophonous arrival eventually supported by a D major triad in bars 362-3 (ex. 5.6).

The recomposition of this passage frustrates the easy reading of formal function which characterised its model. It will be nearly a hundred bars before the peroration of the second subject in A major brings at least the gesture of resolution which hastens the movement to its close. After a development which has continued to present discrete textural blocks of material, these intervening bars form about the longest 'developmental' passage in the movement. They combine motivic material from first and second subjects in a tonal progression from D major to E minor, this dominant degree swerving through E♭ minor and C major before reaching the tonic. The idea of reserving the development of the second subject material for the recapitulation or coda has precedents, beginning of course with Beethoven; but there it is usually part of the integration of the material into the tonic. Here, the

Example 5.6

development interrupts the A minor that seemed to have arrived at bar 309, restoring A major at bar 449; but the intervening musical progress hardly presents the image of wholeness suggested by the prominence of the adoption of sonata form in the movement.

If a code of musical narrative is necessary here, then it is appropriate to consider the contour that the narrative which has been uncovered up to now might describe. On one level, it arises from the status of sonata form, and is not dissimilar to that found in the Fourth Symphony. Adorno hears the Fourth Symphony as an instance of 'phantasmagoria', where 'the transcendent landscape is at once posited by it and negated' (1960: 82/1992: 57), and this reading, confirmed by the last movement, informs his discussion of the sonata form of the first movement. He then describes the first and last movements of the Sixth Symphony as 'Tragic' precisely because of their adoption of sonata form: the narrative derived from the invocation of the formal model is one of voluntary acceptance of closure, a Freudian death-wish whose literary analogue is the Greek tragedy:

> The structure of the [first] movement may well have been suggested by a notion of the tragic that Mahler's *Weltschmerz* accepted from the aesthetic of the day, without at that stage measuring it against his own formal intention ... In the consciousness of his complete technical mastery he dares to undertake a work of the Beethovenian type. In any case, epic composition was never the mere antithesis of the dramatic but also close to it, like the novel, in its onward momentum, its tensions and explosions. Here Mahler pays tribute to drama in a sonata form that he constructs with paradigmatic firmness as first theme, transition, second theme and closing group. Tragedy refuses a nominalistic form. The totality which sanctions for its own glory the destruction of the individual, who has no choice but to be destroyed, rules unchallenged. Mahler's emancipation from sonata form was mediated by the sonata.   (1960: 123-4/1992: 96-7)

Sonata form, then, is felt to be the signifier of more than traditional formal patterning: in a typical paradox, Mahler's nominalism is revealed in the 'refusal' of a nominalist form (unlike the Fifth and Seventh Symphonies), the presence of sonata form indicating its own lack of necessity. The distance between the conventional significance of the form and the content of the formal sections in this movement, a distance which rests on passages such as the two discussed above, is a genuinely narrative effect, the identification of which underlies any attempt such as Adorno's to map Mahler's musical intertextuality onto a social dialectic.

There are aspects of this reading which remain problematic, however. In particular, Adorno's bracketing of first movement and Finale as 'sonata form' movements, both participating in the narrative of 'tragic' closure, whilst extremely subtle and anti-sentimental, is nevertheless a version of the programme that led to the Symphony's 'tragic' epithet in the first place. As the discussion in chapter 3 made clear, Adorno is in fact far more interested in the Finale, to which he devotes several pages of detailed analysis. This is, in fact, because of the difference in coding strategy that is required to produce the 'tragic narrative' in the two movements. Whereas the Finale actively interrogates sonata form in a way that has perplexed all analysts who have delved into it, the first movement neutralises this code via the clarity of its formal outlines. In other words, the Finale makes semiotic capital out of the convention that musical movements have forms derived from a limited number of historically defined models; its signifiers are intrinsic to the music, and its signifieds intrinsically musical, if intertextual and abstract. But the first movement plays off the formal convention with extramusical factors; the conflict with codes relating to harmonic progression, melodic continuity, motivic working and generic typology can only be brought to light by looking beyond the formal organisation as such to the ideology of form, the narrative about form told by the process. Adorno's dialectic of 'epic' expansion and 'tragic' closure in the Finale is absent from the first movement. In its place is the introduction of the narrative substance of the symphony, a drive towards closure. This narrative organisation leaves the remainder of the work the semiotic space in which to continue the engagement with past music and articulate the codes which are invoked by the first movement.

There are several general points which can now be made, before a more detailed analysis of these features is undertaken. First, a semiotic view of the music enables analysis of musical detail to invoke the larger issues of meaning, aesthetic statement and sociopolitical engagement which writers on Mahler have always sought to address. Secondly, the complexity of the enterprise enables the definition of what it is that separates the sentimental view (fostered by Alma amongst others) of the symphony as tragic autobiography from the sophisticated, Adornian concept of tragedy. Thirdly, a related issue is that of the 'collapse of tonality' or 'dissolution of symphonic form' which has been more or less taken as a received fact by writers on Mahler.

Rather than explaining away the features which led to early accusations of incoherence, or seeking to view them as part of a critique admitting no positive terms (the strategy, as John Williamson points out, of virtually all recent German scholarship: 1991: 360), a set of identifiable codes can be seen to create a Mahlerian vocabulary that has a self-aware intertextual status. In this way, moments of incoherence can be used to 'create the text' without the necessity of viewing these as negation; and the continuing rise in popularity of Mahler's works, including this symphony, can hardly be rigorously viewed either as misguided or as indicative of enduring Viennese *Weltschmerz* in the succeeding *fin de siècle*.

This discussion has so far defined a few points at which a narrative code may be invoked in analysis of the symphony. The next step is to see how far a view of musical narrative such as that promoted by Newcomb might apply to this movement.

A SECOND NARRATIVE (THE NARRATIVE OF TRAGEDY)

If Newcomb's use of specific novelistic schemata is left somewhat undeveloped in his discussions of Schumann, his view of Mahler's Ninth Symphony is highly specific: a *Bildungsroman* plot such as that of *Oliver Twist* or *Great Expectations* is mapped onto the succession of the movements. This produces the following general outline (the quotations are from Newcomb 1992: 123-30):

First movement:	Childhood and adolescence ('a farewell to childhood and primal innocence')
Second movement (scherzo):	Youth and increasing sophistication or socialisation ('the young personality buffeted by various types of distractions')
Third movement (rondo):	Adulthood ('the bright, competent, hard adult') and moment of revelation (equivalent to Aristotelian *anagnorisis*)
Fourth movement:	Maturity ('[representing] the possibility of a renewed harmony to heal the wounds inflicted by mankind's alienation from nature')

There are several distinctly appealing features of this analysis, even though its musical observation often boils down to a rather disappointing reliance on the straightforward opposition of 'pure' diatonicism and 'subverting' chromaticism. It avoids the pitfalls of 'biography in notes' as an explanatory paradigm, provides a historically defensible interpretation, and views the entire symphony as participating in a single narrative sweep. In particular, awkward moments such as the end of the first movement, inscribed by Mahler with the valedictory '*Leb! wol, Leb! wol!*' are explained without appearing to make the rest of the work superfluous. And Newcomb is far too subtle a writer to appear to make the claim that this is straightforward 'programme music'; the comparison of 'narrative archetypes' involves a claim that these archetypes have a cultural existence independent of specific genre.

To turn again to the Sixth Symphony, the narrative here cannot be quite that of the 'spiral quest' of the *Bildungsroman*. In particular, the repeated gesture of the major/minor triad 'fate' motive and Mahler's own description of the hammer-blows of the Finale leading to 'the felling of the hero' suggest a different schema, once again leading us to the 'tragic' epithet and Adorno's 'totality which sanctions for its own glory the destruction of the individual'. Indeed, the impulse towards negativity in assessing the overall contours of the symphony can best be discussed in terms of an alternative literary paradigm, one in which closure is the catastrophic denial of the possibility of 'openness', of hypothetical continuation, which is essential to the *Bildungsroman*. It is this feature, indeed, that makes the latter genre such an appealing choice as an analogue to a musical style in which cadential closure is no longer presented as an inevitable and legitimating component.

A suitable set of models is not hard to find. The story of the protagonist struggling with forces that crush his or her individuality, promising and then denying freedom, is one which recurs in several nineteenth-century works. Such are the outlines of *Madame Bovary* or *Anna Karenina*. Moreover, the way in which both these novels problematise both the portrayal of the central character and the relation of the individual to the social world makes them in many ways comparable works to Mahler's own: he too problematises the various institutional oppositions (including music associated with incompatible social groups) which underlie the nineteenth-century symphony.

Just as with Newcomb's study, this is a seductive game once begun. The sort of outline suggested by the above titles might be:

First movement: Adolescence and first realisation of social forces (Emma Bovary's and Anna Karenina's marriages)

Scherzo: Engagement with society, constraining personal choice (Emma's encounter with the viscount, Anna's rise in society)

Andante: The promise of freedom and attempted escape through personal fulfilment (Emma's affairs, Anna's affair with Vronsky)

Finale: *Peripeteia* and ultimate extinction (betrayal for Emma, Anna's illness and abandonment by Vronsky, suicide for both).

Immediately, this suggests solutions for a couple of interpretative tight corners. For instance, the order of the middle movements can work equally well either way round, since the opposing routes of social obedience and personal freedom are developed simultaneously in the novels. In this reading, each movement functions in the manner of a subplot, bearing complex relationships to the other components of the work. Such a view accounts for the moments of resemblance between movements: the *altväterisch* episodes of the Scherzo can be heard as the promise of escape thematised in the Andante, whilst the dominance of falling motivic patterns in the latter movement indicates the impossibility of the Utopian E major episode. On the other hand, the opening and closing sections of the novels typically present reciprocal experiences for the protagonist, which are mirrored by the adoption of sonata form and a larger scale in the opening and closing movements of the symphony. The relationship between the three theme complexes of the first movement and the corresponding themes in the Finale, which is noted by Sponheuer (1978: 305), makes this interpretation even more seductive. In *Madame Bovary*, Charles' courtship of Emma seems to her to be the nearest fulfilment of her romantic dreams possible; her ultimate betrayal and suicide is a similar clash of desire and social reality, resolved by death rather than acquiescence. Similarly, Anna Karenina is first seen reconciling the Oblonskys' marriage; the book ends with her own inability to accept or sustain this social pattern.

If, as this comparison suggests, there is a reciprocal relation between the opening and closing movements, which might be summarised as promise and negative fulfilment, with the first movement leading to a temporary (though real) resolution and the Finale opening with a moment of crisis or *peripeteia*, then there are several points in the structure whose musical features one would expect to bear the signs of this schema.

The concluding bars of the first movement are an affirmatory, major-mode section, the sort of Mahlerian positivity which is a source of anxiety to commentators influenced by Adorno. Williamson describes the strategy necessary for an unwaveringly negative assessment as 'the scarcely definable idea of "musical positivism in indirect speech", positivism as it might be if only it were possible; the deciphered message of the work becomes apparent in the destruction of the *Formimmanenz* in the Finale' (1991: 360). Here too, then, the message of these bars is felt to be in some way connected with the contrast between them and the ending of the symphony as a whole. However, it should be possible to find some more substantial ground for this comparison than hazy metaphysics.

To look at the section in some detail, there are several features of these bars which clearly signal closure. Quite apart from the thundering arrival of A as tonic degree in bar 449, with timpani and low strings adding E to increase its resonance, thematic closure is indicated by the presence of versions of all three subsidiary themes: the secondary theme from the first subject group, the chorale, and the second subject proper, combined contrapuntally in a fashion which foregrounds their common motivic content (bars 453-62).

In addition, the harmonic outline of the section also presents a synoptical, summarising sequence: the prolongation of the A major triad involves two harmonic detours, firstly to a brief F major harmonisation of the high A at bar 468, and then to the *Höhepunkt* of the whole movement, the D triad at bars 478-9, whose harmonic function as IV supersedes the local V of bars 472-7 within this final prolongation. Thus the F major of the second subject's exposition and the D major of its recapitulation (the subdominant degree is also prominent at bars 203-21 and bars 315-22) are now made the explicit supports of the final tonic.

The two bars of climax also contain a final appearance of the major/minor triad, supporting the thematic resolution just described. The climactic moment is achieved by one of the strongest idiolectical techniques of the Mahlerian style: the F♯-E appoggiatura is preceded by a G♯-F♯ appoggiatura. This 'doubling' of function is always an index of intensification, and often occurs at a culminatory moment (the opening of the chorale subject in the Finale of the of the Ninth Symphony, with the three-note descent of the melody 'doubled' by a harmonic drop through a major third, is a memorable example).

Example 5.7

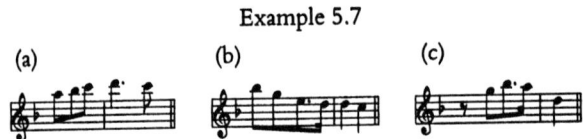

If there are thematic, motivic and harmonic gestures towards closure in this section, though, there are additional features which are less clearly end-directed and which make the reading of the section's function more problematic.

In terms of contrapuntal working, one further feature of these bars is the use of motivic dissolution, often in imitative textures. The second subject is decomposed into three motivic units (ex. 5.7a-c); these form the basis of the texture at points of climax: 5.7a at bars 455-7, 5.7b at bars 469-71, and 5.7c with 5.7a at bars 481-4. What is particularly interesting is the use of 5.7a and 5.7c in immediate half-bar repeats, and their association with each other.

The repetition at pitch or at the octave does of course combine the illusion of motion with harmonic stasis, either at the very local level (bars 455b-456a) or larger spans (bars 480-3). Added to this is the fact that these two motives are originally those most associated with forward movement at the first appearance of the second subject. The three-quaver anacrusis to bar 77 leads to an appoggiatura and the continuing, sequential motive; both the latter are first heard supported by wide-ranging chromatic harmony in bars 78-84. Adorno would say that these motives have become reified, their original function reversed and denied by their commodity-like repetition; this is particularly clear in the concluding bars where the last note of each motive, rather than being an unpredictable leap, is harmonically stable: F♯ as the ex. 5.7a shape, and E♮ as the ex. 5.7c shape, maintaining the $\hat{6}$-$\hat{5}$ appoggiatura as a non-progressing simultaneity. Within this process, then, there is a symptom of unease: in contrast, for instance, to the more genuinely 'closural' final sections of the Third Symphony or Eighth Symphony finales, the motivic activity is maintained right up to the double bar line. This is a similar technique to the use of contrapuntal imitative scales in the section of the Fourth Symphony discussed above: a presentation of motives as fetish objects, not here as an archaism of style, but as a reification of form.

The feature which does most to undercut the reading of the other codes, however, is the voice-leading of this passage. As noted above, no-one could miss the arrival of a structural I in the bass of bar 449; but the melodic voice-leading maintains the F♯-E, as an upper neighbour-note to a structural $\hat{5}$ throughout its progress. Indeed, the F♯ becomes the occasion for a local tonicisation in bar 458. The attempt to let it pass chromatically through F♮ to E and a structural descent is avoided both here (in bars 461-2) and at the *Höhepunkt* (bar 479), by restating F♯ and transforming the F♮ into a neighbour-note of a neighbour-note (another Mahlerian functional doubling). As noted above, the very last bars of the movement present F♯ and E simultaneously, and the arpeggaic rush to the final unison A♮ (bars 485-6) is an odd resolution for the high F♯ held for seven quavers in bars 484

Musical narrative and the suicide of the symphony

Example 5.8

and 485 as the goal of the antiphonal motivic statements. The F♯ is left hanging, so to speak, at the end; the second subject melody, here recomposed out of its elements, is again a reified object. These observations are summarised in ex. 5.8. This ending is, of course, a piece of motivic working which only makes sense by reference to the $\hat{6}$–$\hat{5}$ neighbour-note motive which has been prominent in the first subject (first heard in bar 9, and most memorably as F–E in E minor at bar 395). The treatment of a $\hat{5}$–$\hat{6}$ motivic feature leading to a simultaneous $\hat{5}$ and $\hat{6}$ at the cadence was to provide the serene close of *Der Abschied* in *Das Lied von der Erde*; but here there is no similar redefinition of the diatonic scale by the pentatonic; the gesture remains equivocal in its status as resolution.

It is the interaction between these features that becomes the signifier of the narrative code. There is no other way of articulating the conflict of closure and unclosure here; any description of formal model, motivic process, thematic occurrence, harmonic progression, or even the 'secondary parameters' of Hopkins' study of the Ninth Symphony (1990), will only find a fulfilment of the myth of sonata form. But the appeal to a 'narrative code' involves much more than the idea of 'musical indirect speech'. It is through the existence of this sort of excess to the other 'classic' codes of the symphonic style that the narrative of the movement is composed. It is this moment of excess, this neurosis about the institutional conventions invoked by the Symphony, that is so unerringly picked out by Adorno; but it is also left uncodified and its workings unexplained by his approach. And once again here, just as in the Fourth Symphony, the narrative moment is signalled by an aporia manifested as a general pause. The conclusion of the passage leading up to the coda moves through a memorable chromatic sequence of $^4_2$ chords (bars 436-40), then an F♯ minor triad which makes prominent the motivic F♯/F♮ - E motion; it finally settles on an E major triad playing the (B-)C♯-D♯-E anacrusis in double augmentation, repeated by the brass (twice as fast) after the double bar line. Dividing this repeated motive is the general pause at the moment of tonal resolution, broken not by the A in the bass, but by the percussion (triangle, side drum and cymbals). Once again, the weight of expectation brought about by the preparation cannot be fulfilled by any continuation.

To return to the Newcombian narrative structure outlined above, what sort of narrative structure does this code identify here? Certainly there is closure, a cadential section quite in proportion and keeping with the movement up to that point; and the features which taint the positivity of the musical surface can only amount to a genuine deconstruction, an exposure of the conventions as fictions. However, this is not an unfamiliar situation within the paradigmatic novel-plot suggested above; as with Emma Bovary's marriage, the moment of resolution of the 'plot so far' – which is both genuine resolution in the sense of being wished for, and tainted in the sense of awaiting its negative counterpart in the catastrophic *dénouement* at the end of the novel – is a necessary part of the narrative curve. What is fascinating here is that the sense of unease, the cracks in the mirror, arise from the same sort of invocation of convention (the marriage of the heroine) and problematisation of the conventions of form in the literary narrative, as in the Mahlerian symphony. The musical analysis does not need to posit a mapping onto an extramusical idea in the sense of programmatic signifieds; it can remain steadfastly within the domain of description of 'purely musical' features. The narrative code instead identifies an intertextual construction which it can read as a signifier of a state of affairs analogous to that in the contemporary novel.

Other passages fall conveniently into this reading, once this concept of intertextual signification is accepted. In particular, the section of the development following the first introduction of cowbells exhibits a subtle network of references within and outside the movement and work (bars 217-50). The texture and stable (if chromatically inflected) major-mode harmony here invoke Wagnerian pastoral: an image of freedom which clearly foreshadows the Andante. At bar 225, the key of the later movement, E♭, is established, and the solo horn carries a version of the second subject which strongly resembles the passage at bars 28ff of the Andante. Most cleverly, though, Mahler bases the section on an upward-rising melody (ex. 5.9a) which is both a straightforward inversion of the first subject (ex. 5.9b) and a reference outside the work to the E major 'Gesang' theme from the first movement

Musical narrative and the suicide of the symphony 155

Example 5.9

(a) Sixth Symphony, first movement

(b) Sixth Symphony, first movement

(c) Second Symphony, first movement

of the Second Symphony (ex. 5.9c). It also preserves the motivic $\hat{5}$–$\hat{6}$ neighbour-note: both here and at the end of the movement, Mahler signals the emphatic major mode more by the raised sixth degree than the raised third degree; partially to keep the motivic code intact by 'leaving room' for the major/minor triad, and partially as yet another instance of 'functional doubling'. Freedom and reconciliation are the signifieds of the thematic working here, too; in addition to being given in inversion, the first subject is combined melodically with motivic material from the second subject, for the only time in the whole movement.

The point to be made here is that the hermeneutic recuperation of this passage within the movement and symphony as a whole relies on a narrative code, one which relates the indices of freedom and escape (such as the cowbells) to an overall narrative scheme. But this reading arises precisely out of intertextual features of the passage; only the intersection of different levels of reference and different sorts of code can produce the material out of which a narrative can be constructed.

It might be objected that the plot archetype proposed here is an arbitrary choice, and is in any case founded on only two examples, distorting the structure of each in order to produce a general comparison. But before the limits of this interpretation are reached, it is worth looking at the archetype in a little more detail. Although the objection is well founded in the sense that *Anna Karenina* and *Madame Bovary* obviously differ from each other greatly and in fundamental respects, the plot type that involves closure and death is one that they share with many other novels. Of course, it also appears in many nineteenth-century opera plots, although here the question of gender is more complex (and has been the subject of several recent studies). As will by now be obvious, this is an interesting fact not least because the plot archetype is one that virtually necessitates a female protagonist. Indeed, the identification of death with the feminine, and of the social customs associated with death with that part of life controlled by women, is a common one in bourgeois nineteenth-century society (a fact detailed briefly in 'Death and the Individual',

Seigneuret 1986). Thus a new level of complexity in the musical narrative suddenly forces itself on the attention.

The fact that the modern novel has in many ways been an art form bound up with the representation of women ever since its origins, is one that has increasingly attracted the attention of feminist literary theorists. Nancy Miller, discussing eighteenth-century works, adapts A. J. Greimas' typology of 'euphoric' and 'dysphoric' plots to argue that the myth of the problematic heroine is one that is central to the formation of the novel: the 'euphoric' plot ends with social integration through marriage (*Moll Flanders*) and the 'dysphoric' with her social destruction, usually through early death (*Clarissa*; see Miller 1980). This typology of plot relies solely on ending; it is the desire for closure, for creating a coherent story, that necessitates the narrative control of the heroine and her ultimate effacement. The only way of making her story end is by marrying her or killing her (unlike, for instance, Robinson Crusoe's return to civilisation, or Oliver Twist's inheritance of his estate, or the typical 'story of the artist's life' in the German *Künstlerroman*). Thus the problematics of the novel form are structurally bound up with telling the story of a woman; the most discursive narrative form, the one which more than any other is able to imply action beyond its end, tends towards plot archetypes which emphasise the inevitability of their endings.

If the plot archetype which tends towards inevitable closure – Adorno's destruction of the individual for the glory of the totality – is in the novel incarnated more often in the life of a heroine rather than a hero, then this is further complicated in the nineteenth-century novel by the frequency of the heroine's suicide, most famously in the two examples above, but also found in popular works (Kate Chopin's *The Awakening* of 1899 being its *locus classicus*). Margaret Higonnet (1985) identifies a shift in the interpretation of suicide at the end of the eighteenth century, away from the classical, masculine 'noble death' towards a feminine, medical 'fatal malady'. Its representation is thus an ideologically conditioned phenomenon, which Higonnet claims to involve fragmentation of identity, oppression by masculine social forces, and the desire for rest and independence. Thus the suicide is an image both of the extremity of the desire to choose freely, and of the denial of individual choice to women by nineteenth-century society.

This 'feminisation' of suicide extends, Higonnet argues, also to the most famous male suicide of the Romantic novel, Goethe's Werther. She focuses on the way in which Werther describes what she terms his 'fatally feminine susceptibility' as 'a fatal illness', both feminising and medicalising the narcissism that will drive him to suicide (Higonnet 1985: 107). This context for one of Mahler's literary heroes provides some encouragement for the present reading of the symphony. Like Werther, Emma Bovary and Anna Karenina both yearn to achieve self-determination and fulfilment, but end by being left only with 'solipsism', their deaths representing 'the horrifying obverse of individualism' (Higonnet 1985: 111), the final outworking of the Romantic ideal of selfhood. And here there is a genuine connection between the novels and the symphony. It is precisely the desire for individuality within formal convention that causes the semiotic conflict between function and content identified in the discussion above. Just as the musical outworking of this tension drives first to a positive conclusion (in the first movement) created out of reified musical objects, and then to a negative conclusion (in the Finale) created out of the patient working through of each developmental possibility of the material, so, in the novel, suicide is both willed and forced upon the heroines. The corporeality of suicide as a terminating narrative gesture brings the body into play as the locus of a social and political violence. Only with a female protagonist can the conflict between the natural and cultural, the corporal and ideal, serve to deconstruct the narrative conventions of the novel form. Higonnet comments on Emma Bovary:

> We are not surprised that in her last moments 'she asked for her mirror and remained bent over it for some time'. Her suicide reflects back on her life in a way that unmasks her transcendental desires as narcissistic ...Flaubert doubles the image of a transcendental quest with one of sensuous needs, as extreme unction is applied to what we may call her erogenous zones, upon the mouth that had 'cried out in lust', upon the nostrils 'that had been so greedy of the warm breeze and the scents of love'. (Higonnet 1985: 111)

At the risk of a glib aphorism, it might be said that Mahler's Sixth represents the suicide of the Romantic symphony. In particular, the desire for sensuous gratification and Romantic individuality resides in the profile of the *Schwungvoll* second subject. This (as every recording's sleeve note points out) was even described by Mahler as a portrait of Alma, who was at the period of composition very much the embodiment of both the private and social ideal of Viennese womanhood. This is not to fall back into describing the symphony as biography-in-notes; the chance comment of the composer marks a point of intersection between his personal circumstances and the problematics of the composition. It has to be the second subject that provides the positive coda to the first movement, for reasons of narrative coding as much as formal convention; and it is no accident that the opening melodic material of the Finale is a hybrid of both first and second subjects from the first movement (ex. 5.10).

Temporary or promised integration, and final extinction through effacement: these two narrative tropes describe equally well the characters of Tolstoy's and Flaubert's novels, and the fortunes of 'Alma's' theme in the Symphony (or, by a short hermeneutic leap, the idea of 'symphony' itself). There are several lessons to be learned from this end to the search for a Newcombian narrative in this symphony. The reading is both appealing and disturbing. It is appealing because it offers a set of literary parallels which illuminate the sociopolitical discourse of the symphony. It is also disturbing because the claim that the narrative is essentially a feminine one is on the face of it wildly at odds with the composer's own stated views (despite the foregoing co-option of Werther to the cause), and with the entire tradition of narrative hermeneutics in music. But it is not necessary to insist on this simplistically as a 'feminine' work, or to invoke the recent arguments of feminist musicologists concerning tonal practice (for instance McClary 1991), in order to establish the usefulness of the analysis. Rather, this enterprise makes the

Example 5.10

claim that Mahler is addressing the question of the symphony as a canonic institution in ways analogous to Tolstoy's and Flaubert's engagement with the novel; and that this process has social and political implications as well as aesthetic ones. The overall narrative schema towards closure (but without the false security implied by the conventional concluding cadence) is one that can be replicated in literary narrative only by the problematic engagement of a female protagonist with the conventional world of the realist novel. And at this point yet another narrative suggests itself, not so much as an alternative to the Newcombian narrative, but as a consequence of it. For if the problematic identification of a feminine narrative indicates nothing else, it introduces the body into the discussion as the feature that animates this reading, defining both its disturbance and its appeal.

A THIRD NARRATIVE (THE THIRD MEANING)

It should be no surprise that the use of contemporary critical thought should lead to the appearance of the body as the agent of meaning in the text. Terry Eagleton's comment that 'few literary texts are likely to make it into the new historicist canon unless they contain at least one mutilated body' (1990: 7) indicates the extent to which corporeality has been brought into the apparently cerebral realm of textual criticism. Eagleton, indeed, sees the entire history of aesthetics since the Enlightenment as the desire to unite the body with the intellectual sphere. The bodily violence of narrative closure in *Madame Bovary* and *Anna Karenina* is typical of the late nineteenth century in that they arise from a lost struggle with system and authority: a similar story is told by Michel Foucault's *History of Sexuality*, in which the torturing of the body by regime and system is chronicled with relentlessly dispassionate detachment. From this perspective, it seems more plausible that the similarly violent end of Mahler's Sixth Symphony might also bring the body into the musical text.

Mention of the body in this context inevitably suggests Roland Barthes once

Musical narrative and the suicide of the symphony 159

Example 5.11

again as a point of reference. For Barthes, the body became increasingly important as the site of meaning in the encounter with texts: 'What does my body know of photography?' he asks at the beginning of *Camera Lucida*. To know something in one's body is to know it unconsciously; not as the Romantic chimera of unmediated direct experience, but as a signifying structure beyond both illocutionary reference and symbolic interpretation. This 'third meaning' is one identified by Barthes first in relation to film (the 1970 essay 'The Third Meaning' is reprinted in Barthes 1985: 41–62), but above all in relation to music, where the body cannot but be involved in any act of understanding. Music for Barthes is pure *signifiance*, 'signifying', the obtuse meaning that evades the obvious *signification* (the French title of *The Responsibility of Forms* was *L'Obvie et l'obtus*). Barthes' most intriguing comments are made in relation to his favourite composer, Schumann (for a detailed study of his writings on Schumann, see Brown 1991). The 1975 essay *Rasch*, which takes the vernacular performance directions of the *Kreisleriana* as the occasion for an extended search for the Schumannian body, opens with a disconcertingly brutal paragraph:

> In Schumann's *Kreisleriana* (Opus 16; 1838), I actually hear no note, no theme, no contour, no grammar, no meaning, nothing which would permit me to reconstruct an intelligible structure of the work. No, what I hear are blows: I hear what beats in the body, what beats the body, or better: I hear this body that beats.
> (Barthes 1985: 299)

Playing on the multiple meanings of the verb *battre*, Barthes delineates the Schumannian body as an irreducible corporeality which protests against its imprisonment in the codes of tonality and rhythm. Musical meaning is bound up with the body. This is partially because in Schumann the experience of the music can be obtained only by the physical action of playing it at the piano (an idea pursued in 'Musica Practica', Barthes 1985: 261–6), and partially because of the 'rage' and 'panic' that the music contains in its engagement with conventional musical expression (this is analysed at greater length in Samuels 1994).

In order to trace this idea in Mahler's Sixth Symphony, it is necessary to turn to the functioning of a recurrent motive: a major triad inflected to the minor, accompanied by a powerful, irregular rhythm, initially ♩ 𝄾 ♩ ♩. ♪| ♩ ♩ ♩ 𝄾 (ex. 5.11). The consideration of this figure as a narrative component may seem belated: it has been termed the 'fate' motive almost since the première of the work. It is the

Mvt	Bar numbers	Pitch of triad	Comments	Unit no.
I	57-61	A	Rhythm + triad (ex. 5.11)	(1)
	128-40		Rhythm only (combined with motives from first subject)	(2)
	157-66		Rhythm only (development based on first subject)	(3)
	208-9, 213-15	C, G	Triad only (horns, trombones)	(4)
	337-40	A	Rhythm + triad (horns and trumpets)	(5)
	395-400		Rhythm only (analogous to 128ff)	(6)
	478-9	D	Triad only (*tutti*, supporting second subject climax)	(7)
II	261-6	A	Triad + adapted rhythm (from scherzo's opening)	(8)
	419-26; 432-9	A, G, F; A (three times)	Triad + adapted rhythm (B♭ trumpets; horns + clarinets)	(9)
III	127	D	Suggestion by horn melody (in A major tonal region)	(10)
IV	9-14	A	Triad + rhythm (horns, F trumpets, trombones; then flutes and bassoons)	(11)
	65-6	G	Triad + rhythm (F and B♭ trumpets)	(12)
	338-9	G	Triad only (horns)	(13)
	401-2	C	Triad only (F trumpets)	(14)
	530-6	C	Triad + rhythm (horns, F trumpets, oboes, bassoons; then woodwind)	(15)
	622-5		Rhythm only	(16)
	668-9	A	Triad + rhythm (horns, F trumpets)	(17)
	686-7	A	As 668-9	(18)
	696	A	Triad only (horns)	(19)
	754-9		Rhythm only	(20)
	783-9	A	Triad + rhythm (full brass; third hammer blow falls here)	(21)
	820-2	A	Minor triad + rhythm (horns, F trumpets, woodwind)	(22)

Figure 5.2

I	II	III	IV	V	VI	VII
			(1)			
		(2)				
	(3)				(4)	
			(5)			
		(6)				(7)
(8)				(8)		
(9)					(9)	
						(10)
			(11)			
			(12)		(13)	
					(14)	
			(15)			
	(16)					
	(17)				(17)	
	(18)				(18)	
						(19)
	(20)		(21)			
			(22)			

Figure 5.3

motive that comes closest to leitmotiv in the work, and may be related to a history of similarly striking rhythmic devices, from *Don Giovanni* to *Lulu*.

There are many ramifications to the effect of this motive: the bald alternation of major and minor (as Adorno comments) is a kind of radical compression of a general alternation of mode in the piece, as in most of Mahler's works: for instance, the A major of the first movement coda counterbalances the A minor of the recapitulation of the first subject. Indeed, this Schubertian modal technique is in a way betrayed and undercut by the motive. Slipping from major to minor is normally a subtle process, involving retrospective recasting of experience and ambiguity of chord progression. This is often true in Mahler, as for instance at the opening of the song 'Rheinlegendchen' or at the beginning of the second stanza of 'Um Mitternacht'. The stark presentation of a major triad in close spacing and its minor version banishes the possibility of such effects.

The motive appears in all movements of the work, although only vestigially (at bar 127) in the Andante. It is capable of division into two parts, the (more or less unpitched) rhythm, and the triads. Figure 5.2 charts this motive through the work. This table of occurrences enables a paradigmatic graph to be constructed in the manner of previous chapters, but this time covering the whole work (figure 5.3).

Here the central column (IV) contains the occurrences of the 'model', more or less literal repeats of ex. 5.11. On either side, the columns represent less direct uses of the material, with rhythmic features to the left (I-III) and triadic features to the right (V-VII). The criteria for inclusion are as follows: columns III and V indicate the motives used on their own; columns II and VI indicate their use in conjunction with other motivic material (generally in developmental passages); columns I and VII indicate adaptations or more distant variants. As the graph shows, there is an alternation between the model and increasingly distant forms of it: the opening of the Finale and its close recall the paradigm to its first form. This makes the point that this motive, which sounds incapable of development (being defined by a strict rhythm and a single chord) is put to a wide variety of motivic uses in the work. It is especially prominent as model in the expositions and recapitulations of the outer movements, and as a developmental motive in their development sections.

In itself, this analysis does not say very much; but in the context of tracing a narrative code, it is interesting that the use of the motive does follow the contours of the symphonic form. It is less of an interruption than it seems: rather, its distribution shadows the progress of the form of the entire work. In particular, it connects the first movement and Finale, but in a specific sense not evident from other features. Whilst the motive appears at the close of the first movement first subject, and at the corresponding point of the recapitulation, and then again (although as a distant variant) at the close of the Scherzo, it *opens* the Finale, a gesture which incorporates the closure of the earlier parts of the Symphony into the initiation of the last movement. This reinforces the narrative scheme uncovered above, of temporary fulfilment subjected to *peripeteia*. The motive returns at bar 530 in another initiatory gesture; its double appearance either side of the coda to the work is truly a double closure, both bracketing the formal process of the movement, and reinforcing the passage as the closure of the whole symphony.

But a distributional analysis of the occurrence of this motive can be of use only in discussing the 'third meaning' embodied by it if the specific impact of the different instances of the motive and its variants is analysed. This motive truly brings the body into the music by its brutally physical impact: it always appears on wind instruments (in greater than normal numbers) and percussion, and the musical effect of the single harmony and rhythm cannot be divorced from the fact that the instruments are blown and hit at full force, a theatrical image of mob violence. This is true too of the hammer-blows in the Finale, although here the image is of a single agent of physical force (a headsman or tyrant) rather than concerted forces. And on each appearance, Hopkins' 'secondary parameters' are employed to emphasise this corporeality. This is particularly true of the timbral fade from trumpet to flute in units (5), (11) and (15), and of the repeated quaver trombone triads in units (17) and (18). The motive signifies both directly, as a tonal triad, and symbolically, as a sign of closure; but there is also an obtuse 'third meaning' arising from its physical, theatrical profile which is a symptom of the corporeality of the narrative code.

And this brings the present discussion, quite literally, to its end. For the narrative reading of the symphony is determined by the presence of the motive at the coda to the work. It is important, as the foregoing implies, that it occurs at the end of the first movement, where the climax of the movement incorporates the most highly varied instance of the figure (unit (7) of figure 5.2). But the last appearances (units (21) and (22)) are literally conclusive. There is an obvious point to the fact that the last unit contains only a minor triad: in functional terms, the concluding part of the motive is used to conclude. And the sense in which this is a double close (to movement and work) was mentioned above. But what is it that causes the work to end? It is, in fact, remarkably difficult to identify the A that constitutes structural closure in voice-leading terms at the end: the melodic descent to bar 772 is somewhat compromised by the Neapolitan tremolando wash and bleak counterpoint of the last bars. We know that the work has ended, not so much because of a cadence, as because all the developmental material has been worked through, and because the motive signals closure through its narrative coding. Where on its first appearance (unit (1)) it was integrated into the voice-leading succession, its 'closural' significance arising solely from its position in the form, here this state of affairs is reversed: the motive stands outside linear succession, which simply accepts the bass note A as conclusive. This constitutes a brilliant solution to the problem of making the work end: there is no comforting (but false) cadence or culminatory resolution, yet the work truly ends, and ends with corporeal violence which completes the narrative scheme rather than just breaking off the progress of the music. This infliction of violence on the aesthetic subject, manifested in the mob action that threatens the social metaphor of the symphony orchestra, is unique in Mahler's output. The 'third meaning', the appearance of the body in the musical text, again and more clearly delineates suicide as the narrative trope.

It is a comment on the complexity of this schema that this is the only one of Mahler's works to have this narrative structure; elsewhere, the ending is never as resolutely negative or final, although the engagement with convention is pursued no less rigorously. A fitting conclusion to this comparison of symphonic and novelistic form is provided by George Lukács' comments on Tolstoy. The Utopian world occasionally glimpsed in Tolstoy's novels, Lukács claims, is that of the 'renewed epic', where the conflict between social convention ('motley inessentiality') and individual 'abstract interiority' is finally transcended:

If ever this world should come into being as something natural and simply experienced, as the only true reality, a new complete totality could be built out of all its substances and relationships. It would be a world to which our divided reality would be a mere backdrop, a world which would have outstripped our dual world of social reality by as much as we have outstripped the world of nature. But art can never be the agent of such a transformation: the great epic is a form bound to the historical moment, and any attempt to depict the Utopian as existent can only end in destroying the form, not in creating reality.

(Lukács 1971: 152)

It is in the Sixth Symphony that Mahler refuses more than anywhere else to 'destroy the form'; and the result is closure as problematic as it is inevitable.

THE LIMITS OF NARRATIVE

To return to the 'second narrative' described above, this is an interpretation that has both virtues and limits. One virtue is that it goes some way towards avoiding criticisms of Newcomb's approach voiced by Hayden White (1992: 295-7). White takes Newcomb to task over the 'state of ambiguous uncertainty' given as a description of the conclusion to Mahler's Ninth Symphony. On the one hand, White points out, this formulation fails to clarify whether the plot archetype claims to bring to light Mahler's ideology or Newcomb's. On the other hand, there is an assimilation of the 'conflict' in the work to what White describes as 'a *metaphysical* enemy: time, death, mortality', rather than anything which might require an answer: 'the problem is "time" rather than our social condition' (White 1992: 297). The 'ambiguous uncertainty' is Newcomb's as much as Mahler's; its enjoyment a Romantic fallacy.

This slipping back into the aesthetic which was to be criticised is avoided by exploring the social critique implicit in the narrative archetype discussed above. However, no narrative can make explanatory claims without invoking ideological choices, and if the suicide plot is defensible as a reading of the content of the Symphony, it brings costs with it. In particular, this is a narrative which uses the figure of a central character, a protagonist, to describe the formal contours of the whole work; the plot archetype is actually an archetype of character. It is hard to avoid the conclusion that this involves a covert claim to unity of origin for the heterogeneous materials of the symphony: in other words, a single 'meaning' is being posited for states of plurality and non-integration, neutralising their force in the work. Of course, there is no reason for a narrative hermeneutic strategy to involve this assimilation to a single character; the more common comparison between themes and characters, pursued so subtly by Adorno, preserves the heterogeneity of musical and novelistic materials as a point of similarity between the two. But to the very extent that the plot archetype of a central female protagonist is illuminating, it threatens to close off some of the narrative features which first suggested it: the lack of integration between different coding structures; the dislocating effect of the contrasting sections within movements; the great dissimilarity of the individual movements themselves. Even if it is pursued as 'a' meaning rather than 'the' meaning, this democratic approach to interpretation has to involve holding the reading in tension with its generating structures in an Adornian forcefield or constellation. The deconstructive move to dismantle any reading that makes exclusive claims is never far away, whilst the narrative semiotics of the work makes such readings necessary to any investigation of its signifying structures.

The same might also be said of the 'first narrative' proposed above: the dialectical engagement with formal models marked at the boundaries of formal sections. This formalist reading is in many ways at odds with the subsequent attempt at a non-biographical subjective programme. In fact, it is a narrative which appears to do the reverse, emphasising the historical and social conventions as the stuff of narrative reference, and threatening thereby to obliterate the possibility of an aesthetic subject in the work.

The costs and benefits of narratological analysis have recently been explored by Alan Street (1994). In a discussion of Schoenberg's *Five Orchestral Pieces* Op.16, he pursues formalist, programmatic and psychobiographical narrative possibilities in turn, before finding that each ends by being compromised by the others. This final aporetic state of affairs is both the limit of interpretation – an inherent shortcoming of language as a hermeneutic medium – and a definition of the essentially fluid significatory capabilities of music itself:

> On the one hand, the collapse of intention cuts off any direct route to the notion of an authorial subject. And on the other, the failure of reference to redeem rhetorical self-reflexivity questions whether language can ever be called on to articulate phenomenal experience. ... But representation does provide something in the way of compensation for the charge it levies, for the divorce it opens. One of the things it gives us is music.
> (Street 1994: 183)

This final observation returns us to the point of departure. The possibility of 'producing the text' narrated by music is located in the desires of the interpreter; the code of narration is the trace of desire within the musical text. And the path from the detection of isolated 'moments of narration' within the movement, through the more holistic treatment of literary archetypes, to a final, thoroughly deconstructed, ironically self-aware state of aporia, is itself a suspiciously Romantic narrative of increasing mastery of the musical substance, or at least of the substance's signifying potential; and as such it too should perhaps be resisted. However, if every interpretant in some way necessitates fresh interpretive effort, this chapter has at least brought to light the location of some of the most elusive and yet most potent signifying features of Mahler's work. Only by invoking musical narration as a semiotic code can some of the most fruitful hermeneutic possibilities of contemporary critical theory be deployed in the service of an analytical project.

6

CODA

Now that the end of this study has been reached, it is not difficult to discern the narrative that has animated it. The progress of chapter after chapter through increasingly wider contexts of sign function has told at least two stories. The first narrative is a quest, involving the search for mastery of signifying strategies. The patient tabulation of detail in the analysis of the Andante has given way, by the end of the 'third meaning' of the Finale, to a mode of commentary that can only proceed by imaginative leaps. The second narrative is the reverse: it is the story of the progressive dissolution of the categories of semiotic theory. In many respects, this is a well-trodden path. It might, for instance, be discerned in Barthes' career after *S/Z*, perhaps through *Le plaisir du texte* to *La chambre claire* (Barthes 1973, 1980). The activity of 'producing the text' to be analysed in each chapter has described an arc from the objective description of segmented units, to a deconstructive narrative concerning first the necessity, and then the impossibility, of identifying the signs that make up the system.

It is a moot point whether the overall pattern of this study is a universal narrative of human sign production, or a reflection of the essentially Viennese *Angst* shared by the music of Mahler, the drama of a Schnitzler, or the visual art of a Klimt or a Kokoschka. It is hard not to historicise the simultaneous promise and deferral of meaning found in the articulating codes of the Sixth Symphony. Certainly the methods of chapters 4 and 5 provide a contextualisation of Mahler, by situating the work within the cultural intertexts represented by the Dance of Death or the novel of the tragic heroine. It has been all too easy, for many earlier commentators, either to write Mahler off as an irrelevance to the cultural history of the birth of modernism, or to co-opt him willy-nilly to the aesthetics of the New Music. It is only by attending to the detail of how the distinctive harmonic and melodic language leads to the invocation of the cultural text that the music can be made to signify. And, despite the pursuit of free interpretation in the methods of this study, the sheer capacity of this symphony to impel the hermeneutic effort is testimony to the fact that the author is not quite dead after all.

Carl Schorske, in a fascinating comparison of Mahler and Klimt, contrasts the reactions of the two men, both *parvenus* in the Viennese Ringstrasse society, to their conflict with the bourgeois establishment. Klimt's early radicalism, which culminated in the ceiling paintings for the University, gave way to an increasingly private and aestheticised exploration of representation. Mahler, on the other hand, became if anything more radical as time went on. He, too, shows an increasingly idiosyncratic style, but it retains its power of critique by a relentless opposition of this 'private' utterance to the 'public' world of tonal process, formal design and institutionalised tradition. The brilliance of Mahler's accomplishment rests in no small measure on the success of the technique described in chapter 2, whereby the common coin of musical expression is taken over and subordinated by the Mahlerian idiolect, in a reversal of private and public coding which amounts to a deconstruction in sound. Whether read as an immanent critique of bourgeois ideology, or as an Oedipal slaying of the father, this is a remarkable exploitation of the historical moment of the turn of the century. It is this feature of Mahler's music that makes Adorno comments that 'the tonal, profoundly consonant music of Mahler's late style ... sometimes has the air of absolute dissonance, the blackness of the New Music' (1960: 141/1992: 105). From this dialectical engagement, too, springs Mahler's timeliness for the postmodern West. For an age which ceaselessly recycles nineteenth-century artworks, aesthetic clichés and, let it be said, political rhetoric, Mahler has become an ironic totem. His refusal either to acquiesce in received modes of signification, or to lapse into solipsism, is emblematic of the deconstructive project which aims to keep alive the prospect of disinterested truth, despite the tendency of the postmodern condition to reduce value to commodity. The semiotic profile of Mahler's works relentlessly struggles against both ideology and incoherence. Every interpretive move finds itself unable to close off the process of signification, whilst on the other hand, the articulation of the various levels of coded signs is always clearly delineated. Meaning is preserved, if at times at great cost. There is, indeed, a double irony in the mass reproduction and distribution of Mahler's works, since the task of engaging with the cultural forces that work against the possibility of meaningful utterance has rarely been more pressing.

This study may not have succeeded in describing 'every configuration recognisable in the score' of the Sixth Symphony. But it has demonstrated that a theory of musical semiotics is capable of articulating the analysis of the most complex musical works, and that established techniques of analysis can be made to serve the end of understanding music as a means of cultural production. The recognition that musical works are texts, situated in the same web of relations as other cultural products and therefore susceptible to comparative analysis, is the most likely means of advancing our understanding of the human sciences in the current *fin de siècle*. Such understanding is the aim of any analysis which is both truly semiotic and truly musical.

BIBLIOGRAPHY

Abbate, C., 1991: *Unsung Voices: Opera and Musical Narrative in the Nineteenth Century.* Princeton: Princeton University Press.

Adorno, T.W., 1960: *Mahler: Ein Musikalische Physiognomik.* Frankfurt: Suhrkampf.
  1992: *Mahler: A Musical Physiognomy*, translated E. Jephcott. Chicago: University of Chicago Press (translation of Adorno 1960). Note: quotations in the text do not always follow this version exactly. Any deviation is the author's own.

Banks, P., 1982: 'The Early Social and Musical Environment of Gustav Mahler'. D.Phil. dissertation, University of Oxford.

Barthes, R., 1970: *S/Z*. Paris: Seuil. Translated (1974) by R. Howard. Oxford: Blackwell.
  1973: *Le plaisir du texte*. Paris: Seuil. Translated (1976) by R. Miller as *The Pleasure of the Text*. London: Jonathan Cape.
  1977: Image-Music-Text: Essays selected and translated by Stephen Heath. Oxford: Fontana.
  1980: *La chambre claire*. Paris: Gallimard. Translated (1981) by R. Howard as *Camera Lucida*. New York: Hill & Wang.
  1985: *The Responsibility of Forms*, translated R. Howard. Oxford: Blackwell.

Bekker, P., 1920: *Gustav Mahlers Sinfonien*. Berlin: Schuster & Loeffler.

Bernard, J., 1986: 'On *Densité 21.5*: A Response to Nattiez', *Music Analysis* vol. 5: 2/3, 207–32.

Brown, A., 1991: 'Music's Body: Some Notes on Barthes and Schumann'. Unpublished paper delivered at Cambridge University.

Carner, M., 1981: 'Ländler', in S. Sadie (ed.), *The New Grove Dictionary of Music and Musicians*. London: Macmillan.

Chatman, S., 1978: *Story and Discourse: Narrative Structure in Fiction and Film*. Ithaca: Cornell University Press.

Clark, J., 1950: *The Dance of Death in the Middle Ages and Renaissance*. Glasgow: Jackson, Son & Co.

Culler, J., 1975: *Structuralist Poetics*. London: Routledge.
  1981: *The Pursuit of Signs: Semiotics, Literature, Deconstruction*. London: Routledge.
  1983: *On Deconstruction*. London: Routledge.

Dahlhaus, C., 1982: *Esthetics of Music*, translated W. Austin. Cambridge: Cambridge University Press.

1983: *Foundations of Music History*, translated J. B. Robinson. Cambridge: Cambridge University Press.

1988: *Schoenberg and the New Music*, translated D. Puffett and A. Clayton. Cambridge: Cambridge University Press.

De Man, P., 1983: 'The Rhetoric of Blindness: Jacques Derrida's Reading of Rousseau', in *Blindness and Insight: Essays in the Rhetoric of Contemporary Criticism*, 102-41. London: Routledge.

Derrida, J., 1979: 'Living on/Border Lines', translated J. Hulbert, in *Deconstruction and Criticism*, ed. H. Bloom. New York.

Dougherty, W., 1985: 'An Examination of Semiotics in Musical Analysis: The Neapolitan Complex in Beethoven's Op. 131'. Ph.D. dissertation, Ohio State University.

Dubrow, H., 1982: *Genre*. London: Methuen.

Dunsby, J., 1983: 'Music and Semiotics: The Nattiez Phase', *The Musical Quarterly* vol. 33.

Eagleton, T., 1990: *The Ideology of the Aesthetic*. Oxford: Blackwell.

Eco, U., 1977: *A Theory of Semiotics*. Bloomington: Indiana University Press.

1986: *Semiotics and the Philosophy of Language*. Bloomington: Indiana University Press.

1992: *Interpretation and Overinterpretation*. Cambridge: Cambridge University Press.

Eggebrecht, H.-H., 1981: *Die Musik Gustav Mahlers*. Munich: Piper.

Eigeldinger, J.-J., 1988: 'Twenty-four Preludes op. 28: Genre, Structure, Significance', in *Chopin Studies*, ed. J. Samson. Cambridge: Cambridge University Press.

Epstein, D., 1979: *Beyond Orpheus: Studies in Musical Structure*. Oxford: Oxford University Press.

Flaubert, G., 1981 [1857]: *Madame Bovary*, translated Gerard Hopkins. Oxford: Oxford University Press.

Floros, C., 1977: *Gustav Mahler* (vols. I and II). Wiesbaden: Breitkopf & Härtel.

1985: *Gustav Mahler* (vol. III). Wiesbaden: Breitkopf & Härtel.

Forte, A., 1985: 'Middleground Motives in the Adagietto of Mahler's Fifth Symphony', *Nineteenth Century Music* 8:2, 153-63.

Frow, J., 1990: 'Intertextuality and Ontology', in *Intertextuality: Theories and Practices*, ed. M. Worton and J. Still. Manchester: Manchester University Press.

Gasché, R., 1986: *The Táin of the Mirror: Derrida and the Philosophy of Reflection*. Cambridge, Mass, Havard University Press.

Godzich, W., 1978: Review of Eco (1977) and Nattiez (1975), *Journal of Music Theory* vol. 22:1, 117-33.

Goehr, A., 1982: 'Schoenberg and Karl Kraus: The Idea behind the Music', *Music Analysis* vol. 1:3.

Goethe, J. W., 1959 [1831]: *Faust: Part Two* translated P. Wayne. Harmondsworth: Penguin.

Greene, D. B., 1984: *Mahler: Consciousness and Temporality*. New York: Gordon and Breach.

Hammerstein, R., 1980: *Tanz und Musik des Todes: Die mittelalterlichen Totentänze und ihr Nachleben*. Berne and Munich: Francke Verlag.

Hansen, M., 1980: 'Marsch und Formidee: Analytische Bemerkungen zu sinfonischen Sätzen Schuberts und Mahlers', *Beiträge zur Musikwissenschaft*, vol. 22, 3-23.

Hanson, E., 1986: 'Gustav Mahler and the Will: Tracing a Motive through the Symphonies'. Ph.D. dissertation, University of Washington.
Hatten, R., 1982: 'Toward a Semiotic Model of Style in Music: Epistemological and Methodological Bases'. Ph.D. dissertation, Indiana University.
Higonnet, M., 1985: 'Suicide: Representations of the Feminine in the Nineteenth Century', *Poetics Today*, vol. 6:1-2, 103-18.
Hopkins, R., 1990: *Closure and Mahler's Music: The Role of Secondary Parameters*. Philadelphia: University of Pennsylvania Press.
Huizinga, J., 1924: *The Waning of the Middle Ages*. London: Edward Arnold.

Istel, ed., n.d. [c.1910]: *Mahlers Symphonien*. Berlin.

Jankelévitch, V., 1976: *Debussy et le mystère de l'instant*. Paris: Seuil.
Jülg, H.-P., 1986: *Gustav Mahlers Sechste Symphonie*. Munich: Emil Katzbichler.
Kallberg, J., 1988: 'The Rhetoric of Genre: Chopin's Nocturne in G Minor', *19th-Century Music* vol. 11:3.
Karbusicky, V., 1986: *Gustav Mahler und seine Umwelt*. Darmstadt: Wissenschaftliche Buchgesellschaft.
Keiler, A., 1981: 'Two Views of Musical Semiotics' in *The Sign in Music and Literature* (ed. W. Steiner), 138-68. Austin: University of Texas Press.
Kerman, J., 1981: 'How We Got into Analysis, and How to Get Out', *Critical Inquiry*, vol. 7, 311-31.
Klemm, E., 1977: 'Notizen zu Mahler', in P. Ruzicka (ed.), *Mahler: ein Herausfordung*. Wiesbaden: Breitkopf & Härtel.
Koller, E., 1980: *Totentanz: Versuch einer Textumbeschreibung*. Innsbrucker Beiträge zur Kulturwissenschaft, Germanistiche Reihe, X. Innsbruck: Institut für Germanistik der Universität.
Kurtz, L.P., 1931: *The Dance of Death and the Macabre Spirit in European Literature*. New York: Columbia University Press.

Laske, O., 1977: *Music, Memory and Thought: An Exploration in Cognitive Musicology*. Ann Arbor: UMI Research Press.
Lewis, C.O., 1984: *Tonal Coherence in Mahler's Ninth Symphony*. Ann Arbor: UMI Research Press.
Lidov, D., 1981: 'The *Allegretto* of Beethoven's Seventh', *American Journal of Semiotics*, vol. I: 1-2.
Lukács, G., 1971: *Theory of the Novel*, translated A. Bostock. London: Merlin Press.

McClary, S., 1991: *Feminine Endings: Music, Gender and Sexuality*. Minneapolis: University of Minnesota Press.
McGrath, W., 1974: 'The Metamusical Cosmos of Gustav Mahler', in *Dionysian Art and Populist Politics in Austria*. New Haven.
Miller, N., 1980: *The Heroine's Text: Readings in the French and English Novel*. New York: Columbia University Press.
Mitchell, D., 1961: 'Gustav Mahler: Prospect and Retrospect', *Proceedings of the Royal*

Musical Association vol. 137, 83-95.

Molino, G., 1990: 'Musical Fact and Semiology of Music', translated J. Underwood, *Music Analysis* vol. 9:2, 105-52. A translation of 'Fait musicale et sémiologie de la musique', *Musique en Jeu* 17 (1975), 37-62.

Mounin, G., 1970: *Introduction à la sémiologie*. Paris: Minuit.

Nattiez, J.-J., 1975: *Fondements d'une sémiologie de la musique*. Paris: Union générale d'éditions.

   1982: 'Varèse's *Density 21.5*: A Study in Semiological Analysis', translated A. Barry, *Music Analysis* vol. 1:3.

   1985: 'The Concepts of Plot and Seriation Process in Music Analysis', translated C. Dale, *Music Analysis* vol. 4:1-2.

   1987a: *De la sémiologie à la musique*. Montreal: Cahiers du département d'études littéraires de l'Université du Quebec à Montreal, 10.

   1987b: *Musicologie générale et sémiologie*. Paris: Christian Bourgois éditeur.

   1989: 'Reflections on the Development of Semiology in Music', translated Katharine Ellis, *Music Analysis* vol. 8:1-2, 21-76.

   1990: 'Can One Speak of Narrativity in Music?', *Journal of the Royal Musical Association* vol. 115:2, 240-57.

   1991: *Music and Discourse*, translated C. Abbate. Princeton: Princeton University Press.

Newcomb, A., 1984: 'Once More "Between Absolute and Programme Music": Schumann's Second Symphony', *19th Century Music* vol. 7, 233-50.

   1987: 'Schumann and Late Eighteenth-Century Narrative Strategies', *19th Century Music* vol. 11, 164-74.

   1992: 'Narrative Archetypes and Mahler's Ninth Symphony', in S. Scher (ed.) *Music and Text: Critical Inquiries*. Cambridge: Cambridge University Press.

Ratz, E., 1968: 'Musical Form in Gustav Mahler', *The Music Review* vol. 29. Translated from *Die Musikforschung*, vol. 9 (1956).

Redlich, H., 1963: 'Mahler's Enigmatic Sixth', in *Festschrift Otto Erich Deutsch*. Kassel: Bärenreiter.

   1968: *Mahler: Symphony No. 6* (edition of the score). London: Eulenberg.

Ricoeur, P., 1980: 'Narrative Time', *Critical Inquiry* vol. 10, 169-90.

   1983: *Time and Narrative*, translated K. McLaughlin and D. Pellauer. Chicago: University of Chicago Press.

Riffaterre, M., 1978: *Semiotics of Poetry*. Bloomington: Indiana University Press.

   1979: *La production du texte*. Paris: Seuil.

   1984: 'Flaubert's Presuppositions', in *Flaubert and Postmodernism*, ed. N. Schor and H. Majewski. London: University of Nebraska Press.

Rosen, C., 1975: *The Classical Style*. London: Faber.

Ruwet, N., 1966: 'Méthodes d'analyse en musicologie', *Revue belge de musicologie*, vol. 20 65-90; Translated (1987) by Mark Everist as 'Methods of Analysis in Musicology', *Music Analysis* vol. 6:12, 11-36

   1972: *Language, musique poésie*. Paris: Seuil.

Samson, J., 1989: 'Chopin and Genre', *Music Analysis* vol. 8:3.

Samuels, R., 1986: *Motivic Development in Der Abschied*. Paper read to the Royal Musical Association, Reading.

1994: 'Music as Text: Mahler, Schumann and Issues in Analysis' in *Music, Analysis and Meaning in Music* (ed. A. Pople). Cambridge: Cambridge University Press.
Saussure, F. de, 1916: *Cours de linguistique générale*. Lausanne and Paris: Librairie Payot et Cie.
Schmitt, T., 1983: *Der langsame Symphoniesatz Gustav Mahlers*. Munich: Wilhelm Fink.
Schoenberg, A., 1967: *Fundamentals of Musical Composition* ed. G. Strang. London: Faber and Faber.
  1975: *Style and Idea* ed. L. Stein. London: Faber and Faber.
Schorske, C., 1982: 'Mahler and Klimt: Social Education and Artistic Development', *Daedalus* vol. 111:3, 29–50.
Seebass, T., 1980: Review of Hammerstein 1980 and Koller 1980, *Journal of the American Musicological Society* vol. 33:2, 329–34
Seigneuret, J.-P., 1988: *A Dictionary of Literary Themes and Motifs*. Westport, Conn. Greenwood Press.
Sponheuer, B., 1978: *Logik des Zerfalls: Untersuchungen zum Finalproblem in den Symphonien Gustav Mahlers*. Tutzing: Hans Schneider.
Stefani, G., 1987: *Il segno della musica*. Palermo: Sellerio.
  1989: 'A Theory of Musical Competence'. *Semiotica* vol. 66:1-3, 7–22.
Straus, J., 1990: *Remaking the Past: Musical Modernism and the Influence of the Tonal Tradition*. Cambridge, Massachusetts, and London: Harvard University Press.
Street, A., 1994: 'The Obbligato Recitaive: Narrative in Schoenberg's *Five Orchestral Pieces* Op. 16', in *Music, Analysis and Meaning in Music* (ed. A. Pople). Cambridge: Cambridge University Press.

Treitler, L., 1989: *Music and the Historical Imagination*. Cambrige, Massachusetts: Harvard University Press.

Warren, F. (ed.), 1931: *The Dance of Death* (with introduction, notes, etc. by B. White). London: Early English Text Society.
Webster Goodwin, S., 1986: 'Emma Bovary's Dance of Death', *Novel: A Forum on Fiction* vol. 19:3.
  1988: *Kitsch and Culture: The Dance of Death in Nineteenth-Century Literature and Graphic Arts*. New York: Garland.
White, H., 1987: *The Content of the Form*. Baltimore: Johns Hopkins University Press.
  1992: 'Commentary: Form, Reference and Ideology in Musical Discourse', in S. Scher (ed.) *Music and Text: Critical Inquiries*. Cambridge: Cambridge University Press.
Williamson, J., 1975: 'The Development of Mahler's Symphonic Technique in the Period 1899-1905'. D.Phil. dissertation, Oxford University.
  1991: 'Mahler, Hermeneutics and Analysis', *Music Analysis* vol. 10:3, 357–73
Winter, R., 1989: 'The Bifocal Close and the Evolution of the Viennese Classical Style', *Journal of the American Musicological Society* vol. 42:2, 275–337.

INDEX

Abbate, Carolyn 136-8, 140, 144
Adam, Adolphe, *Giselle* 129
Adorno, Theodor 16, 48, 59-62, 66, 69-71, 74, 76-83, 87-9, 91, 94, 101, 109, 112-15, 117, 127, 131, 133, 137, 140-3, 145, 147-9, 151-2, 154, 156, 161, 164, 167
aporia 86, 141-2, 154, 165
Augustine, St 8
Austen, Jane 123

Bailey, Robert 86, 117
Bakhtin, Mikhail 123, 136
Balzac, Honoré 12, 126
Banks, Paul 95, 109, 130
Barthes, Roland 12-15, 19, 83, 126-7, 133, 134, 143, 158-9, 166
Baudelaire, Charles 121
Beethoven, Ludwig van 65, 136, 146; Third Symphony 125-6; Fifth Symphony 138; Seventh Symphony 57; Ninth Symphony 64, 93; String Quartet (Op. 135) 76
Bekker, Paul 59, 69-70, 82-3, 85
Berg, Alban, *Wozzeck* 123; *Lulu* 161
Berio, Luciano, *Sinfonia* 126
Berlioz, Hector, *Symphonie fantastique* 76, 110, 125-6
Bernard, Jonathan 11
Bildungsroman 138, 149-50
Boulez, Pierre 9
Brahms, Johannes 35, 46; First Symphony 76; String Quartet (Op. 51, no. 2) 19; First Piano Sonata 66
breakthrough (Adorno) 16, 35, 64, 80, 89, 137
Brown, Andrew 159
Bruckner, Anton 46

Carner, Mosco 130
Chatman, Seymour 134-5
Chomsky, Noam 7

Chopin, Frédéric 92, 132
Chopin, Kate 156
Clark, J. 120
cliché 115-19, 126-32
code: generally 6-8, 11-15, 29-32, 85, 89-90; formal code 64-90 *passim*, 100; generic code 89-90, 91-132 *passim*; harmonic code 20, 93; melodic code 20, 24, 51, 61, 76, 78, 83-4; motivic code 18-63 *passim*, 64, 71-2, 78, 83-4, 93; narrative code 27, 51, 58-61, 67, 76-8, 85, 88-90, 133-65 *passim*; non-sequential code 12-13, 19, 24, 55, 80, 84-5, 88, 143; s-code 6-7, 10-11, 19, 34, 53, 63, 110, 116; sequential code 12-13, 83, 143
Croce, Benedetto 92
Culler, Jonathan 4-6, 12, 134, 137

Dahlhaus, Carl 91-2, 109, 114, 138
Dance of Death 119-31
De Man, Paul 1
Debussy, Claude 46
deconstruction 1, 54, 78, 86-7, 90, 132, 135, 154, 164, 167
Defoe, Daniel 156
Délibes, Léo, *Lakmé* 136
Derrida, Jacques 1, 4, 10, 78, 135, 139-40
Dickens, Charles 149, 156
Dougherty, William 14
Dubrow, Helen 92
Dukas, Paul, *L'Apprenti sorcier* 135-6
Dunsby, Jonathan 9

Eagleton, Terry 158
Eco, Umberto 2, 4-8, 10, 15, 19, 63, 110, 139
Eggebrecht, Hans-Heinrich 28, 85
Epstein, David 19
esthesic analysis 8, 10, 12, 70

Fitzgerald, F. Scott 123

Flaubert, Gustave, *Madame Bovary* 127-8, 150-1, 154-8
Floros, Constantin 69-70, 79-82, 84-5, 90-1, 95-7, 100-1, 108, 110, 113, 129-30
Forte, Allen 49
Foucault, Michel 158
Freud, Sigmund 128, 138, 147
Frow, John 139-40
fulfilment (Adorno) 16

Gasché, Rodolphe 140
general text 4, 139-40
Godzich, Wlad 7
Goehr, Alexander 19
Goethe, Johann 121, 156
golden section 58, 69
Greene, David B. 114-15, 131
Greimas, A. J. 156
Grundgestalt 19, 25

Hammerstein, Roland 121
Hansen, Mathias 89-90
Hanson, Eric 48
Hardy, Thomas 136
harmonic code see code
Hatten, Robert 14, 55
Haydn, Joseph 66, 130, 141
Higonnet, Margaret 156-7
Holbein, Hans 121, 131
Hopkins, Robert 117-18, 153, 162
Huizinga, Jan 120

iconic sign 7, 112
ideology 4, 6, 15, 66, 140
idiolect 34-49, 53-4, 63-4, 84, 88, 100, 167
intertextuality 1, 13-14, 34, 48-55, 63, 70, 81, 85-6, 89-90, 128-9, 132, 139, 141, 143, 147-8, 154-5, 166
irony 115-19, 132

Jackendoff, Ray 48
Jacobsen, Jens Peter 77
Jankelevitch, Vladimir 46
Jean Paul (Richter) 138
Joyce, James 13
Jülg, Hans-Peter 79, 89

Kallberg, Jeffrey 92, 109
Karbusicky, Vladimir 130
Keiler, Allen 9
Kerman, Joseph 5
Kidd, Robert 116

Klemm, Eberhardt 80
Klemperer, Otto 65
Klimt, Gustav 166
Kokoschka, Oskar 166
Koller, Erwin 120
Kundera, Milan 16

Langlois, Eustache 122
langue / parole 3
Lanner, Joseph 130
Laske, Otto 9
Le Fèvre, Jean 120
Lerdahl, Fred 48
Lévi-Strauss, Claude 10
Lewis, Christopher 70, 86
lexie 12
Lidov, David 56-7
linguistics 2, 5
Lukács, George 163

Mahler, Alma 2, 81, 101, 148, 157
Mahler, Gustav, First Symphony 16, 84, 109; Second Symphony 34, 58, 64, 86, 107, 136, 150, 155; Third Symphony 50, 86, 150, 152; Fourth Symphony 58, 86 140-5, 150, 152, 154; Fifth Symphony 18, 34, 49-50, 58, 65, 94-5, 107, 110-18, 128-9, 143, 147; Sixth Symphony: first movement 26, 80, 85, 89, 100-1, 143-8, 150-7, 159-63; Andante 18-63 *passim*, 69, 81, 84, 154-5, 159-62; Scherzo 2, 81, 91-132 *passim*, 159-62; Finale 58, 64-90 *passim*, 100, 147-8, 151, 157, 159-63; Seventh Symphony 18, 94, 107, 147; Eighth Symphony 58, 152; Ninth Symphony 58, 70, 107, 138, 149, 151, 153, 164; *Das Lied von der Erde* 58, 153; *Kindertotenlieder* 18, 26; *Rückert-Lieder* 18; *Revelge* 78, 131; *Rheinlegendchen* 107, 161; *Um Mitternacht* 161; *Wo die schönen Trompeten bläsern* 130
Marchant, Guy 119
Marx, A. B. 65
McClary, Susan 157
McGrath, William 48
melodic code see code
Miller, Nancy 156
Mitchell, Donald 90, 117
Molino, Jean 8-10
motivic code see code
Mounin, Georges 6
Mozart, Wolfgang 65, 130, 140-1; *Don Giovanni* 161

narrative code see code

Index

Nattiez, Jean-Jacques 8-12, 17, 19, 24, 27, 48, 63, 67, 70, 134-6
Naturlaut 28-32, 58
neutral level 8-10, 24, 70
Newcomb, Anthony 137-9, 149-50, 154, 158, 164
Newlin, Dika 117
nominalism 77, 79, 88, 91, 114, 145, 147
non-sequential *see* code

parody 115-19
Peirce, Charles Saunders 3, 5-6, 10, 18
pitch-class set theory 5
Plato 3
poietic analysis 8, 10, 70
positivism 5, 13-14
programme music 77, 85-6, 93, 131, 133-40, 149, 164-5
proportion 55-61, 69
provisional analysis 24, 101

Ratz, Erwin 69-73, 75-6, 78-82, 85, 89
Ravel, Maurice, *La Valse* 125-6
Redlich, Hans 26, 69-70, 73-6, 78-9, 81-2, 84, 89
reification 48, 112, 114-15, 117, 119, 152, 157
Richardson, Samuel 156
Ricoeur, Paul 135, 137, 139
Riffaterre, Michael 6, 128, 130, 143
Rosen, Charles 65, 93
Rousseau, Jean-Jacques 78
Rowlandson, Charles 125
Ruwet, Nicolas 11-12, 17, 24, 27, 63

s-code *see* code
Saint-Saëns, Camille 129
Samson, Jim 93
Saussure, Ferdinand de 2-3, 5
Schenker, Heinrich 5, 13-14, 17, 48, 65
Schmelzer, J. H. 130
Schmitt, Theodor 28-32
Schnitzler, Arthur 121, 166
Schoenberg, Arnold 14, 16-17, 19-20, 25, 48, 61, 65, 99; *Five Orchestral Pieces* 165
Schorske, Carl 166
Schubert, Franz 130, 161; Ninth Symphony 89
Schumann, Robert 137, 149, 159; Second Symphony 138; *Kreisleriana* 159

Scott, Walter 121
Second Viennese School 8
Seebass, Tilman 119
segmentation 10-11, 21-4, 54-5, 63, 67-9, 95
Seigneuret, J.-P. 156
semiotic triangle (Peirce) 3-4, 10
sequential *see* code
seriation process (Nattiez) 67
Shakespeare, William 116
sign production 6-7, 15, 19, 55, 63-4, 139
signifier / signified 2, 6, 12, 55
Sponheuer, Bernhard 66, 69-70, 79-82, 85, 88-9, 150
Stefani, Gino 14
Straus, Joseph 65, 70
Strauss, Richard, *Salome* 66; *Elektra* 66; *Ein Heldenleben* 81; *Tod und Verklärung* 81, 90
Stravinsky, Igor 145; *Rite of Spring* 9, 125-6; *Symphony in C* 64
Street, Alan 165
Strindberg, August 121
structuralism 10, 139
suspension (Adorno) 16, 113, 116-17, 137

Tchaikovsky, Peter 85; Fifth Symphony 110
text production 85, 90, 143-4
Tolstoy, Leo 163; *Anna Karenina* 126, 150-1, 155-8
Treitler, Leo 93
tripartition 8-10

Ursatz 5, 66, 70

Varèse, Edgard, *Density 21.5* 11, 15, 19, 63
Verdi, Giuseppe, *La Traviata* 125
voice-leading 5, 13-14, 24, 49-52, 62-3, 82-8, 106-8, 112, 118, 132, 141, 145-6, 152-3, 163

Wagner, Richard 28, 66, 85, 154; *Siegfried Idyll* 32; *Tristan und Isolde* 67
Warren, Florence 119
Webster Goodwin, Sarah 121-4, 127-8
Weigl, Alois 94
White, Hayden 135, 164
Williamson, John 54, 67-9, 83, 86-7, 133, 148, 151
Winter, Robert 140

Printed in the United Kingdom
by Lightning Source UK Ltd.
102205UKS00001B/89-92